THE MIND OF
KIERKEGAARD

The MIND *of*
KIERKEGAARD

by

JAMES COLLINS

Professor of Philosophy
Saint Louis University

PRINCETON UNIVERSITY PRESS
PRINCETON, NEW JERSEY

Published by Princeton University Press, 41 William Street,
Princeton, New Jersey 08540
In the United Kingdom: Princeton University Press,
Guildford, Surrey
Preface and Bibliographical Note (1983) copyright © 1983
by Princeton University Press

First Regnery edition, 1953
First Princeton Paperback printing, 1983

LCC 83-60464
ISBN 0-691-07279-5
ISBN 0-691-02027-2 pbk.

The following publishers have kindly given their permission to
make quotations from books to which they hold the copyright: The
American-Scandinavian Foundation (Kierkegaard's *Concluding Un-
scientific Postscript* and *Philosophical Fragments*); Augsburg Publishing
House (Kierkegaard's *The Gospel of Suffering*); Gyldendalske Bog-
handel Nordisk Forlag (Kierkegaard's *Samlede Vaerker*); Oxford
University Press (Gerard Manley Hopkins' *Notebooks and Papers*;
John Keats' *Letters*; Kierkegaard's *Christian Discourses, Journals, The
Point of View, The Present Age* and *Training in Christianity*); Prince-
ton University Press (Kierkegaard's *The Concept of Dread, Either/Or,
Fear and Trembling, The Sickness Unto Death, Stages on Life's Way* and
Works of Love); Charles Scribner's Sons (George Santayana's *The
Idea of Christ in the Gospels*); Vision Press (Kierkegaard's *Consider the
Lilies* and *Purify Your Hearts*).

Clothbound editions of Princeton University Press books are printed
on acid-free paper, and binding materials are chosen for strength
and durability. Paperbacks, while satisfactory for personal collections, are not usually suitable for library rebinding.

Printed in the United States of America by Princeton University
Press, Princeton, New Jersey

This Edition is for
Michael Collins and Kay Funk
My son and daughter-in-law

Preface

SEVERAL THINGS have been brought home to me during the years since *The Mind of Kierkegaard* was first published (1953, updated 1965). Concerning the significance of studying Kierkegaard, I will present my reflections under three headings: persistence, scholarship, and values.

Persistence

Even as late as 1950, it was not unreasonable to surmise that interest in Kierkegaard in the English-speaking world might be grounded only in extrinsic considerations. Perhaps people were paying attention to him mainly as an author of exotic origin, someone to put alongside Hans Christian Andersen in the small company of Danish writers known abroad. There was ground for curiosity about Kierkegaard due also to the large number of his books translated in so brief a span and the multitude of pseudonymous spokesmen represented in them. It was fascinating to delve for a while in this literary and religious Hobbitland, before one moved along to other and more fashionable landscapes.

Speculations of this sort have had to give way, however, to the actuality of continued and indeed broadened attention being paid to Kierkegaard's ideas in their own right. Not only students in philosophy and theology but also those in psychology, comparative literature, and social sciences are drawn to his writings. University courses in these and related fields regularly examine his thought as a major general conception of the complex relationships in human life.

Kierkegaardian problems turn out to be recurrent human ones that help liberally educated persons to understand their situation and the options open to them today.

From the standpoint of history of philosophy, I am specially interested in the links of Kierkegaard with existentialism. Undoubtedly, one of the considerations initially drawing attention to him was his contribution to that movement. Jaspers counted Kierkegaard, along with Nietzsche, as a forefather of the philosophy of existence. Many of Heidegger's analyses of revelatory human moods took their point of departure in the descriptions made by St. Augustine and Kierkegaard. The latter's account of the difficulties of interpersonal living under modern conditions supplied Sartre and Marcel also with plentiful material for reformulating within their respective contexts.

Such grounds of debt and comparison do supply incentives for including Kierkegaard among one's own source readings. But they also raise the question of his fate, once the existentialists had rounded out their own creative work. Does the role of Kierkegaard in our intellectual life become reduced to that of an adjunct to a historical movement, of an aid useful only to researchers specializing in that field?

This is an abstract possibility. Yet it gets progressively canceled out as each new generation of readers learns to appreciate his work primarily for its own sake and only secondarily for its contribution to other standpoints. Thus Kierkegaard's relationship with existentialism has had two clear benefits. First, this association drew initially toward him many people who might otherwise never have made his acquaintance. And next, they eventually learned to perceive that Kierkegaard follows his own path and develops his own account of the human condition, its tensions and resources.

Across the almost 130 years since Kierkegaard's death, his writings have exhibited a durable quality, a remarkably resilient capacity to show new significance for different times. This classic trait of persistence encourages us today to make our own soundings in the source works. The latter can refresh us in new ways without ceasing to maintain their own shape or exhaust their power.

Scholarship

Kierkegaard would not still continue to intrigue and nourish us, however, were no advances made beyond the first wave of English translations and general introductions. His continued pertinence depended upon a refusal to remain content with those earlier efforts, indispensable though they were. Among the community of Kierkegaard scholars, a conviction gradually took form in the nineteen-sixties and -seventies that much more work had to be done from every aspect. New standards of rigor had to be applied and new relationships explored, so that Kierkegaard studies could keep pace with other scholarly advances and thus continue to attract fresh readers to Kierkegaard himself.

Current research is being conducted along a broad front and often involves co-operative activities. Fortunately, textual problems are relatively minor, permitting continued use of the splendid Danish editions of Kierkegaard's collected works and his papers and letters. These editions furnish a reliable basis for preparing the tapes of a machine-readable text used in computer studies. Alastair McKinnon and others have published computer-generated indices, tables, and graphs. These tools furnish information on Kierkegaard's vocabulary, the frequency and variation of his primary terms, their immediate contexts and their correlation with different groups of his writings. Not only stylistic and comparative literary approaches are aided thereby, but also a sound textual footing is supplied for linguistic and conceptual analyses of his thought. Kierkegaard's subtle modulations of language enable him to make maximum reflective use of some favorite concepts and imagery, vary his avenues of communication, and thus enrich his entire authorship.

Whereas previously it was only the rare scholar who read Kierkegaard in the Danish, such acquaintance with the original language is now a commonplace requirement for advanced study. One consequence has been to increase dissatisfaction with the first series of translations and to launch the new translation of *Kierkegaard's Writings*. It is a co-operative enterprise being executed under Howard Hong's general editorship and under the sponsorship of Princeton University Press. As in the case of new translations of Descartes and Hegel, there will result some profound changes in our understanding of the familiar Kierkegaardian themes. Vocabulary is being readjusted, texts corrected, and connections shown with other writings of Kierkegaard and events in his life and times. While there is no total break with previous versions, the fresh translations do bring readers of Kierkegaard in English much closer to his own statements and the context affecting their precise intent.

Recent scholarly tendencies in secondary studies are incorporated in the *International Kierkegaard Commentary*, under Robert Perkins' general editorship. It recognizes that every new translation of Kierkegaard is itself an interpretive act, inviting and even demanding some re-interpretations in our understanding of him. Hence each volume in this series is devoted to the corresponding volume of *Kierkegaard's Writings*. Furthermore, the commentary is a joint effort of many specialists. This reflects the international nature of contemporary Kierkegaard research, the diversity of viewpoints, and the need to place students in direct contact with these different readings of the text. Hagiography is being replaced by measured analysis. Essays in each volume are not solely expository, but include critical evaluations and comparisons. Work on Kierkegaard is thus employing the well-tried methods normally used in research on major source thinkers.

New findings in any one historical field usually affect the adjacent intellectual territory. A case in point is the Hegel-Kierkegaard relationship. During the past two decades great strides have been taken in Hegel studies, which yield a more experiential and developmental view of this great German philosopher. There is a more sympathetic atmosphere for examining both the affinities and the real grounds of difference between him and Kierkegaard. This has prodded such scholars as Niels Thulstrup to fill in some important gaps in our knowledge of just which works of Hegel were studied by Kierkegaard, as well as to describe in detail that second-generation Danish Hegelianism which colored his interpretation and was the direct object of his criticism. The intellectual matrix is complex enough to require that comparisons avoid the simplistic alternative of either regarding Kierkegaard as an unwitting Hegelian or of contrasting the two figures so starkly that their real relationships disappear and the crucial intervention of Danish Hegelianism is forgotten.

Values

The earlier and the more recent studies on Kierkegaard maintain continuity through their shared appreciation of his reflections on the three spheres of existence: esthetic, ethical, and religious. Whatever similarities are noted between other thinkers and Kierkegaard on this theme, his own development of it is commonly recognized to be distinctive and compelling in its internal statement. His portrayal of these existential attitudes arouses a ready and sympathetic response today from people of many cultures and conditions. They find here the unifying center of values in his thought and the guiding thread for their study of his many writings.

Investigators today offer helpful perspectives for improving our grasp upon Kierkegaard's existential modes and relating them anew to our own problems and interest. Three promising avenues are (a) the psychological, (b) the ontological, and (c) the social-religious interpretations of his scheme of values.

(a) Kierkegaard provides a stimulus for students searching for a philosophical anthropology. Taken in conspectus, his spheres of existence give a concrete view of the chief components and drives in human life. There is a general unity in his account, in the sense that no one of the spheres can be eliminated without somehow unbalancing and impoverishing all the other resources and choices. To bring out this interconnection, such psychologists as Kristen Nordentoft give a more contemporary ring to Kierkegaard's own description of his pseudonymous "psychological" findings. The descriptions of anxiety and other moods furnish materials for psychiatrists interested in relating Kierkegaard to modern theories of the self, its dark features of repression, and its search for therapies.

(b) Under what conditions can the existential relations provide an ontological image of human nature and its growth? Without transforming Kierkegaard into a speculative philosopher, we can discern in his stages of life some permanent structural implications concerning man's temporal being and aims. In Kierkegaard's pseudonymous writings, there are several presuppositions about how our ways of existing express the maturation process of our own reality and its orientation toward God. The opportunity to render these points more explicit and to compare them with historical and comtemporary positions in ontology is an attractive prospect for many investigators today.

(c) More careful attention is now being given also to Kierkegaard's later writings and his papers. As John Elrod observes, these sources have a social significance sometimes overlooked. Kierkegaard's ethical and religious concerns are not confined to the lonely self in search of God. Instead, the themes of communication and love involve a revaluational attitude toward the political and ecclesial establishment. They manifest Kierkegaard's reforming care for the quality of our interpersonal life in its esthetic, moral, and religious modes of value. This societal motif underlies his lifelong preoccupation with the many forms of mutuality and radical equality in human existence.

The present book is a reissue of the 1965 edition of *The Mind of Kierkegaard*, with the substitution of this new Preface and the addition of an annotated Bibliographical Note covering work done in the intervening years. It is intended to introduce students to Kierkegaard's basic thoughts and to point out many of the scholarly aids available for making an independent study of his writings.

Saint Louis University   James Collins
January, 1983

Contents

CONTENTS

Chapter One

Kierkegaard the Man

FAR more has been established with certainty about the public life of Kierkegaard than about his intellectual development. For every well-charted step in his social relations, there are ten steps taken in his interior life which still remain obscure to us. His biography is, however, a dramatic one chiefly from the standpoint of the clash of spiritual values. We are fortunate in having at our disposal some excellent biographies and Kierkegaard's own revealing *Journals*. These sources tell us about the manner of man Kierkegaard was, and—inevitably, in the case of one who lived so intense an inner existence—they also reveal a good deal about his mind and its motor principles. Without some understanding of his life, not much sense can be made of the thoughts which stem so immediately from his personal situation.

The purpose of this introductory chapter is to sketch this personal history and furnish the background details about Kierkegaard's frame of mind, just before he began his literary activity. If this biographico-psychological approach were to be taken as a substitute for independent analysis of his works, it would defeat its own ends. There is a real danger today of deflecting interest and critical judgment from the general standpoint represented by this disquieting nineteenth-century Dane. Yet this is not a sufficient reason for neglecting to consider Kierkegaard the man, since such a study provides the most natural pathway to a grasp of his teachings. It is only necessary to respect his own request that his position be judged by its actual content, as well as by the personal cost at which it was acquired and maintained.

I. SKETCH OF HIS LIFE

Kierkegaard has aided his biographers not only by providing a rich deposit of details and reflections on his personal growth but also by indicating the cardinal events around which these materials can be arranged. His autobiographical essay—*The Point of View for My Work as an Author* (written in 1848, published posthumously)—calls attention to three central peaks in his life and prepares the way for the fourth and final crisis, which only ended with his death.[1] His formation at the hands of his father, the unhappy love affair with Regine Olsen, his collision with the press and the mob, and his open struggle with the Established Church of Denmark—these are the major situations in which he was implicated and which conditioned his outlook. The four ages of his life were: son, lover, polemical author, witness to the truth. At each stage, a unique and indelible set of traits was stamped on his mind and communicated to the books in which that mind found its natural flowering.

Danish national pride and national frustration had equal shares in Kierkegaard's makeup. He never ceased to regret the fact of having been born in Copenhagen, the provincial capital of a country lying on the fringe of European civilization. Especially galling to him was the remoteness of his national tongue from the common stream of cultural communication, for he rightly surmised that this would hinder the spread of his views. The political and economic backwardness of Denmark, following on its ill-fated policy of armed neutrality during the Napoleonic era, did not help to arouse respect abroad for Danish achievements in the arts and sciences.

At home, this weakness was reflected in an unhealthy concentration of talent, wealth and energy in Copenhagen, which nevertheless retained all the petty traits of a market town. The country's inferior status was only confirmed by the predominance of German literary and philosophical ideals. In the background lay a constant threat from Prussia, whose ambition was not confined to cultural infiltration but was ready to take the form of concrete military and territorial encroachment.

Probably in reaction to this state of affairs, Kierkegaard was always quick to pour scorn upon the German philosophical windbags, who concocted pompous theories with such ease, and upon the dupes among his own countrymen who were willing to swallow them. On the other hand, he had a keen appreciation of native Danish geniuses like Thorwaldsen, the sculptor, and Oehlenschlaeger, the poet, who were trying to create a modern national tradition. And amidst his complaints about his isolation from the rest of Europe, Kierkegaard was not blind to his own considerable contribution to his country's critical and literary heritage. The impulse which he gave to Danish literature bore immediate fruit in the writings of Brandes and Ibsen. It is difficult to calculate the full effect of his impact upon the religious life of Denmark and the rest of the Christian world. In the long-range view, his own corner of earth was as sound a springboard as could be found for his projects.

The Son

Naively but honestly enough, Kierkegaard was accustomed to boast of his descent from the purest strain of Danish blood. His father, Michael Pedersen Kierkegaard, was born in Jutland in 1756, moved across its bleak moors as a shepherd lad, and came to Copenhagen at the age of twelve. From an apprenticeship with his mother's brother, he rose rapidly in the hosier's business and soon became a leading wholesaler in wool and foodstuffs. His business success was proverbial in Copenhagen, being supplemented by shrewd investments in government securities. Rather dramatically, M. P. Kierkegaard retired in his early forties, in order to devote himself to meditation and the training of a large family. His first wife had died childless in 1796. The next year he was forced to marry his servant and distant relative, Anne Sørensdatter Lund, whom he had gotten with child. The last of the seven children of this marriage, Søren Aabye, was born on May 5, 1813.

In later years, Søren made little mention of his mother, but he never ceased to ponder on the character and mystery of his father. Physically, Søren was never very robust. This frail condition he attributed in part to his being the child of his parents' old age (the father and mother were respectively fifty-six and forty-five years old at his birth). In addition, he was born with a hunched back and uneven legs. This fact, together with his status as youngest child, gave him numerous privileges in the household and in his father's heart. His native wit and sharp tongue were encouraged, earning for him at home the sobriquet "the fork" and at school the respect, although not the affection, of his companions. In accord with his father's wish, Søren always kept well within the upper rank of his class. He compensated in learning and repartee for his physical weakness. A sense of intrinsic superiority developed quite soon, but his teachers were not sure whether he would ever devote his curiosity and undeniable originality to serious, constructive ends.

Beneath this surface brilliance of learning and liveliness, Søren's real education was going on at an unnoticed depth, with his father as tutor. Running throughout all his reminiscences of the boyhood years is an acknowledgment of three basic dispositions inherited from his father: imagination, dialectic and religious melancholy. The father deliberately cultivated these powers in his son. When inclement weather prevented them from taking their usual walk through the streets of Copenhagen, father and son would set out together on a spirited, imaginary excursion. Friends would be greeted, gossip exchanged, notice taken of passing traffic, obstacles avoided, and none of the small details left unobserved. Søren became accustomed to searching the faces of strangers and guessing at their hidden stories. These exercises, along with his wide literary readings, developed his psychological acumen and habit of visualizing all the possibilities of a situation. Imagination was disciplined, however, by an equally precocious development of intelligence along logical lines. M. P. Kierkegaard was well acquainted with the rationalist philosophy and theology popular during the latter part of the eighteenth century. This knowledge was not allowed to grow dim or remain merely a private treasure. He would summon his favorite divine, J. P. Mynster, and other worthies to discussion meetings at his home. There, a thorough airing would be given to the most subtle problems in Wolffian philosophy and Lutheran theology. Søren used to sit entranced, while his elders advanced their arguments, pro and con, in technical terms and with all the resources of logic. But the magic moment was always awaited, when his own father would dissolve the fine net of dialectic with a few rapier thrusts and thus assert the supremacy of his position.

The quality of his religious instruction led Søren, later on, to call his home training a crazy and cruel upbringing. His father visited upon him the full force of his own religious moods and troubles, without any regard for adapting his presentation to a child's sensibility. His religious belief had its doctrinal foundation in Lutheran Christianity, with its stress on the sinfulness and inborn depravity of man, his distance from God, and the unutterable mercy of Christ in taking our sins upon Himself. The Redemption of men by Christ crucified was regarded as the central religious doctrine, but it was not conveyed to Søren in a purely theoretical way. The elder Kierkegaard frequented the revival meetings of the Moravians, who centered upon the tears and sufferings of Christ, the wounds inflicted upon Him, and all the details of His crucifixion which would excite emotions of compassion and repentance. Not the infant Jesus but the man of sorrows was held up for worship. Withal, it was emphasized that God is all-powerful love and providence. But this belief did not seem to bring peace to the soul of the old man: he walked about with quiet despair as companion. A powerful melancholy gripped him during his religious meditations, although his son did not guess at a more personal reason for this depressing mood, until he had been at the university for a few years.

Søren matriculated at the University of Copenhagen in 1830, enrolling for the theological course out of deference to his father. Yet during most of his undergraduate years, his academic interests lay in the fields of literature and philosophy. He was an enthusiastic student of Plato, the Romantics, Shakespeare and the latest authorities in philosophy. For one semester, indeed, he did engage as private tutor the most brilliant of the rising young theologians, Hans Martensen. But the man who had sat under Hegel, welcomed Schleiermacher to the Danish shores and assured the world that he could go beyond his illustrious predecessors in reconciling theology with contemporary needs, was unable to impress his young student or lead him to undertake a serious study of theology. Kierkegaard's mode of living during the early 'thirties was not conducive to such interest. Apart from some student speeches in favor of the monarchy and women and against the liberal movement, he distinguished himself chiefly by his wit and his taste for fine food and drink. His favorite haunts were the café and the theater, which he visited in the company of a chosen circle of his student admirers. Not only the sowing of wild oats but also thoughts of suicide, disbelief and despair occupied him during this period.

There was more involved in this moral and intellectual breakdown than the conventionally wild ways of young manhood. About 1835, Søren experienced what he termed a great earthquake.[2] It dawned upon him that his father's melancholy was due to some secret moral defection, and that therefore the blessings of fortune were only the ironical means employed by providence to manifest its displeasure with him. It seemed entirely likely that a divine curse had been laid upon the entire family and would bring them all to untimely destruction. This foreboding was apparently confirmed by a rapid succession of deaths in the family, leaving alive only the old man, Søren and his elder brother, Peter Christian. An "infallible law of interpretation" now suggested itself, in accordance with which the father was to survive his sons, who would not live beyond their thirty-fourth year. Although Søren's habits and opinions had alienated him from his father and led him to establish separate residence, Michael Pedersen Kierkegaard made a supreme effort at restoring an understanding and, along with it, his son's moral health, which had been impaired by the terrible suspicion. He confessed to Søren that, as a boy in Jutland, he had raised his fist in blasphemy against God. Together with his sexual fall, this deed had weighed heavily upon his conscience throughout the latter half of his life. This sense of guilt had led to his melancholy, and now he unburdened its cause to his favorite son.

As a consequence of this heroic confession, prompted as it so evidently was by love and solicitude, Søren was reconciled with his father and led back to an effective belief in God's fatherly love. The most powerful religious experience of his lifetime—one in which a Pascalian sort of religious joy was the predominant note—occurred in May, 1838, a few months

· 7 ·

before his father's death. From this experience can be dated his own dedication to the problems of religious existence. Shortly after his father died (August, 1838), Kierkegaard issued his first book: *From the Papers of One Still Living*, the title of which indicated his surprise at surviving his father. This satirical analysis of Hans Christian Andersen and the esthetic view of life was his first attempt to settle accounts with the principles which had governed his own youth. And to the surprise of all his acquaintances, Kierkegaard now finished his theological course, crowning his studies with a master's thesis *On the Concept of Irony with Particular Reference to Socrates* (1841). Even in this outward way, he sought to pay his debt of piety to his father's memory.

The Lover

Already in 1837, Kierkegaard had met Regine Olsen, at that time only fourteen years old. The sentiment he felt at once toward her apparently caught him off balance. The entries written in his *Journals*, just previous to his introduction to Regine, were filled with thoughts of his sins and need for repentance. Hence his spontaneous reaction to this meeting was an observation that he had been turned back again to the world; he prayed that God would help him in living and improving himself. His courtship was deliberate and steady, and he experienced a triumph in winning Regine from a previous suitor. The engagement did not take place for a full three years after their first meeting, but immediately afterwards Kierkegaard was convinced that he had done wrong and that the engagement could never lead to marriage. Numerous ways of avoiding the inevitable break ran through his head, including taking her as a concubine, tricking her into rejecting him, and marrying her without revealing "his secret." The idea of behaving so outrageously that Regine would voluntarily dismiss him, made the strongest appeal.

But no matter how calloused his talk, he could not dislodge her deep trust in him. Finally, he had to take the responsibility upon himself. In October, 1841, having previously returned her engagement ring with a cold, involved note, Kierkegaard broke definitively with Regine. Not even her appeal to Christ and the memory of his father was powerful enough to deter him from this last step.

Why his one earthly love affair went through this tragic, almost grotesque, course has been answered in diverse ways by Kierkegaard himself. The main points of his testimony hang together, even though they do not adequately explain or justify his actions. There can be no doubt that he loved Regine in some way, but the engagement specified this attachment in terms of married love and family responsibility. This cast a new light upon their relationship, enabling him to view his fiancée and especially himself in a more concrete way. Incompatibilities, which had previously appeared to be minor and corrigible, now became for him indexes of an unbridgeable chasm between them. Thus, her gaiety, frankness and spontaneity had seemed only temperamentally opposed to his own deepseated somberness, isolation and deliberation. But the prospect of marriage led Kierkegaard to think that much more than temperamental differences were present. He interpreted her spontaneous behavior as the sign of a personality which is irremediably unreflective and unspiritual. He felt himself to be "an eternity too old" for her, since she could never accompany him along the ways of critical reflection and resolution. And now he realized that he had never been a youth, except at the distance of poetic fancy and deliberate wish.

It was not an ordinary conflict between an open and a closed type of personality. Even though he might want to do so, Kierkegaard could not give up the fort of his silence and yield the close-hugged secret of his interior life. Even in his *Journals*, he remained evasive about the precise nature of this reserve. Doubtless, it had a physical basis in his hunched back and weak legs. The hesitancy to which this weakness led, was increased by the attitude bred into him by his father that guilt was attached to the sexual act *in se*. He sometimes declared himself to be no full man, since the animal element was lacking. He was incapable of resolving the discord between soul and body, insight and desire. Because of the resultant spiritual bashfulness and dread, Kierkegaard felt incapable of entering into marriage. In this connection, he sometimes mentioned a mysterious thorn in the flesh, a buffet given to him by God. This probably refers both to his physical defect and to his melancholy of spirit, which was reinforced by his solidarity with his father's guilt. Since it is unjust to place these burdens upon another human being, and since secretiveness is incompatible with genuine married love, Kierkegaard saw the way to a complete union with Regine barred by obstacles he could not hope to remove.[3]

In later years, he wondered whether he might not have discovered in religion some basis for the hope of marriage. He confessed that the real failure of the marriage plans was to be laid to his own lack of faith. His melancholy, for instance, betrayed a doubt whether Christ had indeed done perfect satisfaction and so had effectively broken the power of inherited guilt. His introversion was a barring of the doors to human companionship, and even though Christ often enters through closed doors, He comes to rebuke the unbelieving. As Kierkegaard observed about himself, he had the courage to doubt all things but not to know and take possession of all things. Fundamentally, it was his faith that all things are possible to God which was put to the test in his love for Regine.

Yet against these self-recriminations, Kierkegaard invariably balanced another religious consideration: his special calling from God which he did not clearly perceive, until after his commitment to Regine. He came to regard his peculiar psycho-physical constitution as a vehicle used by divine government to confirm his exceptional status among men. As Kierkegaard approached spiritual maturity, he replaced his early sense of superiority by a more humble and demanding appreciation of what it means to be a religious exception. He found himself incapable of converting his fairy princess into a wife, just as he soon found himself incapable of accepting a ministerial post in the Danish Church. In his own language, he was "unable to realize the universal," unable to fit into the common categories of human existence. Yet God's purpose in giving him a thorn was not to make a useless idiosyncrasy, a quaint conceit, out of his life. Rather, Kierkegaard believed that he was asked to forego the security and consolation of the ordinary ways of life, in order to further the positive ends of providence. He had received sealed orders, and those orders read: *Go further!*

The Polemical Author

His first step in this renewed vocational direction was his visit to Berlin, during the Fall semester of 1841. Here, he attended the lectures of Schelling and Marheineke, and discovered that, in forsaking Regine, he had chosen not only "death" but also a literary career. Regine taught him to be a poet and a writer, for she released the first great swell of his esthetic activity. *Either/Or* (1843) was composed as a code message to her. His intention was to break her from a merely romantic and finite attachment to himself, and yet leave the way open for a mature, ethical choice. He sought to wean her from himself, but with the possibility of a reconciliation on the basis of a mutual religious understanding. This twofold aim drove him back to Berlin a second time, after his first book seemed only to have heightened her expectancy for a renewal of love on the same footing. But by the date of publication of his new books, *Repetition* and *Fear and Trembling* (both in October, 1843), Regine had despaired of regaining him and had announced her betrothal to his old rival, Fritz Schlegel. Thereafter, although Kierkegaard retained the tenderest regard for her and sought in vain to keep on friendly terms with her husband, the possibility of marriage was closed to him. However, to Regine and his father were dedicated the numerous writings which he issued during the next decade.

The three books mentioned above belong to the esthetic group of writings, which Kierkegaard issued pseudonymously. They deal with the enriching of human personality at its three levels of esthetic, ethical and religious consciousness. In *Stages on Life's Way* (1845), he summed up this theory of the three spheres of existence in a collection of essays, representative of these viewpoints. On the occasion of a critical review of the *Stages* by P. L. Møller, Kierkegaard became embroiled in a journalistic dispute, which left a deep mark upon him. P. L. Møller (who should not be confused with Kierkegaard's friend and mentor, P. M. Møller) was an esthete and literary critic, who aspired to succeed Oehlenschlaeger in the Chair of Esthetics at the University of Copenhagen. In order to further his claim, he edited a literary annual, *Gaea*, toward the end of December, 1845. In this volume, he made some adverse references to the *Stages*, censuring its author for inserting his peculiar moral and philosophical views into a context which should have remained purely literary. Kierkegaard made an immediate reply in the newspaper *Fatherland*. He not only took exception to Møller's remarks but also revealed the latter's clandestine association with a scandal-mongering paper, *The Corsair*.[4]

Under the talented editorship of Meyer Goldschmidt, *The Corsair* was avidly read in every Copenhagen household. Men of every station discovered their private failings aired in its pages. No political institution or intellectual ideal escaped its cynical, leveling treatment. Until he wrote his counter-attack upon Møller, however, Kierkegaard had been a notable exception to this policy: *The Corsair* had given embarrass-ingly warm praise to his esthetic books. Now, Kierkegaard challenged Goldschmidt to extend his abuse to him, an invi-tation which was accepted with grim enthusiasm. Week after week, Kierkegaard (under the guise of his pseudonyms) was held up for public ridicule. His awkward gait and appear-ance, his daily habits and turns of speech, were made the sub-ject of circumstantial reports and searing cartoons. The at-tack soon degenerated into a street brawl, for even the chil-dren, with whom he liked to talk, began to call him "old man either/or." As "the great philosopher with uneven pant-legs," Kierkegaard took his place among the stock comic characters of the contemporary stage, and certainly under-went the martyrdom of laughter. Yet he also accomplished his practical aim. Møller was forced to leave Denmark per-manently, while Goldschmidt eventually suppressed *The Corsair*, out of shame and chagrin that it had aroused such scorn in a man whom he inwardly admired.

From this incident, Kierkegaard learned how it feels to be trampled on by a flock of senseless geese. Even more, he learned in an empirical way about the corruption of all sec-tions of society through the agency of the press and anony-mous whispering. Throughout the campaign, the so-called better elements in society—the literary people and the repre-sentatives of Church and State—maintained a cowardly si-lence. Ordinary people were alienated from him, either out of a similar fear of majority opinion or because of a failure to discern the true issues in the midst of the calumny. Analyz-ing this situation, Kierkegaard traced it back to the wide-spread contempt for individual, existing men which was in-duced by Hegelian philosophy and its theological counter-

· 13 ·

part. Hence it was appropriate for him to offer the public his sustained attack upon Hegelianism, *Concluding Unscientific Postscript to the Philosophical Fragments*, at the very height of the controversy (February, 1846). The manuscript of the *Postscript* had been completed at the time when he sent off his first article against Møller. Along with the previously published *Philosophical Fragments or a Fragment of Philosophy* and *The Concept of Dread* (both in 1844), this book supplied his contribution to the philosophical discussion about Hegel which was then engaging most German and Danish thinkers. Kierkegaard's method was to analyze the nature and assumptions of Systematic speculation, and to expose its incapacity for dealing with actual existence and the problems of real men.

He had the romantic notion that, after producing these books, he would abandon writing entirely and retire to a country pastorate. But the *Corsair* campaign made such a retreat impossible and, in this way, helped to clarify his mind still further concerning God's designs for him. He came to realize more vividly that, as an exceptional individual, he was obliged to launch out like a Greenlander in his lonely kayak and undergo intense personal suffering for the truth's sake. Indeed, the requirement of individual responsibility and witnessing to the truth, in a way that entails suffering at the hands of the majority, was now regarded by Kierkegaard as the proper standard of Christian existence. Yet this demand had been passed over, watered down or contemplated only in a poetic way by the spokesmen for Christianity in Denmark. It became increasingly evident to Kierkegaard that his future work lay almost exclusively in the religious field, and that it would generate a conflict with the Established Church which might cost him his life, as well as his honor and worldly peace.

The Witness to the Truth

Kierkegaard's notorious assault upon official religion was as carefully premeditated as any other major effort in his life. Behind it lay a long period of debate and calculation of the risk. His later *Journals* record the private struggle behind the scenes, whereas an entire group of religious books gave ample public warning to his contemporaries that a crisis was brewing. From the beginning of his formal authorship in 1843, he had printed alongside of his pseudonymous books a series of *Edifying Discourses,* which openly contained his own convictions. Their common theme was man's moral and religious obligation as an individual, standing before the God Who is no respecter of majorities, establishments or compromises. In the religious discourses composed after his struggle with *The Corsair,* Kierkegaard began to unveil the polemical edge of his reading of the text of Christian existence. *Edifying Discourses in Various Spirits* (1847), *Works of Love* (1847), *Christian Discourses* (1848), and *The Lilies of the Field and the Birds of the Air* (1849), sharpened his criticism in terms of more specific issues. His second great religious experience, which came in 1848 as a conviction that he ought to speak out openly, encouraged him to carry out his program of radical attack. Renunciation of the world cannot mean the same as coming to easy terms with it; God educates the individual through suffering, rather than through dispensation from it; the godly man is he who has the undivided will to do all and suffer all, for the sake of the Good; a faith that does not bear fruit in the works of love is sterile and hypocritical. Only a slightly more concrete and pointed mode of address was needed to make these theses completely relevant to religious conditions in Kierkegaard's Denmark. After making a final exploration of religious psychology (*The Sickness Unto Death*) and the theoretical problems connected with religious authority (*Two Minor Ethico-Religious Treatises;* both in 1849), Kierkegaard was ready to devote his remaining years to an unmistakable indictment of the Church of Denmark.

More precisely, his purpose was to clear the atmosphere of an illusion that surrounded Protestantism, especially in its Danish form. On the ground of simple human honesty, he asked the Church officials to make public admission of the discrepancy between the Christian ideal and their preaching. He called upon them to confess that they were no longer presenting New Testament Christianity in its full rigor, that they were no longer asking men to follow Christ in unconditional discipleship. The three hard-hitting books of this 1850-52 period—*Training in Christianity, For Self-Examination* and *Judge for Yourselves!*—championed Kierkegaard's version of undiluted Christianity. They affirmed the substance of religion to be the following of Christ in His lowliness and heterogeneity with the world. In sharp, scandalous contrast to this Christian message stands the accepted position of Christendom. The latter does away with the need to choose Christ at a sacrifice to oneself, since it simply erases the distinction between the way of the world and the way of the Lord. Whereas Luther had raised his voice in protest against the subordination of holy things to secular interests, Lutheranism has completely integrated the religious life with the bourgeois order. Whereas Luther called for a saving faith, official Christianity dispenses men from the need for asceticism and good works. These facts, Kierkegaard submitted, should not be passed over in silence any longer.

Until the death (January, 1854) of Bishop Mynster, the Primate of the Danish Church and old friend of his father, Kierkegaard contented himself with demanding an admission of the difference between Christianity and Christendom. But Martensen's panegyric of Mynster as one who belonged to the line of venerable witnesses to the truth, aroused Kierkegaard to make a reply, in which the full requirement of the following of Christ was placed upon all who professed to be Christians. In order to exclude the personal factor, Kierkegaard delayed publication of this article until December, 1854, by which time Martensen had been safely installed as Mynster's successor in the See of Zealand. But in the short period from December to the following September, twenty-one articles appeared in the *Fatherland*, and nine pamphlets were printed in the *Instant* series.[5] A controversy in the strict sense never developed from Kierkegaard's pamphleteering activity, since Martensen (who had once tutored him) refused to join issue with him. Years before, in reply to Kierkegaard's *Fragments*, he had characterized the book as unscientific, unsystematic and unprofessorial—designations in which Kierkegaard had gloried. Now, Martensen suspected that base personal motives were behind the latest attack. And so he remained silent, except for a single angry outburst, which only showed that he had no understanding of the questions at issue or the frame of mind of his opponent.

Kierkegaard took his case against Martensen out of the academic halls and churches into the streets. He extended his criticism and satire to all the parsons, their livings, their families and their sacramental ministrations. He went beyond all bounds, in making a case against the Establishment. In a desperate "midnight cry" of warning, he adjured people to cease participating in official public worship and to withdraw from an established order which is only a counterfeit of New Testament Christianity. At the height of his denunciation, on October 2, 1855, he was stricken down with paralysis of the lower limbs and carried to the hospital. The tenth number of the *Instant* had been prepared but not yet sent to the printer. In his hospital room, Kierkegaard would neither receive his brother, who had always been critical of him and who was now a "royal official" of the State Church, nor accept communion at the hands of any ecclesiastical civil servant. This was the only polemical note sounded on his deathbed.

The touching record of Kierkegaard's last month on earth was kept by his one lifelong friend, Emil Boesen. It shows a man whose earthly task was done and who now summoned all remaining energy to make his death a meaningful act. Having given to Denmark the "dead man" that it needed to stir it up, he now turned himself to God. He prayed that despair might not attack him at death, and that he might soon sit astride a cloud and sing Alleluia! Alleluia! Alleluia! after his own fashion. Asked whether this hope rested on belief in the grace of God in Christ, he replied: "Yes, of course, what else?" [6] Kierkegaard died peacefully on November 11, 1855. But his body was laid at rest only after his nephew protested, at the graveside, against the way in which the Established Church was claiming him as its own in death.

2. HIS EARLY INTELLECTUAL ATTITUDE

Study of Kierkegaard's life is essential to, but not sufficient for, an assessment of his mind. This observation would be superfluous, were it not for some recent abuses of the biographical materials. They have been analyzed from a psychiatric standpoint, with a view to explaining away his thought in function of a neurotic personality. Doubtless, there is room for legitimate psychiatric study of many features of Kierkegaard's character: his relation to his father, his sickliness and melancholy, his unhappy love affair and general attitude toward women and marriage, his inability to communicate with others in a frank and easy way, his extreme sensitivity, and his intensely introspective bent. But psychiatric and psychoanalytic findings cannot rule upon the truth or falsity of his

position. It is sheer nonsense to offer as philosophically con-
clusive the Freudian report that, at his death, Kierkegaard
appears to be no more than a "poor, emaciated, thin schiz-
oid." [7] There is a sense in which Kierkegaard's personality-
traits are just as irrelevant to the question of validity as is the
fact of Nietzsche's insanity—extremely personal thinkers
though they both were. The findings of abnormal psychology
should be kept strictly subordinate to philosophical analysis.

Whatever the peculiarities of Kierkegaard's character and
build, he was himself aware of most of them, recorded them
for us, and tried to make allowances for them in evaluating
his own tenets. Unlike speculative philosophers, he never
claimed to give a complete and rounded theory of the world.
Following the beloved example of Socrates, he concentrated
upon a particular intellectual and moral situation. This led
him to emphasize some forgotten and badly needed truths,
without having regard for the general proportions of a philosophical system. As a moral gadfly, he stung the conscience
of his time, in the places where it needed to be roused. There
is still another sense in which his method is idiosyncratic and
restricted in scope. Not only the views he proposed but also
his manner of supporting them was dictated by his personal
experience. He spoke not as a *doctor* but as a *testis*, a personal
witness to the truth as he was living it. Since his aim was to
urge men to transform their lives morally and religiously,
Kierkegaard presented his thoughts as concretely and individually as possible. Inevitably, his own limitations and
peculiarities were reflected in his writings. These qualifications should always be kept in mind by the reader. They do
not release him from the responsibility of taking Kierkegaard
seriously for his wider import, but they do place upon him
the added duty of making his own transcription of the Kierkegaardian message, of testing it according to the common hu-

man canons of evidence and proof, and of supplementing it by truths which Kierkegaard himself overlooked or deliberately kept in the shadow.

The Testimony of The Journals

Kierkegaard's *Journals* began in 1834, the twenty-first year of his life and the year in which he published his first newspaper article. But whereas he consigned to the *vita ante acta* all the published pieces appearing previously to *Either/Or*, the personal notes constituted, from the beginning, an integral and indispensable part of his authorship. They were not themselves intended for print during his lifetime, but were destined to exert their wider influence in another time and situation. Written both *ad se ipsum* and as a report to readers yet unborn, these jottings strove after honesty, thoroughness and depth, in their presentation of a man's most intimate observations and confessions. From these pages of recollections, work sheets, plans, and prayers can be gathered some notion of the character of their author. No better introduction to the mind of Kierkegaard can be found than the entries in the early journals. We of a later generation have been made his confidant, at least in a dialectical way, where Kierkegaard could not bring himself to confide in his contemporaries (in his own words, "to milk himself" in public).

In a mock serious entry, "given in our study at six o'clock in the evening" of July 13, 1837, Kierkegaard reviewed the first few years' harvest, with the intention of explaining his attitude and improving the quality of his secret efforts.[8] Allowance had to be made for the eventual publication of the notes, a consideration which made him wary of consigning thoughts to paper in their casual and undeveloped state. The ideal of literary perfection was always before him, with its sometimes falsifying effect upon his intimate jottings. Moreover, he could never overcome an innate shyness or modesty of spirit, which prevented him from setting down the very phrases which he used inwardly in religious matters, until their time of spiritual use was over. But his resolution to forget all alien eyes was prompted by a need for practice behind the scenes, for extracurricular activity which would give him as much fluency in writing as in speech. To capture a thought in the warm freshness of mood—"with the umbilical cord still attached"—and to have at his disposal fugitive ideas and elusive overtones: these were the rich rewards to be gained by keeping a journal, even apart from the opportunity to get his due from posterity.

Kierkegaard's basic themes in the early notebooks are few, but they are of great importance for understanding the books published during his lifetime. His notes introduce us at once into the intellectual climate produced by a combination of Hegelian philosophy, Romantic estheticism and the Danish Lutheran Establishment. He groups his reflections around certain striking images and key notions, which recur throughout these pages and soon overflow into the published books. Outstanding among these symbols is that of the Archimedean point, suggested in the opening pages of the journal and constantly employed thereafter in a polemical way. Like Descartes, Kierkegaard was fascinated by the story of Archimedes' longing for a leverage point, whereby to move the world: it hinted at his own search for a stable foundation for a life-view.[9] This unshakeable support was to be found neither in the physical world of the scientists nor in the logical constructions of the philosophers. If there were to be a genuine revolution in human thought, it could not come about merely through a change of standpoints *within* this world of created things and human conceptions. Such shifts were confined within some limited and purely theoretical sphere, whereas Kierkegaard sought an insight into finiteness as a whole and a real, absolute motive for determining his human freedom in a practical way.

It is not worth pretending that a man can fall in love with nature and the present social order, as though Hegel's dialectic had healed the breach between what is and what ought to be, between appearance and the elusive thing-in-itself. It did not take Schelling's Berlin lectures to teach this lesson to Kierkegaard. Long before he listened to Schelling's attack on Hegelian immanentism, the lonely, inquiring Dane had concluded that the Archimedean point, wherever it might finally lie, surely was not to be found within this world of space and time or its ideal laws. This negative conviction set him off uncompromisingly from the nineteenth-century bourgeois mind, as he observed it in his own land. This mentality is characterized spiritually by its stifling comfortableness, arising from an exalted compromise with "things as they are," as being a true expression of an eternal ordering. No more harrowing revenge upon Hegel's sublimely comic spirit could be devised than this suppression of man's incommensurateness with his environment. Even temperamentally, Kierkegaard could never have fitted in unprotestingly with such a compromising attitude. This is one reason why he sometimes acknowledged that his inborn dread and sense of foreboding were fortunate gifts, rather than sheer afflictions of spirit. For, they generated in him a perpetual uneasiness in the presence of any given arrangement or accepted explanation. Locke and the whole empirical school were content with a psychological explanation of this feeling of uneasiness, in terms of a secular morality and esthetic, centering about finite objectives yet to be attained. Even Karl Marx remained sufficiently under the spell of the dialectic to interpret "self-alienation" as a moment in the movement of society towards its final, this-worldly state of satisfaction.

No such easy solutions were acceptable to the young

Kierkegaard, although he was strongly attracted to another contemporary myth of man's reconciliation with the world. By reason of his melancholy but active imagination and his irony, he felt a kinship with the Romantic poets, novelists, and philosophers then flourishing in Germany.[10] The early pages of his journals are studded with references to his readings in, and criticism of, Romantic literature. Especially during the period from 1835 until the renewed closeness with his father in 1838, Kierkegaard was deeply influenced by Novalis, Hoffmann, and the Schlegels. In them, he perceived a strong counteractive force which might save the age from becoming completely Hegelian. Their emphasis upon all that is strange, mysterious, uncharted, and nonconceptual in human experience seemed to open a gaping breach in the side of the impregnable System, and to make room for values which found no place in that imposing structure. Above all, Kierkegaard found congenial the Romantic notion of *Lebensanchauung*, a life-view which must be achieved by each individual as his inalienable task, rather than passively ingested in ready-made textbook form. Against the vaunted objectivity of dialectical philosophy, he opposed this need for subjective activity and personal assimilation and transformation of experience under leading principles, which can stand the test of life's demands. Kierkegaard was never a friend to chaotic, uninterpreted experience and unshaven passion. For a while, he believed that the Romantic outlook might enable him to master the empirical order, without giving way to formalism and arbitrary theoretical constructions.

As it turned out, his enthusiastic allegiance to this school did not survive the reconciliation with his father. But whereas Hegel's critique of the Romantic mood (in his *Phenomenology of Spirit*) has become a philosophical classic, little attention has been paid to Kierkegaard's own searching revaluation. This is due partly to the disguised form in which it is presented in the esthetic works, and partly to the fact that his formal treatment of the problem in his earliest writings (*From the Papers of One Still Living* and *On the Concept of Irony*) has often been overlooked. Professor Hirsch has removed the last excuse for such neglect, by pointing out clearly and at considerable length the relevance of these books and the corresponding sections in the journals of that period.[11] Hirsch's findings show that Kierkegaard's dissatisfaction arose, when he tried to relate the Romantic views to his own religious development.

While Schlegel's *Lucinde*, for instance, lent some support to his own growing concern with inwardness and personal reality, it remained completely within a natural context that was stranger to sin and repentance. These latter experiences were most decisive for Kierkegaard's own character. He belongs in the ranks of the twice-born, for whom a moment of repentance and renunciation is essential for the attainment of personal maturity. When this factor is omitted, the final settlement is only an illusory one, based on a false notion of man's position in the real world. Inevitably, the Romantics tended to overrate man's creative power and, in doing so, disregarded the true conditions of human existence. Their main weapon of irony was wielded successfully against Hegel, reducing his ponderous necessities to thin air, before the agile attack of the ironizing human spirit. But precisely this sense of omnipotence, of destroying and creating anew everything on the horizon of being, tricked the Romantic thinkers into a fantastic world wherein God and the human self are fused and disappear in their distinctive reality.

In the *Journals*, Kierkegaard admitted this danger of losing his selfhood and his awareness of adoring distance before God. Sometimes, while contemplating nature in a Romantic mood, he seemed to lose his selfhood in an all-dissolving pantheistic reverie. Then, he could persuade himself, at least in imagination, that he had the divine power of fashioning the world to his own liking and of bearing on his shoulders the entire burden of human life and sorrow.[12] Such dreams of divinity were shipwrecked, however, upon the bleak, unyielding shoals of his sin, anxiety, and need for forgiveness. Romantic imagination—that fashioning hand within the mind, as Gerard Manley Hopkins called it—must submit to the common prudential discipline exercised by a man over all his powers, in the interest of the whole personality. This personality reveals its finiteness and contingency in a mood of unquiet foreboding, which Kierkegaard now interpreted as a kind of homesickness of earthly life for something higher than the world. Home, he was coming to learn, was not to be found by establishing imaginative relations between himself and his natural environment. During his trip to his father's native province of Jutland in 1840, the analogy between paternal and divine love was borne in upon his soul with the assurance that man's true home, his true Archimedean point, can be nothing other than belief in God's fatherly love for us.[13] And, in later years, he spoke of a man's oratory, where he can pray to God in secret and in silence, as the only fit symbol of the foothold that can move not only mountains but the world itself.

Like Blaise Pascal, whom he resembled both as a man and as a writer, Kierkegaard pondered a good deal upon the grandeur and misery of man. Of the grandeur he was not unaware, nor of his own full share of talents. The problem was how best to understand and assure human dignity, how to treat finite gifts as gifts which might be relied upon. Some of the most moving notes of his trip to Gilleleie (1835) treat of the foundations of true pride, hope, and humility, as they are suggested to an individual who has forsaken the props of Minerva and Parnassus for nature itself. Aided during the period of his greatest despair and dissipation by a critical reading of Fichte's famous *Vocation of Man*, Kierkegaard refused to submerge his spirit in the herd or to receive his imperative in an external way. Yet the reigning poets and philosophers could not bring his mind to safe anchorage, either in the sea of pleasure and ironic imagination or in the snug harbor of Systematic understanding. Logic and poetry have their rights, but only when they can be integrated within a total human life, having its deepest roots plunged far into the soil of the divine. Kierkegaard testified that his own ills and those of his age were of a moral, even more than an intellectual, nature. He was seeking not a truth which could be contemplated disinterestedly and as an external, achieved result, but rather one for which he must live and die. The truth he sought after was "a truth which is true *for me*," one which demanded sacrifice and personal response.[14] Human dignity lay in the direction of a life lived for the sake of an ideal that would arouse a man to free, responsible action. For Kierkegaard, this meant a life spent in the service of, and personal approach to, God.

It also meant inescapable conflict with the established forces and institutions of his day. Most men of the time were content with losing themselves in a maze of scientific or practical details, while their wider destinies were determined impersonally and *en masse*. Even the so-called enlightened minds were powerless to stand forth as genuine individuals, having command over their own temporal careers. Romanticism beguiled one into a state of imaginative ecstasy and grandeur, which was only a prelude to disillusionment, ennui, and despair. Hegelianism required a man not only to drink deep of the cup of wisdom but also, in Kierkegaard's phrase, to fall bodily into it. The individual could do no more than acquiesce before the necessities and accomplished results of history—and then proceed to conduct his private affairs according to quite other categories. The corrective should have been provided

by religion, but in its organized form it also was found wanting by Kierkegaard. His early criticism of the church in Denmark was mild in comparison with the final pitch of his polemic, as his own vocation gradually revealed itself to him in
its full rigor. Nevertheless, several fundamental lines of attack
were laid down during the youthful years of his alienation
from God and his initial, groping efforts to characterize religion, holy and undefiled.

In the journal entries of 1835 and 1836, distantly objective
references are made to "the Christians," as though to a foreign
breed being subjected to scientific scrutiny. Martensen and
the rationalistic theologians are castigated for their hodge-
podge attempt to restate Christian dogma in Systematic Hegelian language. Actually, the bastard result strikes Kierkegaard
as a scandal both to philosophy and Christianity. The former
is made to serve a function beyond its capacity, whereas revelation proves acceptable only at those points where it can
be justified by reason. Consequently, the Christian tradition
has been subjected to a twofold volatilization: by poetic
imagination and by dialectical reason. In the wake of the fashionable craze to "go farther" than the last generation, the
theologians have even submitted sacred dogma to the process
of *Aufhebung*, or the resolution of former stages in a new
synthesis. Factors in Christian belief like faith itself, incarnation, tradition, and inspiration, have been divorced from the
particular, historical facts which gave them distinctive content.[15] A watered-down, generalized explanation of these
truths has been offered, which fits well into the scheme of the
System—but with the slight disadvantage of having emascu-
lated Christianity beyond recognition. No vigorous spiritual
life is possible, unless the shadow of pantheism is removed,
along with every tendency to participate in the religious life
only through the medium of imagination and outward pro-
fession.

Before the publication of his esthetic works, Kierkegaard had already set out along the dangerous road of return to God: conversion of self to God in the most literal sense. Although recognizing the value of the Mohammedan and other forms of religion, he found the supreme expression of the religious way of life in Christianity. Applying the paleo-pragmatic criterion of truth as that which makes a difference in one's life, Kierkegaard believed that Christianity embodies the highest religious truth and inward edification. The union of a man with God and of a man with his fellows is most intensely realized in Christianity, for here the consciousness of such a union is heightened, without dissolving one's own personality in pantheistic ecstasy. Through other religious approaches, the truth speaks indirectly; Christ speaks in his own person, as He who is the Truth. Yet, the latter-day Christians are losing sight of the uniqueness and heterogeneity of this revelation, in their eagerness to trim their theological sails to the most up-to-date winds of philosophical doctrine. In this predicament, Kierkegaard felt need of a voice so penetrating, terrifying, arousing, and flexible, that it would make the self-styled Christian world tremble in sympathy as well as in anger, as he proclaimed anew the consciousness of sin and the paradoxical nature of Christian faith.

No one of the great rebels of the nineteenth century was lonelier and more at odds with his age than Søren Kierkegaard. When one thinks of him, one sees some justification for Crane Brinton's paradoxical thesis that a Nietzsche gave voice to the secret thoughts and tendencies of his time, in a conformist way that belied the belligerency and scorn of his customary mode of address. Kierkegaard's scalpel cut much deeper than Nietzsche's hammer into the fleshy heart of the era. That to continue on his course meant a life of ceaseless strife, was another presentiment weighing upon the mind of this "autumnal man," even in the years preceding his clash with *The*

Corsair and with the Established Church. Careful allowance
was made by Kierkegaard for the part which his natural pre-
dilection for dispute (his "fundamentally polemical nature")
played in setting him against the current. Apart from a bad
disputatiousness, he was glad to recognize a justifiable use of
polemic. All great historical figures—men who fill their age
rather than merely move with the times—must make their
first step one of opposition. In real life, it does not hold true
that something new simply emerges as a necessary consequence of a previous condition.[16] This negative conviction
belongs in common to Kierkegaard, Lenin, and all practical
revolutionists, in contrast to one side of Hegel and Karl Marx.
But what really matters is the nature of the positive source
of reconstruction, and here Kierkegaard parts company with
those who wish to build a revolution on something less radical than a change in a man's inward condition and his relation
to God.

Kierkegaard confessed that his attacks were directed at the
masses, not to arouse them to do anything as a crowd but
rather to single men out, one by one, as individuals. Once
more, his beloved model was Socrates, a thinker who strove
singleheartedly to make people think for themselves, use independent judgment and act with deliberate choice. This
must be kept in mind, especially when the assault upon the
Hegelian System is examined. Its target is not so much Hegel
as the epigoni who set the tone of Danish culture; not so
much theoretical technicalities as the broad practical results
of the Hegelian outlook, as reflected in a people's moral
and religious life. In this sense, Kierkegaard is well classed
along with Pascal, Nietzsche, and Dostoevsky, as belonging
in the great tradition of European moralists. He saw that it
is better to wound deeply, and keep the wound healthily
open, than let an area of rottenness fester in secret. Not with-

out cause did he refer to himself metaphorically as a stormy petrel and a man-of-war, put out far on the deep. If he were not willing to take the risk of openly proclaiming and living by his truly unseasonable thoughts, he knew that his voice would have no right to be heard and would carry with it neither conviction nor existential truth.

One notable feature of Kierkegaard's early offensive is the attention paid to words and their significance. Among the symptoms of nineteenth-century Europe's spiritual bankruptcy is a new confusion of tongues or, rather, a confusion within language itself. Kierkegaard depicts the situation in terms suggestive of semantic anarchy, a rebellion of words against the common meanings assigned to them by men. This revenge of words upon their former masters is attributed to the frenzied endeavor of people to "go beyond" what has already been enunciated. In an age of reflection, a premium is placed upon mediating every absolute, canceling off every thesis by its antithesis. No word can be used in a forthright way to signify an irrevocable decision, since every choice is subject to qualification and limitation. The upshot, as observed by Kierkegaard, is the emptying of all definite meaning and permanence out of words. One fashionable thinker strives to outdo another in attaching novel meanings to terms, in order to achieve a modish eclecticism and temporary domination over the crowd of followers.

Ordinary people either are swept along by each successive wave of opinion or withdraw suspiciously and skeptically from all intellectual pursuits. They content themselves with using a few pregnant words, a few pithy phrases, which at least achieve economy, stability, and some degree of common understanding. Kierkegaard was quite in sympathy with this everyday attitude, to the extent that it distrusted the long-windedness, the esotericism, and the pretentious twaddle which were passing for sound coin in the lecture hall, in the pulpit, and in the press. He was sensitive to a need for resolute and gifted men, who will win back "the lost power and meaning of words." [17] His own work was largely directed toward recovering the true sense of the basic words, expressive of the human situation. This task of reading anew the documents of human existence was specially urgent in the case of traditional Christian terminology. Kierkegaard likened the latter to a magic castle, containing many beautiful princes and princesses now slumbering, but needing only to be awakened and invited to step forth again in their pristine splendor. First, however, the spell cast over Christian dogmatic concepts and the other human treasures has to be broken, and broken by a cunning equal to that which reduced them to the state of confusion and impotence. This strategy of loyal deceit was followed by Kierkegaard first of all in a series of pseudonymous writings, the esthetic works. These works are to be examined in the two following chapters.

The early *Journals* help to prepare the reader for what is to come in Kierkegaard's books. It may be expected that they will come to grips with the accepted modes of thinking in social, philosophical, and religious matters. Kierkegaard combines broad sympathy and insight into the ways of man, with independence of judgment and a crafty sort of criticism. His poetic nature enables him to visualize the kind of universe which appeals to the esthetic mind; his love of dialectics draws him close to Hegelianism. But these attractions are counterbalanced and overbalanced by his religious seriousness. Consequently, human existence is not for him a brilliant play of images and a refined pursuit of pleasure; nor is it a self-identification with the thought of the absolute. The fact is, however, that Kierkegaard's own contemporaries had given their allegiance to estheticism and idealism, even to the point of endangering the uniqueness and supernatural character of Christianity. Hence his first step is, necessarily, a polemical one, directed against the prevailing attitudes in life and philosophy. The stake is not merely a vindication of Kierkegaard's theory about existence but also a justification of his own way of existing and its foundation in a quest of religiousness.

Chapter Two

The Spheres of Existence and the Romantic Outlook

THE first phase of Kierkegaard's serious authorship comprises a group of books which appeared in rapid succession during the years 1843 to 1845, and to which he gave the common designation of "esthetic works." [1] That they were composed so closely together and with such intensity, is due mainly to the part which some of them played in the events following on his broken engagement with Regine Olsen. There was equal pressure exerted upon him, however, by his desire to speak his mind to his contemporaries concerning some disputed issues. He had in distant view his disturbing thoughts about the meaning of Christian faith and living, along with the need of establishing a contrast between Christianity and Hegelian philosophy. More immediately, he felt called upon to deal with Romanticism, as a widespread popular mood and ruling literary fashion. The philosophical aspects of his treatment of Romanticism reveal important traits of his own personality and standpoint.

There are two questions which immediately confront the reader of the esthetic works: what is one to make of the use of pseudonyms, and what is the general import of the doctrine of the three stages of life? These questions will be considered in the first two sections of the present chapter. In addition, something must be said more especially about the first of these

stages on life's way, the esthetic mode of existence. Kierkegaard's treatment of esthetic existence contains his most sustained critique of Romanticism.

I. THE USE OF PSEUDONYMS

Various problems arise in the interpretation of philosophical texts. The more common ones concern the authentic reading of a manuscript and the exact sense of passages which are
sufficiently established but require to be read in their context. Occasionally, however, there are other levels of meaning which must be determined. Some of the Platonic dialogues and Hume's *Dialogues concerning Natural Religion*
present us with the difficulty of deciding which of the inter-
locutors comes closest to expressing the author's own position. In the case of the last-named work, it is likely that Hume
allowed much more weight in public print to the arguments
of orthodoxy than he admitted in private meditation and correspondence. Moses Maimonides' *Guide for the Perplexed*
and Spinoza's *Theologico-Political Treatise* are good examples of works which have an obvious and coherent meaning, and yet which also have an esoteric message accessible
only to those who are properly prepared beforehand by the
use of other sources. Nietzsche comes closest, in recent times,
to the situation presented by Kierkegaard. Nietzsche often
boasted of being a philosopher with many masks, just as
Kierkegaard refers to himself as a *Janus bifrons*.[2] One can
never be sure, at the moment, whether the German philosopher is merely giving a special viewpoint free rein to advocate its case as strongly as possible or whether he is speaking
his own integral mind on a subject. In this trait of cultivated
ambiguity, he proves himself to be a true descendant of the
Romantics.

An analogous situation confronts us in the case of Kierkegaard's esthetic works. Kierkegaard never steps forward *in propria persona* to claim any of the opinions as his own. They are not presented anonymously, since his authorship was common knowledge (and was filed with the government censor) long before his formal acknowledgment in the *Postscript*. But he does attribute the books to pseudonymous "authors" and "editors," and peoples the esthetic pages with a whole company of personages, who give *their* opinions on a variety of topics. Furthermore, in his *Journals*, he quotes and refers to these pseudonyms quite objectively, and warns readers against attributing to himself any statement found in the esthetic writings. What accounts for this tortuous device, and in what predicament does it leave the careful student?

Kierkegaardian scholars have outdone themselves in the cleverness of their explanations and justifications of this procedure, but none has surpassed Kierkegaard himself in this respect. Entry after entry in the *Journals* is consecrated to this problem, which continued to bother him almost as much as his behavior in regard to his one-time fiancée. In addition, he deals with it formally in two of his later books, the *Postscript* and *The Point of View*.[3] It would seem that at first he had resort to pseudonyms out of a natural inclination, and that only later on did reflection reveal to him the deeper significance and purpose of this practice. Sorting through the many references to his employment of pseudonyms, Kierkegaard's reasons can be discussed under three main headings: personal motives, the ends of truth, and religious considerations. It was only gradually and, as he was convinced, under the guidance of Providence that he himself was able to distinguish between these different phases of the problem and its solution.

Personal Motives

Kierkegaard confessed that, from his earliest years, he took childlike delight in mystifying people, in setting them wondering and puzzling about remarks he might let drop. Where he could express himself in less straightforward fashion, without doing injury to the truth or to a serious duty to others, he was prompted to take the path of indirection. He liked to construct intellectual Chinese puzzles, having one compartment cleverly concealed within another.[4] In this penchant for raising dust for its own sake, he detected a feeling of inferiority and a need to compensate for it, by convincing himself of his ability to bemuse less agile minds. Although he brought this motive out into the open and sought to control it, Kierkegaard never succeeded completely in outgrowing or disciplining this secretive and obfuscating tendency. Many passages in the esthetic works and even in his religious discourses simply overwhelm one, with their straining after sheer virtuosity in the statement of difficulties and nuances. At times, this love of mystification defeats the primary aim of communicating truth, because it destroys the reader's confidence and produces an obscurity not dispelled by other means.

On a far different footing is another personal reason advanced by Kierkegaard for using pseudonyms in three of his esthetic writings: *Either/Or, Repetition,* and *Fear and Trembling.* These books were his means of communicating with Regine Olsen after their separation, while Kierkegaard still hoped to become reconciled with her. He clothed his intimate utterances in the guise of poetic experiments, myths, lyric outpourings, biblical exegesis, literary criticism, and memoirs. In these Romantic ways, he hoped to speak to her significantly, without betraying her confidence to the casual reader. He succeeded well in concealing the most immediate personal significance of these publications, by the use of such literary devices. To the extent that these biographical overtones are essential to an understanding of his mind, however, Kierkegaard was under obligation to supply a key for readers of later times. This he did in his *Journals.* After Regine's commitment to another man, this consideration ceased to move Kierkegaard. But other reasons for retaining the pseudonymous medium assumed increasing importance for him, although they had never been wholly absent, even in the earliest esthetic volumes.

Toward the Discovery and Communication of Truth

Due weight has not always been accorded to Kierkegaard's repeated assertion that the esthetic works constituted his own fundamental education and progress toward truth. In writing them, he seems at times to have had his own development more in mind than the profit which his readers might be expected to draw from them. Sometimes the cloudiness of thought and crabbedness of expression are due more to his own hesitant searching for fact than to any attempt at mystification or concealment. Although he insisted that his own final standpoint was always higher than that represented in the esthetic books, still they faithfully mirror his own previous attempts to wrestle with the problems under discussion. While it would be foolish to identify all of the opinions as his own or to accuse him of living in the manner described and praised by some of his pseudonyms, yet it is important to bear in mind that he was intellectually and imaginatively concerned about all the viewpoints which found pseudonymous champions in his books.

Natural endowment, parental upbringing and cultural formation seem to have conspired to fill Kierkegaard's mind with ideal conceptions of various and conflicting ways of life. His own vivid imagination was sharpened, under his father's encouraging eye, to the point where he could develop the slightest hint of an attitude into a full-bodied possibility for an outlook on life. Contact with Novalis' conception of truth as a polar clash between such alternatives, gave him a philosophical basis for working out standpoints to their extreme, antagonistic consequences. The pseudonymous authors and personages are individualized spokesmen for these different solutions to life's problems. His poetic temperament led Kierkegaard to express these views in a concrete, psychological way, rather than in the form of an abstract set of theses and countertheses. This gave him a free hand both in displaying his own sympathy with various types of men and in developing their leading convictions with the utmost consistency and thoroughness. As he phrased it in his *Journals*, this medium of the incognito was his very element, in which he could move about with plenty of elbowroom and a minimum of doctrinal embarrassment.

This observation should caution us against taking literally, as expressing Kierkegaard's own position, every dictum found in the esthetic books. Yet they would be only idle exercises of imagination, were they in no way connected with his own convictions. Sometimes, he evades responsibility too easily, on the ground that the views are proper to the pseudonym in question and his own peculiar character. Some of the published pages contain excerpts transcribed with scarcely a verbal change from intimate, confessional notes in the *Journals*. Kierkegaard does admit his responsibility at least for making these various viewpoints audible: he is not only the secretary but also the author of the pseudonymous "authors." [*] As their author, who yet maintains a certain poetic distance from his creations, he has the right to ask us not to identify any of their statements with his own definitive position. But readers, in turn, have the right to ask him to provide them with some canon for determining his own stand, presuming his purpose to be a serious one. To what extent can any one of the pseudonyms be said to approach the view of Kierkegaard himself? At the time of the composition of the esthetic works, he did not consider himself under any obligation to supply an answer to this question. He pointed out that all these works were written under the sign of "either/or," implying that the decision about the truth is a personal matter, left for each individual reader.

This reply is based on the theory of the indirect communication of truth which he held at that time. In creating pseudonyms, he was seeking to revive the Socratic sense of dialectic, by means of a popular Romantic device. Out of a free clash of sciences—a head-on collision between opposing ways of life—he hoped to induce people to find for themselves some leading principles and clues to the *philosophia secunda* he was then seeking. His refusal to enter the arena with an unmistakable announcement of the truth was not due to any diabolical delight in leaving the issue in suspense. Rather, it was an indirect protest against the Hegelian pretensions to serve up all truth in an objective, cut-and-dried way. He contended strongly that truth is no finished product, which can be handed over the counter of philosophy, quite impersonally and effortlessly. If no conclusions are provided in a book which seriously engages attention, then the reader is forced to argue the issues through to a conclusion of his own finding. Because the pseudonyms can argue their case in a dramatic, engaging way, they lure the reader onwards, until he is forced to judge for himself between them and perhaps even beyond the alternatives they present. Hence Kierkegaard looked upon these books as so many essays in Socratic deceit.[6] Their purpose is to make us discover, first, that truth is a matter of personal insight and assimilation, and then that the full content of truth escapes the range of esthetic minds.

Especially for people who have been trained in a school tradition of philosophy, which lays much stress upon straightforward and comprehensive statement of positions in manual form, it is advantageous to read some of these esthetic books. They serve to remind us that the habit of wisdom is a hard-won perfection and in no way identical with the ability to state and defend a scholastic thesis, whether of Hegelian or Thomist origin.[7] On the other hand, no generalization of the method of pseudonymous communication ought to be made. Kierkegaard himself came to realize, in later years, that it is a human, and even a religious, duty to witness to the truth in as direct and unequivocal a way as possible. This can be done, without denial of the need for personal effort in gaining an insight. Indeed, a motive for such an effort is more strongly provided by a simple but profound sentence in Aristotle or Spinoza than by a good deal of convoluted reasoning on the part of Kierkegaard's pseudonyms. The intellectual response of the independent reader is often diminished, when the truth is clothed in imaginative form or when attention is directed overtly to the need for making a personal evaluation. Kierkegaard's pseudonymous method is more a therapeutic means than a standard procedure to be followed by the philosopher. It is adapted to his own historical situation and to the corrective moral aims in which he was primarily interested.

The Religious Purpose

In the light of his profound religious experience of 1848, Kierkegaard reinterpreted his esthetic writings in retrospect. The results of his reflection are set down in his most intimate book, *The Point of View*, which stresses the religious interest behind the entire esthetic enterprise. In proportion as he gained a fuller appreciation of the religious character of his vocation as a writer, he also came to see that even the pseudonymous books bore a relation to the problem of becoming a Christian. Yet this relation was not evident to the first eager readers of "The Seducer's Diary." They could not understand why a professedly religious writer should introduce himself by a kind of duplicity—the use of the pseudonyms—or why he should use the esthetic genre to attain a religious goal. Kierkegaard's explanations on this point are so many elaborations upon a remark which he once passed on Novalis' use of poetic means: most men can relate themselves to the good and the true only through the imagination. Their view of the world is mediated *de facto* by the imagination or esthetic power, and their natural aspirations toward God are fashioned along imaginative lines. Kierkegaard regarded the Romantic soul as the type of the naturally religious mind, which is attracted to God through concrete symbols, myths, and other poetic representations. Hence anyone who wishes to discuss the religious problem with such a mind, must make the first contact on the level of imagination, through the portrayal of dramatic personalities embodying different positions.

Kierkegaard went on to maintain that the Christians of our day have only an esthetic grasp upon the meaning of Christianity.[8] They accept it along with the other factors in their folkways, but it never becomes for them anything more than a customary way of acting and meeting crucial events, like birth and marriage and death. All the thoughts that really count, the important free decisions, the attitudes which shape and build a man through his deliberate consent and self-formation, are taken from outside the Christian, or even the religious, sphere. This meant for Kierkegaard that Christian religiousness has been transformed into a kind of automatic dreaming, and that people's lives are being shaped by esthetic rather than religious categories. But so omnipresent and resilient is the illusion concerning Christendom, that it cannot be dispelled by frontal attack or blunt denunciation. Hence Kierkegaard thought that indirect tactics were called for, even on religious grounds.

People being what they are, it is best to assume the esthetic standpoint and develop its assumptions and consequences as cleverly and entertainingly as possible, through the pseudonymous characters and their worlds. Having won a hearing, the full import of living according to the rule of imagination can then be pressed home, with an honesty and force seldom allowed in direct discussions. Then, the contrast between this outlook and an ethico-religious one can perhaps be grasped by the readers themselves. Once their interest and reflection are aroused, they can decide for themselves at least that they are *not* patterning their conduct according to genuinely religious standards. Kierkegaard did not expect more from a reading of the esthetic books than this negative sort of self-knowledge and a consequent clarification of the choice which men face.

Christianity is secretly weakened from within, when allegiance to it is founded only on ingrained habit, without a mature appraisal of the alternatives. In our day there is a vast existential compass of life based upon other principles. Kierkegaard provides in his esthetic works a *mappa mundi* for those who wish to know where they stand and what issues really confront them. This is his final justification for his descent into Avernus, a motive which meets the hypercritical attitudes inculcated into modern men, with regard to questions of lesser moment than the individual's salvation. But it must be remembered that this religious reason behind the use of the pseudonyms was neither dominant nor incisive, when the esthetic project was started.

2. THE SPHERES OF EXISTENCE

That there are three stages on life's way—the esthetic, the ethical, and the religious—is Kierkegaard's most influential doctrine, the one contribution with which he is usually credited by general histories of philosophy.[9] It is clearly enunciated in his last purely esthetic work, the *Stages*, is analyzed and refined still further in the *Postscript*, and serves as a handy trichotomy during the heat of battle which filled his last years. It is his way of stating the basic choices which confront

the concrete individual, in his search for mature self-posses-
sion. They are the existential determinants of human character, the general modes of living which serve as rival patterns
and principles. Around this three-fold division, Kierkegaard
organizes the entire argument which runs through the esthetic
works. His later philosophical and religious studies suppose
that this original analysis of central human motives is a sound
one, which can be applied even outside the esthetic context.

Despite his readings in Schleiermacher about life's choices
and his careful study of the Hegelian dialectic of the various
types of minds, Kierkegaard did not take his triple division
ready-made from such sources. Rather, it seems to have been
forced upon him by reflection upon his own experience. Such
an origin makes us wary of generalizing the doctrine of the
three spheres beyond certain special historical circumstances,
but it also tempers the charge of artificiality and triadic mes-
merism which is sometimes brought against it. An examination
of Kierkegaard's early papers and journals reveal that, for a
long time, he groped about in quest of the leading principles
under which he could organize his literary studies, his extensive observation of human characters, and the lessons of his
own life. At first, he applied the terms "stage" and "sphere"
indiscriminately to any field of human activity, such as political or military interests. Gradually, however, he came to reserve these terms, in their pregnant and technical sense, for
the most fundamental commitments and organizing ideals
available to men. In the first of the books which belong to his
formal authorship—*Either/Or*—he states the alternative as one
between the esthetic and the ethical orders. Significantly
enough, no decision is reached in this book, which suggests
that the situation may require the introduction of still another
possibility, a religious one, as indicated by the sermon with
which the book concludes. Regarded schematically, the next

two books in the esthetic series subject both the *either* of esthetics and the *or* of ethics to a fresh analysis. *Repetition* criticizes the *esthetic* life anew, whereas *Fear and Trembling* insists that the *ethical* standpoint is not sufficient to comprehend the realities of religious faith. Thus the way is paved for separate treatment of the *religious* sphere in the *Stages* and the *Postscript*, as well as in the religious works proper. There is a gradual development of this theory of the three spheres of existence, rather than an a priori deduction.

There are still other indications that this schema is regarded by Kierkegaard more as a supple tool for the intepretation of experience than as a rigid and absolute formula. He was always convinced that the distance between spheres of existence is bridged, not by any gradual merging or by a necessary transformation of one into another, but only by a "leap" or free decision on the part of the individual. He recognized certain states of soul, nevertheless, which indicate that a person has plumbed one of the inferior stages to its depths, and has reached the extreme limit of that mode of life—what Karl Jaspers calls a limit-situation. A cynical and despairing irony marks the man who has lived an esthetic life through to its bitter end, and is consequently placed at the borderline, where a leap into the ethical sphere is possible. At first, Kierkegaard regarded humor as the proper attitude of the Christian in regard to the things of time, a kind of protective covering or incognito, useful in dealing with worldly fortunes and with individuals who do not see the world through the eyes of faith. But by 1845, he felt that humor is not so much a religious as an ethical passion—indeed, that it signifies that one has reached the borderline of ethical life and is faced with the choice of becoming religious in a plenary way or of thwarting the natural inclination of ethical existence to surmount itself.[10] During this same year, which marked the composition of the *Postscript*, the distinctive nature of Christianity was so strongly impressed upon him that he ceased to speak of the religious sphere in an unqualified way, and thereafter distinguished sharply between all natural modes of the religious and the unique Christian religious spirit. This distinction between "religiousness A" and "religiousness B" is equivalent to designating four stages in the dialectic of life. The immanent modes of religious existence do not exhaust or naturally blend with the transcendent kind of religiousness, which comes only with the gift of Christian faith.

Attention has been called to a misconception to which the term "stage" can give rise.[11] It may be thought that an individual is required to begin with the esthetic rung of the ladder of life and then mount up, in succession, to the ethical and religious rungs. But Kierkegaard did not intend this schema to be understood according to any temporal order, nor did he mean that one way of life is left completely behind, as one would leave behind the lower steps of a ladder. In this respect, the term "sphere of existence" is less misleading, since spheres may well be treated as simultaneously present and as overlapping. Once this erroneous interpretation is pointed out, however, the appropriateness of the term "stage" must also be recognized. Since Kierkegaard holds that everyone in Christendom is in some degree infected by the esthetic outlook, the process of self-criticism and self-edification must begin with a reflection upon this ubiquitous esthetic attitude. Furthermore, the different stages are distinguished from each other, and solicit our allegiance as rival viewpoints, precisely in so far as each makes an *absolute* claim upon our life. We may indeed *consider* these conflicting modes of existence together, but it is impossible to *live* them together. In the order of choice and existence, there is no straddling and no compromise between these mutually exclusive outlooks. From this standpoint, one does leave the other stages behind in consenting to some particular mode of existence, although there is no special order which must be preserved in making the transition or in consolidating one's original position.

But there is a further problem, for which Kierkegaard provided no satisfactory answer either in the esthetic works themselves or in his later remarks about the spheres of existence. Granted that there is a mounting hierarchy of existential fullness, passing from the esthetic through the ethical to the religious life, what remains of the lower stage after a man has chosen a higher or the highest? Kierkegaard admits a decisive difference between a particular stage, considered as advancing a claim to autonomy, and this same stage considered after this element of absoluteness has been removed by a definitive choice in favor of some other sphere. The "dethroned" sphere of existence does not simply disappear, for there are esthetic and ethical needs and powers in every man which cannot be eradicated. But Kierkegaard is unwilling to make the flat statement that all lower values, once they are recognized to be genuine and yet inferior, can be incorporated on the higher level and made to serve the higher ends. He is not reluctant, indeed, to admit that an ethical sort of existence can appropriate esthetic values or that the entire content of the ethical sphere can be taken over by the naturally religious man. His real difficulty centers about the relation between *esthetic* and *religious*, especially Christian, existence.

His own experience, rather than any theoretical requirements, convinced Kierkegaard that man's real predicament is to be placed between a thoroughly esthetic way of living and a thoroughly religious one. No permanent footing can be maintained on a purely ethical basis, and in this respect Kierkegaard stands opposed to all efforts to make morality self-sufficient. Ethical principles are intrinsically ordained to the religious outlook, and a secular morality is either unaware of its religious significance or only an esthetic discourse

· 46 ·

about being moral. The genuine alternatives are still the world and the cloister, the esthetic and the religious kinds of existing. Recollecting his own bout of playing the Romantic genius and also the tremendous upheaval involved in his return to faith, Kierkegaard was inclined to state the contrast as being one between "perdition and salvation"—between which there can be no compromise or reconciliation.[12]

On the other hand, he was convinced at times that esthetic values are redeemable, once the claim to absoluteness has been rejected. The question was not merely an academic one for him, since on the esthetic side he counted his own literary and psychological powers. These he certainly employed to good use in his religious discourses, and yet he was always troubled about whether his vocation as a writer was a religious vocation or not. Because he hesitated on this point, Kierkegaard also maintained an ambivalent attitude toward the possibility of a Christian humanism. Especially during the period of composition of the pseudonymous works, human values suffered the same fate in his eyes as did esthetic values. They are both reconcilable with the immanent form of the religious, but so great is the gap between the latter and Christian religiousness that Kierkegaard (or at least his "philosophical" pseudonym, Johannes Climacus) sometimes denied that anything from the esthetic and human order survives the leap of faith. He lacked full confidence in the power of the supernatural order to transform natural abilities and perfections, without compromising its own transcendent character.

Apart from personal reasons, Kierkegaard was probably led to stress the antithesis between the esthetic and the religious modes of existence, because of a desire to differentiate his teaching on the spheres of existence from Hegel's triadic theory of thesis, antithesis, and synthesis. Kierkegaard profited a good deal from a study of Hegel's logic, but he concluded that Hegel's identification of the structure of thought with that of being was contradicted by human experience. Hence he sought to ally the dialectical principle with the movement of concrete human choices, rather than with the supposed unfolding of the absolute *Begriff* or rational concept. The individual in his personal character and freedom, rather than the individual as the locus of universal and necessary laws, is the responsible agent in the Kierkegaardian dialectic of the modes of existing. The culmination of Hegel's dialectic is the complete self-consciousness of the absolute Notion, whereas the culmination of Kierkegaard's dialectic is the relating of the finite individual to the transcendent but loving God.

This contrast in the basic orientation of the two dialectics, the absolutist and the existential, leads to other differences on more particular points. The most important contrast is expressed by Kierkegaard in a twofold negation.[13] The three stages of life are *not* to be distinguished in an abstract way, so that the third will be the synthesis of the first two; the triple division does *not* remove the necessity of facing an ultimate "either/or." The meaning of the latter negation has already been explained, when it was pointed out that the ethical stage never achieves complete independence, and that, consequently, the individual is never relieved from making a final choice between the esthetic and the religious mode of existence. This also implies that the highest or religious sphere cannot be regarded as the mediating synthesis between the first two, the result of an *Aufhebung* of thesis and antithesis. For one thing, the Hegelian explanation of thesis and antithesis, as being opposed because of their limited and hence abstract nature, does not obtain here. As Kierkegaard views them, each sphere embodies in *concrete* form a *total* way of life. Furthermore, the passage or leap from one to the other is not due to any internal necessity and sudden transformation, generated by what Hegel liked to call "the power of negativity."

Negativity of this sort can lead our minds from one extreme proposition to an opposing one and sometimes to a resolving judgment, but this is not the same as the real commitment of an individual existent. Personal choice is made in finite, personal freedom, not in the quasi-freedom of a total system. And it involves a deliberate rejection of other ways of determining one's existence, rather than their higher reconciliation.

It is evident from his preoccupation with Hegel that Kierkegaard could not find, in his doctrine on the spheres of existence, an adequate solution to the problem of a Christian humanism and the place of esthetic factors in Christian life. His dialectic seemed to be clearly distinguishable from Hegel's, only if no traffic were allowed between the ultimate *either* and *or*. Yet when the esthetic life is no longer admitted to be absolute, there still remains the task for Christians of renewing the face of the entire earth and hence of reckoning in a positive way with humanistic values.

Finally, a comparison is required between Kierkegaard and Marx, even though these strict contemporaries had no direct historical relation. Although both subjected the Hegelian dialectic to sharp criticism, they moved far apart in their methods and results. For the father of modern Communism, it was mainly a question of righting the position of the dialectic: Hegel's thought had to be inverted and placed back on its feet, in order to secure the right order required by a materialistic outlook. This corrective would seem to Kierkegaard to be only a superficial tinkering with a System which is radically vitiated by its confusion of thinking with existing. Kierkegaard did not suggest any further manipulations in regard to the proper order between spirit and matter, original and derived activity. His proposed reform had nothing to do with the problem of putting the head and the feet where they belong, for the simple reason that a dialectical process has neither head nor feet, top nor bottom. It has no self-sufficiency or actual inevitability, no matter how it is viewed or for what ends it is employed. Instead of reshuffling the Hegelian dialectic from within, Kierkegaard quietly called attention to the fact that every sort of dialectic is a tool of the individual man, and achieves results only in his hands and through his free decisions. Any really drastic criticism must begin with the nexus between the dialectic and the free individual.

3. "THE ACOUSTICS OF THE ROMANTIC SOUL"

A discussion of Kierkegaard's estimate of the esthetic mode of existence is complicated by the fact that his treatment is itself placed within an esthetic and pseudonymous framework. Except for some retrospective notes in the *Postscript*, together with the criticism passed on esthetic life by the pseudonymous protagonist of ethical values, Judge William, most of his views on estheticism are presented through the agency of characters in the esthetic writings who themselves represent this way of life. He thought that the most effective way of presenting this attitude was to provide a sampling of typically Romantic effusions. But among all the moods cultivated by the Romantics, three seemed to Kierkegaard to voice the major chords of the esthetic sensibility: sensual immediacy, doubt, and despair. These he associated with three figures, who had fascinated the imagination both of the common people and of great artists: Don Juan, Faust, and Ahasuerus, the Wandering Jew.[14] From his student days, Kierkegaard had been closely attracted to these figures and, at one time, had proposed to write a "natural history" of the Middle Ages around them. They represent the various possibilities of life outside the religious sphere, and it is significant that they all belong to the esthetic order. Because they both had a folk origin and served as inspirations for major works of art in various mediums, they corroborated his thesis that the esthetic approach .makes a universal appeal to men of different interests and talents. By grouping his reflections upon esthetic existence around these personages, we can retain something of the concrete richness of Kierkegaard's investigations, without losing sight of the dialectical ends which he always kept in mind.

Don Juan: Sensual Immediacy

Following in. the Romantic tradition, Kierkegaard saw in Mozart's *Don Giovanni* the supreme artistic expression of the esthetic ideal, in all its strength and weakness. The pages which he devotes to the music and libretto of this opera are among the finest passages in musical criticism. What Nietzsche was to do for Wagner in the sunny days of their friendship, was done by Kierkegaard for Mozart with sustained brilliance and in a generous spirit of gratitude which he never repudiated. He regarded Mozart's music as the best example of that intimate co-operation of refined sensibility and concrete intelligence, which the esthetic life in its sounder aspect tends to promote. His comments are a happy combination of detailed objective analysis and broad interpretation; they neither use the occasion as a mere sounding board for his own pet theories nor bog down in the trivialities of program annotation. This section of Kierkegaard's work is a model for sane, philosophical treatment in the field of art.

Seeking to account for the rise of the Don Juan story, Kierkegaard indulges in the Romantic counterpart of the "world-historical speculation" which he later ridiculed Hegel for employing. A Don Juan could take his origin only in such a situation as prevailed during the high Middle Ages, when the powerful forces of morality and religion were withdrawn from the world, in a flight to God.[15] Kierkegaard took most of his one-sided information about medieval Catholicism from Görres's famous work on Christian mysticism, from Baader, and from the Romantic novels. Hence, at this time, he looked upon mysticism as a kind of spiritual estheticism, which seeks impatiently to leap over time and the finite in its yearning for the divine. The result of such an abandonment of secular life would be to leave a clear field for the powers of the world and the flesh. Just as St. Paul declares that sin came into the world with the Law, in so far as the Law aroused a consciousness of sin, so Kierkegaard attributes the appearance of an embodiment of sensuality, such as Don Juan, to Christianity, in the sense that it directed attention away from the essentially good, sensuous aspect of man.

At least when he is speaking through his pseudonyms, Kierkegaard grants that many basic features of esthetic existence are intrinsically good and fitted for integration with higher principles. The sensuous side of human nature makes two important contributions to Kierkegaard's view of existence. It is only through sense perception that the individual is brought into contact with the existent material world, and hence only through this medium that man obtains a sensuous intuition of real movement. Our dependence upon an empirical source for our perception of actual becoming is one of the cornerstones of his polemic against Hegel's idealistic and absolutist theory of mind. Furthermore, neglect of the flesh is the first step toward neglect of the passional element in man and reduction of desire, will, and resolution to aspects of thought. A Don Juan is there to remind us that no conception of human existence is adequate, which cannot find a distinctive place for sensuous experience and the full play of the passions. This phase of Kierkegaard's anti-Hegelianism brought him into momentary alliance with a more balanced view of the human self, but it was offset by his extreme Lutheran notion of the order of grace as being in contrast with a corrupt human nature.

In any case, although there is nothing deordinate about the

passions and the sensuous level as such, they do introduce disorder into existence, when they are taken in isolation from other human forces. The sensuality of which Don Juan is an incarnation, is a kind of counterkingdom of the flesh, in counterdistinction to (and, ultimately, in opposition to) the kingdom of the spirit. He represents the mode of living which results when an individual is abandoned by, and eventually himself turns away from, the ethical and religious principles of right order. Taken by himself, Don Juan has all the exuberance and primitive drive which are present in a man, before reflection sets in. His is the first phase of esthetic life, which begins innocently enough in isolation from, but not deliberate revolt against, motives which might regulate and discipline sensuous desire. Kierkegaard characterizes this naive sensuality as a kind of *Schweben*, a hovering or tension between extremes which is best translated by a musical theme. This is the characteristic attitude of the Romantic soul, when it is healthy and well poised.

Unfortunately, men often make distinctions, not in order to achieve a more rational unity, but as the first step on the road to progressive disintegration. In Don Juan, there is implicit the tendency to make esthetic interests primary and even exclusive; he has revolted from the rule of the spirit, even before he reflects upon it and raises his own proper standard. The very virtues advocated by Romanticism help to corrupt men by their narrowness and their inhumane resistance against being supplemented by other perfections of man. Kierkegaard finds this to be the case especially with the two features which he most admired among the Romantics: their stress upon the fresh and original aspects of existence and their praise of the passions.

At a time when most literary men and philosophers were priding themselves upon the reflective character of their existence and their facility in calling into question every direct and uncriticized position, Kierkegaard turned to the Romantic appreciation of belief and frank sentiment. It is vain to suppose that speculation can ever become completely reflective or mediated, in the sense of dispensing with every foundation in what is directly given. But on the other hand, he agreed with Hegel that nothing is to be gained by wandering off into the night in which all cows are black. Reflection can be directed upon the immediately given factors of existence, without denying or destroying their immediate character. In fact, this is just what the Romantics were doing, in their deliberate cultivation of original states of feeling. While admitting the importance of such immediate feelings, Kierkegaard was not willing to surrender the entire guidance of human living into their hands. In addition to recommending the discipline of reason within its proper bounds, he pointed out that the Romantics understand the term "immediate" in too univocal a sense.[16] Thus, Novalis declares that every action and thought motivated by original feeling is an act of religion, and that the religious outlook is encompassed within the esthetic. To Kierkegaard, this is a token of the confusion of categories induced by the Romantic mood. One of his major contentions is that religious faith is a kind of immediacy which is beyond both immediate existence and the scope of philosophical reflection.

Just as the Romantic philosophers fail to see the distinction between various sorts of immediacy, so they fail to appreciate the full scope of the life of the passions. This is the main objection raised against estheticism by the ethical representative in the esthetic writings, Judge William. He observes that the average esthete is troubled by an inability to make a prompt and permanent decision.[17] This impotence is due, in part, to the fact that the esthetic sphere makes no provision for the moral will, which is among the deepest passional principles and the source of our resolution and fidelity. Either the good is identified with the pleasurable, or it is opposed in the degree that it is recognized as having more than an esthetic and hedonic significance. The Romantics are willing to champion the passional aspects of human life only up to the point where the passions minister to the imagination and the pleasure principle, but what is needed is a radical accentuation of this passional side of man's nature. Hence Kierkegaard's stress upon the passions—upon the will and faith, as well as sensuous desires in their proper place—is a double-pronged weapon, aimed against Romanticism as well as Hegelianism.

Sensual immediacy is the basic state of the esthetic individual. When passion is admitted only at the sensuous level and apart from the moral will, it inevitably turns into abstract and selfish lust. The individual loses power over himself and is made prisoner of the search for the pleasurable moment, a moment which can never be realized to complete satisfaction. This accounts for the ennui, the restlessness, the instability, and the other secondary aspects of esthetic life which phenomenological analysis reveals. Kierkegaard describes these phases of esthetic life in detail and with great psychological and literary skill. His studies in this field are pioneer essays in phenomenological description. But he subordinates them to his main purpose of providing materials so that we may judge for ourselves about this kind of existence, when it pretends to organize all values around its standard. His principal charge is that estheticism cultivates imagination and concrete intelligence at the expense of the will and genuinely reflective reason. As a consequence, the esthetic personality cannot grow to maturity and cannot even realize the full promise of the esthetic urge itself.

Faust, Man of Doubt

Great care was taken by Kierkegaard to study the Faust legend, not only in its classical form in Goethe, but also in obscure medieval chapbooks, which record the popular versions of this story. He criticized the second part of Goethe's poem as a kind of sentimentalized surrender of Faust's true personality, which either remains true to its own daimonic ideal or vanishes away, when conversion is attempted. Kierkegaard pictures Faust as forever loyal to the esthetic ideal and hence as a lost soul. But he sometimes softens the outlines and complicates the situation by discussing his own relation to Regine Olsen in terms of Faust's relation to the unfortunate Margaret. Moreover, he often reflects in the *Journals* upon the Faustian element in his own character. The transformations which the Faust-character undergoes in his mind are subtle and many-leveled, reminding one of Coleridge's road to Xanadu. Kierkegaard's Faust is a splendid example of how the esthetic works are open to several different, but related, interpretations.

Kierkegaard includes Faust as a component of the Romantic mind, because of his own experience of doubt during his early years. He had witnessed, in his own case, that passage from confident buoyancy to skepticism which he expresses imaginatively as a transition from Don Juan to Faust. There is a stamp of authentic personal attestation attached to his observations about the terrible inward hunger of the doubter for truth, if there be truth, and for the passing solace of ordinary life and happy immediacy.[18] Another introspective item is that, even in his search after untroubled happiness, the doubter cannot cease to criticize the false kind of tranquillity based upon unexamined foundations. Like the music critic who cannot play a note, the esthetic doubter is at least sure that existence is not firmly grasped, until it has passed the test of a critical spirit. Even though the result be the abandonment of all hope in our human predicament, the fundamental questions must at least be posed.

This same sort of critical courage animates Kierkegaard's

examination of the ways of life which are antagonistic to religious existence. He felt in himself a Faustian relish for the mystery of sin, for experiencing and probing the whole range of human possibilities. But he adds—what a Faust could not add—that the attendant perils of such an exploration are sometimes balanced and overcome by faith in the holiness of God and the goodness of all forms of existence, as standing open to Him. This is the kind of certainty which, in its lineage, is poles removed from the craven and uncritical quest for certainty-at-all-costs which John Dewey rightly asks us to forego, but which Dewey unaccountably equates with every sort of faith in a transcendent God.

Faust is a rebirth of Don Juan, a second phase in the esthetic dialectic. Anyone who reflects upon the futility of trying to satisfy the human spirit in the sheer flow of immediate feeling and pleasure is liable to become skeptical about every supposed certainty, resting place, and moment of joy. Speaking "historically," Kierkegaard considers Faust to have made his appearance still later in the Middle Ages than did Don Juan, at the moment when reflection began to take the place of direct pursuit of pleasure, in an abandoned age. Indeed, he takes Faust as the symbol of Western man left unguided to work out his life-plan by himself, after revolt from the Catholic Church.[19] He is a one-sided, since a purely negative, figure of the men of the Reformation searching individually and in vain for solid ground, in a period when the principle of authority had been put aside and all was shifting sand. Kierkegaard does not allow that Faust approached Mephistopheles as a higher authority, upon whom he could finally rely. A true skeptic remains suspicious even about superhuman deliverances, especially when he had once been a believer in divine revelation. Although the esthetic person thinks that his life is conducted beyond the range of good and evil, a moral element of pride is essential to his standpoint in its skeptical phase. Even though he will not turn to God for guidance, he nevertheless thinks that his store of wisdom can be augmented only by some preternatural aid, rather than by ordinary human means. For all his critical objections to religious truth, he is often an easy victim of superstition and diabolism.

The Faust problem presents some special difficulties for Kierkegaard's general doctrine on the esthetic stage. It forces him to reconsider the meaning of immediacy, to state his position in regard to the Romantic notion of daimonia, and to distinguish Faustian from ordinary philosophical doubt. These issues help to clarify his stand concerning the philosophical situation of his day, since they were in the forefront of discussion among his contemporaries. They also make his portrait of the esthetic soul more sharply etched.

We have noted already how Kierkegaard tried to combine the best features of the Romantic stress upon the immediate with the Hegelian insistence upon mediacy or a dialectical appraisal of the given situation. But since he was out of sympathy with the idealistic postulates of the Hegelian dialectic, he had to present another account of the meaning of the mediate. It is not merely the logical antithesis of the state of immediacy and not a product of some mysterious, absolute power of negativity. On the other hand, it is not achieved by becoming reflective in just any sort of way about one's original placement in being. This latter conception of the critical attitude was popular among the Romantics, who felt that they had overcome the limitations of the life of feeling, once they could look with disillusioned eyes upon all of life's affirmations and polar opposites. Both the Hegelian and the Romantic accounts suffered in Kierkegaard's eyes from excessive abstractness: the first advocates a mediacy only in pure thought, whereas the second advocates one which is confined to the imagination and the skeptical mood. Kierkegaard was convinced that no radically critical attitude toward oneself can be achieved, except through a moral and religious sort of appraisal and through an actual change of heart. Hegelianism is foreign to the order of real changes in the mode of existing, and in any case its standard is always an immanent and deterministic one. Romanticism deals with men under real conditions but does not take all the relevant conditions into consideration. No matter how subtly refined the seducer or how exquisitely reflective the doubter, he cannot enter into full possession of himself, as long as he fails to view himself in the light of moral standards and religious demands upon existence. Hence Kierkegaard regarded a Faust or a pseudonymous Johannes the Seducer as men still caught in the web of fate and still immature in regard to the further aspects of existence. The only sort of reflection which he deemed capable of removing this state of unfreedom is moral and religious reflection, for it is only through this agency that a man can relate himself freely to a transcendent principle of existence.[20]

In *Fear and Trembling*, Faust is represented as coming to Margaret under the impulse of an intellectual daimonia. Kierkegaard's study of the Romantic writers led him to reflect upon the notions of genius and the daimonic.[21] Eventually, he gave this trend of thought an original direction, by relating it with the ideas of dread, the exceptional individual, and the religious sacrifice. In his earlier esthetic writings, however, he contented himself with defining the general meaning of daimonia and stating the moral principle implicit in it. A daimonic life is one based deliberately upon an all-absorbing idea. The daimonic person relates himself immediately and individually to his leading idea, repudiating by implication the ordinary conventions and attachments of the human community. Such a person need not undergo any visible change to correspond with his distinctive inner state.

Kierkegaard liked to underline this discrepancy between shadow and substance, as providing a vivid refutation of Hegel's repeated contention that the inner has no more reality than the outer, that the self can and ought to be adequately expressed in visible form. Although he recognized that a deliberately fostered concealment can be morally dangerous, Kierkegaard refused, at least in the esthetic books, to regard the daimonic principle as intrinsically evil. It was too closely associated in his mind with the Christian teaching on individual vocation and, more particularly, with his own sense of a special calling from God.

But he did not agree with the Romantic philosophers that any and every daimonia is legitimate and worth cultivating. Here again, he wished to point out the moral implications behind the esthetic principles, even when these implications are denied by esthetes. When the individual seeks to rule his life according to a paramount principle, he institutes a moral relation with that principle, and determines his life as good or bad in conformity with the nature of the ideal which is chosen. Moreover, the manner in which he accepts his exceptional calling has a moral consequence. Certain individuals seem to be set aside and marked by nature for this special relation to an absorbing task. Either they can accept this distinction as a gift from God or they can pretend that they are completely *sui generis* and creators of their own destiny, in an absolute sense. Faust is a daimonic character of the latter sort and does not escape from moral judgment, on this score. His pride is duplicated on a smaller and fundamentally ridiculous scale by all esthetic individuals. Kierkegaard justifies this assertion by making an analysis of modern man's pitiful attempts to rise above the herd and its featureless mediocrity.

The anonymous character of modern life can be traced directly to its foundation in esthetic existence. When esthetic standards are accepted as ultimate, personality fails to develop along normal lines of moral and religious growth. Failing to realize himself integrally and in his proper dignity, the individual has no grounds for distinctive development. The upshot is a contradictory cross movement toward both excessive standardization and the cultivation of idiosyncrasies. In modern civilization, both tendencies have received institutional sanction, in the honor paid simultaneously to mass uniformity and private hobbies. Kierkegaard's thoughts on this problem have been developed by the existentialists in their critique of the appeal to the impersonal "one says," as well as in their satire upon individual busyness. They recognize that both uniformity and the craze for fads and for hoeing one's Candidean garden are only dim memories of the reality of community and person. But some existentialists have forgotten that, for Kierkegaard, this esthetic condition is not the full report on existence. They have accepted the tale of social frustration and private meaninglessness as though it characterizes human life essentially, whereas in fact it only marks our existence, when the experiment is made of grounding it eccentrically on an esthetic basis alone.

There is a sense in which Kierkegaard considers a Faust to be preferable to a dozen university professors, who begin their annual lectures with the academic nursery formula: "Once upon a time there lived a man named Descartes, and he was a great doubter." The existential doubt of Faust is only parodied by the methodic, textbook doubt of the dons.[22] The latter sort of doubt is only cultivated as a theoretical exercise, leaving the rest of one's life untouched and serene; for, somehow, the "provisional morality" is never replaced or even critically justified. In sharp contrast, Faust illustrates the difference between doubt as a qualified despair of thought and doubt as a thorough, "substantial" despair of the whole personality. But Kierkegaard conceives of Faust as never fully acknowledging the hopelessness of his mode of existence and the depths of his own despair. Faust is willing to continue searching for the happy moment which is worthy of being arrested, even though he is skeptical of ever finding it. He would like to return to academic doubt, even when he knows it to be only a ritual and not the kind of doubt which he represents or, rather, *is*. For an open acknowledgment of despair, without any possibility of relief, Kierkegaard evokes another legendary figure, the Wandering Jew.

The Despair of Ahasuerus

In the Wandering Jew, Kierkegaard saw the truest symbol of his age and the outcome of a closed esthetic existence. Beneath the tranquillity and exaltation of the erotic and beneath the steady intensity of doubt, he found silent despair as the last word of esthetic existence. He concurred with Hoffmann's remark that Ahasuerus must be conceived as endlessly wandering through the world in dull indifference and complete absence of hope in God or man.[28] This is the last reef upon which the esthetic life founders, despite its many evasions of such an issue. It is important to recognize for what they are, the various attempts made by individuals to conceal despair or avert their own eyes from it. Kierkegaard describes these dodges with considerable perspicacity, proving at the same time that he could outdo the Romantics in the discernment of hidden attitudes. They include the hustle and bustle of everyday life, the search for diversions, the reducing of all actual events to the status of imagination and memory, the cultivation of the arbitrary whim, the search for a repetition of happy events, and irony. From the philosophical standpoint, the latter two artifices are most significant. None of these methods, however, is successful in avoiding the fundamental despair which shipwrecks the esthetic claim to determine human existence and values according to its exclusive perspective.

The pseudonymous "author" of *Repetition* is a brilliant psychologist and esthete, Constantine Constantius. He seeks to avoid the fate of Ahasuerus by means of the esthetic category of "repetition." The profoundest wisdom of the Greeks was contained in the conviction that what is now, has also been from all eternity. Constantine is interested in testing the counterthesis that what has been in the past, can receive new being in the present. Far from taking panic at a possible repetition of events and the boredom it might entail, he looks to a reflux of eternity into time as the true source of originality and freshness, as the only reliable support in a world of constant change. He makes an experiment in test of this hypothesis, but he approaches the possibility in a purely speculative and "objective" frame of mind.

He tries in vain, on a second and a third night, to recapture the magical delight of a first night's performance at a Berlin theater.[24] He is aware that real repetition is quite other than dull sameness and uniformity, but he cannot determine the conditions under which it may occur. At this point in his investigation, he is consulted about an unhappy love affair by a young man. His acumen is sufficient to tell him that the young man is really undergoing a religious crisis and that his own ministrations can be of no avail, in such a situation. At the same time, he assures the youth that neither will he find guidance from the professional philosophers, since they do not concern themselves about existential situations and changes or about a genuinely religious relation of man to God. This is an equivalent confession that both Hegelianism and the Romantic outlook are impotent before the question of time and eternity. Even the esthetic mind must eventually conclude that esthetic principles are insufficient to relate temporal existence to the eternal and the transcendent. If there be a kind of repetition or participation in the eternal mode of being, it can only be attained by breaking through the limits of the esthetic sphere. By remaining within these confines, Constantine condemns himself to a life of despair and bondage to chance and fate. He intimates that other spheres of existence are more important for man, but he himself lacks the resolution to venture out to explore them.

The final refuge of the despairing esthetic mind is in the attitude of irony, the favorite pose of the Romantics. Kierkegaard is formally concerned with this attitude in his master's thesis *On the Concept of Irony*, the results of which are accepted in the esthetic books.[25] His position is that esthetic irony has a good side and a bad side. It has a salutary effect in preventing people from regarding their own viewpoint as an absolute, which lies beyond all comparison and criticism. Similarly, it provides a strong weapon against the Hegelians' identification of the absolute God with their thoughts about the absolute, as well as against their systematic ignoring of the problem of the individual systematist *qua* individual man. But Romantic irony provides only a negative liberation from error; if taken as an end in itself, as a sufficient determinant of existence, it is stultifying and leads to despair.

The danger of irony is that it tends to reduce all things, including the individual self and God, to the status of possibilities and points in the polar field of imagination. It levels all values to indifference, and discovers that good and evil and other contrasts are at bottom the same. Paradoxically enough, this abstractness brings the Romantic position close to that of Hegel. The lesson of Kierkegaard's analysis of the esthetic stage is that it ceases to be a genuine mode of existence, when it seeks to be self-contained. This is borne out quite exactly by the rightful, positive place of irony in human life. Although the esthetic order governs the content and expression of irony, it does not provide its basis. This basis is found only in an infinite reality, not in indifference to the articulations and distinctions of reality. Irony results when the finite is brought into comparison with the infinite and its standards. This supposes, however, that both terms in the comparison are real and that the self, which employs irony against its own pretensions and those of others, is a real member of the finite order. Irony tells us that the finite is not the absolute, rather than that the difference between them is only a moment in a speculative dialectic or one phase in the play of imagination. Romantic irony is incapable by itself of securing the foundations of human existence, for the introduction of God's infinite reality and man's relation to him is possible, only if existence is acknowledged to be a moral and religious affair, as well as an esthetic one.

In many ways, Kierkegaard is most convincing in his treatment of the esthetic phase of existence. One reason is that his own temperament and gifts gave him an intimate understanding of this view of things. He was justified in referring to himself customarily as "a poet and a thinker," a combination which is employed effectively in the esthetic writings. Kierkegaard had mastered the literature of the Romantics, which saved him in this instance from chasing phantoms of his own creation. Furthermore, there was good opportunity here to employ a descriptive method and to suggest conclusions, rather than establish them directly. We can see for ourselves that an exclusively esthetic sort of existence is a humanly intolerable abstraction. Such an admission is all that Kierkegaard asks of us, at this point in his argument. For, it is sufficient to dispose our minds for a sober consideration of the claims of ethical and religious life. This is the purpose of the first stage in his existential dialectic.

Chapter Three

The Ethical View and Its Limits

I. KIERKEGAARD'S APPROACH TO ETHICS

THE book upon which Kierkegaard expected his literary reputation to rest and the one, in fact, which does win the favor of contemporary readers most readily is *Fear and Trembling*. In the subtitle, he announces that the book is to be regarded as "a dialectical lyric." Its dialectical preoccupations reach out in two directions: it contains an examination of the Hegelian claim to have surpassed Christian faith through the new philosophical synthesis, and it makes a criticism of the ethical form of existence. Our concern here is mainly with the second of these dialectical discussions, and the first noteworthy point is that the discussion is carried on in a "lyrical" or poetic way. This fact is further emphasized by the attribution of the work, on its title page, to a pseudonymous author, Johannes *de silentio*. These hints are sufficient to locate the book among Kierkegaard's esthetic works, and hence to place certain qualifications upon the standpoint which it takes toward the problems of ethical life. Any interpretation of the text should respect these circumstances, for otherwise a false report will be given of Kierkegaard's own position.

Unfortunately, some popular studies ignore this caution, give a direct, literal account of the work, and as a result distort Kierkegaard's mind on this important issue. Especially

· 66 ·

his teaching on the possibility of suspending ethical duties has been given a sensational twist, so that a Sartre can conclude that a consistent existentialist must strictly be the creator of his own moral values and obligations. This inference is possible only when Kierkegaard's ethical reflections are cut off from their context in his overall study of the various modes of existence. If they are replaced in this broad setting, then a quite contrary conclusion is required. The purpose of the present chapter is to furnish the background for understanding both the poetic and the dialectical nature of the ethical argument in *Fear and Trembling*.[1]

As the record actually stands, one rarely meets with an unblocked, harmonious development of human character, such as is ideally possible. Men as we find them are more likely to insist upon the sufficiency of the esthetic or ethical mode of existence than upon their integration in a common, unified view. These stages then become closed circles within which the individual tries to live autonomously and fit his experience, repressing any tendency to overflow the boundaries set by his original commitment. Kierkegaard is interested, not in the pathology of character which might be described here, but rather in the direct clash of viewpoints and the dialectical relations between poetically conceived representatives of the rival spheres of existence. His treatment is highly dramatic and betrays a constant underswell of concern about the religious predicament of individuals. His statements about ethical life are distinguished in two ways from the usual treatises in this field. They are not primarily concerned with ethics as a distinct philosophical discipline, and they do not envisage the distinctive problems which arise when the ethical side of human nature is regarded moderately as but one aspect of man. Undoubtedly, these are shortcomings, if his approach is to be regarded as a rounded treatment of the matter.

Kierkegaard never tires of warning his readers that he is to be taken as a corrective rather than as a norm, but he is seldom taken seriously in this caution and occasionally he himself forgets about it. This warning should be kept in mind during the investigation of his ethical stand, however, since the latter is quite evidently conditioned by, and in some respects limited to, his historical situation. His models for ethical inquiry are Socrates and the Aristotle of the more tentative and empirical sections of the *Nicomachean Ethics*, although he had no plan of returning to the Greek conception of human conduct. Ethics as a formal philosophical standpoint and prevalent attitude meant for him Kantian ethics. Because he saw the danger to religion in an autonomous conception of morality and yet was unacquainted with any philosophical treatment which escapes this pitfall, Kierkegaard did not reach any rigorously philosophical solution of the problems of moral life. He was prevented from constructing his ethical thought upon a metaphysical basis because of his opposition to Hegelianism—which he accepted as the definitive form of metaphysical speculation—and because of a prejudice against "objective theorizing" about practical ethical matters. The only way in which he envisioned a scientific and moderate treatment of ethical problems was through a sort of moral theology, which is formally integrated with the truths provided by revelation. The exact nature of the positions which would be determined by this *philosophia secunda*, under the guidance of revelation, is never stated in detail. As a "corrective," Kierkegaard was more interested in the immediate practical question of dealing with people who do not acknowledge any subordination of ethical thinking to a standard provided by religious transcendence.

His own method is the existential dialectic, which informs the esthetic works. Apart from the general difficulty of interpreting the pseudonymous writings, there is an additional reason why his ethical view is not likely to meet with widespread acceptance in America today. The philosophical climate has so changed since Kierkegaard's time that Kant and Hegel are no longer the reigning masters, and another ethical doctrine has been proposed as an alternative to acknowledging the Christian interpretation of existence. The great hope of naturalistic empiricism is to place ethics upon a completely naturalistic basis, by providing an explanation of obligation and the other aspects of moral life, without making an appeal to a transcendent God. Naturalists are convinced that the same method employed with such striking success in the physical and biological sciences, can be extended to include all the content formerly covered by the humanistic sciences and philosophy, including ethics.[2] They argue that, if this claim is well founded, there is no need to posit a distinctively religious interpretation of existence or to admit a place for supernatural faith and the order of grace.

The naturalistic hypothesis cannot be dealt with adequately, on the basis of Kierkegaard alone. This is due in part to his lack of any strict philosophy of human conduct, and in part to his lack of familiarity with the scientific and empiricist traditions developed up to his own day. But he can be of some aid in this discussion; his suggestions should not be written off as entirely outmoded and irrelevant to present day issues. For one thing, he gives reasons for not accepting an ethical view based wholly upon man and upon immanent, finite considerations. This suggests that there is a postulate shared in common by the philosophies Kierkegaard had in view and by naturalism. Although a naturalist like John Dewey repudiated many features of his early attachment to Hegel, he still retained the organic view of reality and the monism of method which characterize absolute idealism. These are precisely the assumptions which seem to permit a univocal extension of scientific method to the field of ethics, in the manner recommended by the naturalists. And they are subjected to criticism by Kierkegaard both here, by implication, and more formally in his works directed against Hegelianism.

Furthermore, Kierkegaard is not entirely a stranger to the methodological question, upon which the naturalists so strongly insist. He spoke out against two trends, which were just starting in his day, but which have contributed heavily to the naturalistic cause, in recent years.[3] The first of these is the policy of basing standards of conduct upon social tendencies or the interests of a particular group, a policy present in germ in the texts of Hegel and Feuerbach which Kierkegaard consulted, and brought to full bloom by Hegelians like Marx and by the positivists. He deemed this attempt at founding a social morality to be an attack upon religion and upon an ethic of the categorical-imperative type. For, it dispenses both with God as the foundation of the moral law and with an absolute obligation placed upon the human will. Recognizing that this conception could not make headway, unless the human personality were submerged in a quasi-divine, totalitarian social unit, Kierkegaard preferred to reserve his criticism of this theory of morality for his discussion on the nature of the individual.

The second current in ethics comes closer to contemporary naturalism. Using as his example the attempt to explain human actions according to laws of statistical frequencies, Kierkegaard expressed the foreboding that some day physics would supplant ethics as the science of human conduct. Should this occur, he foresaw a science of man which would be accurate, as far as it went, but which could deal with the sphere of freedom and reflection only by analogies and not in terms of what is proper to man. Although the natural sciences can recognize that man is different from other beings in nature, they cannot deal formally with the principle of this difference. Hence it is not enough for naturalism to proclaim its opposition to a reductionist theory of man: it is in principle prevented from examining man's distinctive mode of existence and must remain subordinate to a way of thinking which *can* grasp this distinctive mode. Kierkegaard works out the differences between the scientific and the "subjective" or "existential" approaches in his philosophical discussion of truth on the human or existential plane.

2. THE ETHICAL REVALUATION OF ESTHETIC LIFE

The ideal of an ethically centered life is viewed from a double perspective in the second part of *Either/Or,* which contains the report of Judge William, the pseudonymous representative of the ethical viewpoint. The Judge tries to justify his own stand not only in itself but also as an answer to the claims made for hedonism and Romanticism. The Judge's criticism is both negative and constructive, for he seeks to show how an ethical life supplies what is lacking at the esthetic stage and also redeems everything of positive worth found at the lower level. Indeed, this ethical pseudonym supposes that there is a much greater degree of harmony between the three spheres of existence than Kierkegaard himself is willing to allow. To this extent, the discussion in *Either/Or* can be misleading, unless one adverts to the fact that everything transpires there as if the esthetic and ethical alternatives are the sole possibilities, whereas Kierkegaard in his own right intends to show that the life of religious piety opens up an entirely new set of existential values. In the later works of the esthetic group, he suggests that religious motives elude the grasp of both the esthetic and the ethical mind. And in the religious writings of his last period, he emphasizes to the point of exaggeration the disjunction between the entire order of immanent values—esthetic, ethical and religious (man's natural piety)—and the highest expression of a religious view of existence: the attitude of Christian faith.

What Esthetic Existence Lacks

When ethical standards are taken as ultimate, however, it seems an easy task to reconcile the first two spheres of existence, once the deficiencies of the Romantic outlook have been remedied. The major shortcoming is expressed functionally in the Judge's remark that a Romantic individual remains a victim of despair, without ever having chosen to despair.[4] Behind this obscure observation lies Kierkegaard's fundamental judgment on the Romantic ideal. The man of poetic sensibility, and nothing more, is responsive to all the determinants of his being: his own natural endowment, the active forces of nature, the cultural heritage of the past, the flow of moods, dreams and chance occurrences. He is so sensitive to these various influences that, for all his praise of freedom, he remains fascinated by the conception of himself as a locus and outcome of unknown, determining powers. His view of freedom is that each individual is a wholly unique complexus of effects: he is more a passive rebel against public standards of conformity than an active champion of reasonable self-determination. His search for pleasure and esthetic harmony will issue in despair, but this attitude is more a cast of mind into which he is driven, despite his buoyancy and irony, than a deliberately chosen standpoint. He embodies certain moods and sings their praises, rather than achieves a state of character through acts of deliberate choice and persevering effort.

In sharp contrast, stands the ethically disciplined individual. Whatever his moral condition, he can at least boast that he is the accountable source of his own state and knows himself for what he really is. In opposition to the Romantic stress on the underside of life, its mysterious forces and the dark pools of opaqueness in the soul, an ethical mind insists upon the lucidity of self-knowledge. He believes that he has followed the Socratic maxim successfully, and that both self-understanding and self-mastery are the rewards of shaping his conduct in conformity with the moral good. His decisive advantage lies in his appeal to an unconditional standard of moral perfection. By measuring his own actions and character against this criterion, he can overcome his partiality and deception toward himself. The eye of the soul should be cast upon the moral ideal graven in our conscience, rather than upon the elements in our nature which lie beyond our direct ken and control. Or rather, one should first take heart from the former and then set out to conquer the latter with its aid. Freedom is the chief good which ethical existence brings with it, as a supplement to the esthetic foundations of life.

Kierkegaard does not attempt to settle any question by means of this phenomenological analysis of contrasting viewpoints. By highlighting the opposition, however, he shows his awareness of the vast differences between what Karl Jaspers has colorfully designated as the Passions of Night and the Law of Daytime. Before the event, he charted the tendency of Romanticism to issue in a Freudian anthropology, based upon the power of the unconscious, the notion of a group mind, and laws of physical and historical determinism. In this drift, he recognized a strong challenge to the previous rationalistic view of man. His ethical protagonist, significantly enough, is not an uncomplicated, rationalistic individual, but one who hopes to reinstate the rights of practical intelligence in the face of the Romantic version of our inner life. Kierkegaard's contention is that *both* approaches to man uncover genuine elements in our nature, but that the tension between these views will lead to the disintegration of personal and social life, unless the religious principle of unity be introduced into our treatment of man.

This general contrast can be specified along more particular lines. Among the major points of difference is that between the concealment advocated by the esthetic mind and the openness counseled by the ethical mind. In *Either/Or*, the poetic youth glories in his ambiguity, his ability to deceive and the close reserve which surrounds his life, whereas his ethical counterpart strives to be frank, openhearted and simple in his dealings with others. This reflects the difference between following one's personal whim or taste and governing one's life by a moral standard, admitted to be binding upon all men. In the one case, the shifting individual circumstances and talents are made decisive, whereas in the other case these are subordinated to universal factors, which obtain for all individuals and times. The ethical ideal is to bring every aspect of an individual's being into conformity with the universal law, so that what is essentially human may be expressed in the individual instance.[5] The presence of a common standard tends to promote an attitude of self-revelation and co-operation among men, as a counterbalance to the inclination to refuse to communicate in thought and conduct with others.

This antithesis between the Romantic and Kantian outlooks, in regard to self-expression and communication, is not easy to resolve. Kierkegaard felt attracted toward both views. As a young man, he resolved to cultivate a *communicatio idiomatum* concerning his innermost feelings, and the entire enterprise of the pseudonymous works testifies to his native preference for reserve and indirectness. But he also appreciated the moralist's aim of permeating every aspect of individual life with the influence of duty and the moral good. The problem is to preserve the integrity of the individual without falling into an antinomian position, and to further a common participation in the good life and its rule of law without end-ing in an artificial universalism. Kierkegaard deemed these twin dangers unavoidable, unless common duty and private conviction are both regarded in the light of the religious teaching on vocation, which is a call from God to the individual for the sake of the entire people of God.

Finally, ethical existence is able to supply the greatest lack of esthetic life: a strong will. The absence of this factor accounts for a tendency of esthetic individuals to be irresolute and ineffective in practical affairs and skeptical in matters of intellect. They become sealed off in the private world of possibilities and their own images, passing from one to the next in endless succession, without being able to terminate the imaginative comparison in a definite plan of action. Kierkegaard touches here on one of the prime sources of abnormality in modern life. Yet his appeal to the will as a remedy has often been misunderstood as a plea for anti-intellectualism and the cult of power. He does not advocate that we *suppress* imagination and intellect, but only that we *integrate* them with will and the sense of concrete conditions of action which it heightens. Indeed, under the broad term "will," he includes not only the power of resolution itself but also the operations of intellect and the passions, in so far as they are governed by a concern for the actual world and the actual condition of the individual. He looks to the enlightened and passionate will to secure the proper good of the individual against the deordinate concentration upon feeling and the waking dream which Romanticism cultivates.

What Can Be Salvaged from Romanticism?

This question is not posed in its full force at this point in Kierkegaard's inquiry; rather, it is asked from the standpoint of a Kantian moralist, who is sensitive to an ineradicable esthetic side of human nature and to the need for its incorporation into an ethical world view. Such an individual would seek to reinstate the rights of beauty and simple enjoyment, once the autonomy of esthetic life is renounced. What is perhaps peculiar to Kierkegaard's ethical pseudonym, Judge William, is the central place which he accords to marriage. He regards the married state as the concretion of the whole ethical ideal and as the human condition within which alone legitimate esthetic claims can be honored and brought to fulfillment. Here is an instance in which Kierkegaard's personal problems determine his line of thought, both to its advantage and to its disadvantage. The crisis induced by his engagement and estrangement occasioned his sustained and subtle reflections upon love and marriage, but it also led him to make of marriage the test case and center of ethical life. This had an unbalancing effect upon both his conception of marriage and his conception of ethical life. For, he came to regard married love, as that component in ethical existence which converts it into an independent, self-satisfied sphere, and hence which serves as an obstacle to the full development of the existential dialectic. This is the basic theoretical reason behind his later disparaging attitude toward marriage and women. These later views are colored not so much by Christian teaching or by a reading of Schopenhauer as by Kierkegaard's own over-systematic association of women with estheticism and marriage with moralism.

Judge William demonstrates the esthetic validity of marriage by showing that whatever is beautiful and truly human in the pagan erotic view and in Romantic first love, is incorporated into what he calls the ethical institution of Christian marriage.[6] He substantiates this thesis in several ingenious ways. One consideration is that sensual love falls under the ethical censure only because of its selfishness. The latter characteristic is due, in turn, to the over-close attachment of the Romantic soul to the ecstatic, pleasurable moment, to the exclusion of God and universal duty. Once these latter principles are allowed to be of supreme importance, there is nothing to hinder an ethical appropriation of erotic values in married love. What is present by way of hope and natural tendency in erotic love, is transfigured and realized more fully in conjugal love. The ethical contribution is a resolute purpose and sense of obligation to persist in the married union through times and tides, to hold fast to one another in the midst of changing fortunes. The marriage vow is a sign that the ethical will can dominate chance and fate, and hence can liberate the individual from the confinements of esthetic existence.

The claim is made, indeed, that married life uncovers for the first time the true proportions of esthetic life, as freed from selfish distortion. The two essential traits of esthetic existence are the reconciliation of polar opposites and a happy endurance in time. Only the former note is honored by the esthetes, whereas they lack the energy of will and the stability to achieve the latter. Esthetic despair is overcome only in marriage, for this is precisely the state which combines the various poles of existence in harmonious tension and also endures as a reliable, historical reality. This is a bold stroke of interpretation on Kierkegaard's part, for it involves the further judgment that, although esthetes invariably end in despair, the sound energies which they release are not destined to frustration, provided that they are integrated with a more comprehensive outlook. This is the optimistic side of his dialectic, which is sometimes overlooked by students and regarded with suspicion by Kierkegaard himself, from the standpoint of his conception of Christian faith. It is a sound and humane insight, however, one which should not be scrapped, even when the supernatural mode of existing is in question.

A redemptive effort is at work on all levels of life to rescue, transfigure and consummate all the sound aspirations of human nature. What prevented Kierkegaard from extending this sort of reasoning to the sphere of religious transcendence was, in part, the illegitimate use of Christian notions made by moralists like Kant.[7] Kierkegaard feared that such rationalistic treatment would rob Christianity of its transcendent element and hence, as a corrective, he stressed the discontinuity and incompatibility between the Christian faith and the lower stages of religious and secular existence. But his own pseudonymous example in dealing with esthetic and ethical conflicts suggests the need for a more discerning reinterpretation of authentic factors in these other spheres and a greater allowance for God's part in this process of restoration and elevation of man to the status of a sharer in God's own life.

Estheticism may register a final protest against the role of time in moral existence and, more particularly, in married life. It may contend that nothing is more readily conducive to boredom and the deadening of sensibility than the dull round of routine duties. It may object, further, that artistic efforts have seldom been successful in portraying married life and that this indicates a deep incompatibility between esthetic requirements and the ethical ideal. Judge William turns these objections deftly into counterproofs that estheticism fails to comprehend even its own first principles. Unless one approach marriage in the proper spirit, its beauty and the happiness which it brings will remain hidden. Married people take the risk of boredom and mechanical routine, in order to secure the greater good of fidelity to one's original promise and in order to make progress of another sort than that of passing from one momentary attachment to another.[8] This inner enrichment, which accrues from remaining faithful to the presence of the beloved, escapes the notice of esthetes, because of a peculiarity of artistic representation. The latter tries to compress esthetic significance into an intensive moment, which foreshortens or cancels out altogether the long stretches of time. Such concentration is not always possible, especially when the subject matter belongs to what Kierkegaard calls "internal history" and what Dilthey and Bergson have familiarized us with as *Lebenszeit* or "qualitative personal duration." In this realm, it is literally true that "every moment counts."

Despite the Romantic emphasis upon history, times past and the *Volksgeist*, this philosophy cannot deal with ordinary historical continuity and the virtues of temporal existence, as found in actual individuals. But far from supporting the estheticist position, this limitation suggests that, at a certain point, there should be a dissociation between esthetic values themselves and their artistic representation. The latter medium is not adequate to express all that is beautiful and happy in existence. Whenever fidelity and the other perfections connected with inner temporal duration and the resolution of will are involved, the appropriate mode of representation must be ethical. The gracefulness and joy of moral living indicate that certain reaches of beauty are better expressed through one's actual way of existing than through one's poetic representation of possible existence. Only the moral person "solves the great riddle of living in eternity and yet hearing the hall clock strike." [9] Nietzsche would have recognized the poise, healthy courage and serenity of Kierkegaard's ethical individual as approximating to his own conception of the Apollinian man. Kierkegaard himself likens such a person to a dancer, capable of making the most daring leaps and covering the widest ground, without betraying any sign of extraordinary effort. This theory of the artistry of life accords with the general view of the ethical pseudonym concerning the harmony between the various phases of existence, but it is supported by an extremely weak explanation of the relation between ethical reflection and esthetic immediacy. [10]

3. THE ETHICAL CHOICE AND THE FINAL END

Most of the positive features of the ethical life-view have been brought out in the previous comparison with estheticism. Separate treatment is required, however, for two further aspects of Kierkegaard's account: the nature of ethical choice and the *telos* of ethical life. The former problem must be considered separately, because of its essential place in the formation of the ethical attitude and because the key text is so obscure. The second problem is singled out here, because its significance is apt to be missed by the casual reader, who may not see here a self-condemnation of the ethical pseudonym and hence a convenient bridge to the study of Kierkegaard's criticism of ethical autonomy.

The Nature of Ethical Choice

Judge William's ethical wisdom can be compressed within a single precept: *Choose thyself.* He speaks of "choosing" as his unique category and the favorite subject of his meditation. Yet whether Kierkegaard intended it deliberately or not, the fact remains that this central concept is discussed in very hazy, metaphorical language and in reliance upon the paraphernalia of German idealism. It is likely that this is an instance in which Kierkegaard has not succeeded in delivering either his thought or his terminology entirely out of the hands of his professed enemies. This defect is the more serious for the fact that the aim of the discussion is to mark out a zone for ethical choice which will distinguish it at once from the empiricist and the absolutist misrepresentations. The thesis is expressed in the following difficult passage:

In choosing absolutely I choose despair, and in despair I choose the absolute, for I myself am the absolute, I posit the absolute and

I myself am the absolute; but in complete identity with this I can say that I choose the absolute which chooses me, that I posit the absolute which posits me.[11]

In our own philosophical atmosphere, one is inclined to dismiss such a statement as mere jargon, cut out of the same cloth which made Heidegger's ruminations an easy target for Carnap's ridicule. But it is not an exaggeration to say that the whole of the second part of *Either/Or* is a commentary upon this text. Its importance is witnessed by its inclusion in some of the better expositions of Kierkegaard's thought, but the clarification of meaning is not promoted by merely quoting it, without providing some sort of explanation and criticism.

Some sort of absolute choice must be made, if the ethical individual is to embody the unconditional practical imperative of duty. But this is an ambiguous proposition, as evidenced by the fact that "an absolute choice" may refer either to the object chosen or to the way of making one's choice. Kierkegaard's noetic thesis that what counts is not the content but the mode of judgment, is foreshadowed here in the ethical thesis that what counts is not the object but the manner of choice. This is one reason why despair is mentioned: it is not so much a definite "object" as a way of regarding the whole field of objects of desire and choice.[12] It refers to the manner in which I will or refuse to will, rather than to a thing which I seek to obtain. To choose ethically means to choose in an unlimited way, so as to assume complete liability for a task to be done. Judge William's contention is that a man can choose absolutely, in this way, only in his own regard. This conception of ethical choice is opposed to that of Sartre, who holds that one cannot choose concerning himself, except as involving all other men and even as assuming responsibility for their destiny.[13] Kierkegaard's view recommends itself more strongly, but must be reconciled with the Kantian theory of moral law, upon which his notion of ethical personality ultimately rests. No matter how universally binding a law may be, the individual can only intend that others should act in the same way *provided that* they are placed in similar circumstances and choose to act morally. No one can actually place another in these circumstances or determine another's freedom from within. It may be added that God is chosen absolutely, only in the sense that the individual commits himself absolutely to obey and seek after God.

It is as difficult, however, to refrain from specifying the manner of choice in some way by its relation to the object chosen as it is to overlook the content of a judgment in discussing the manner of judging. In choosing absolutely, one cannot avoid specifying the absolute—a difficulty which accounts to some extent for the ambiguity and unnecessary juggling of terms in the settlement of this question. When Kierkegaard concentrates upon the subjective intensity and unconditional character of moral choosing, then "absolute self" can only mean the self of the chooser. It is that which is chosen by an act of freedom, binding the chooser under an unconditional obligation to realize fully the ideal nature of the concrete individual. This kind of absolute designates the manner in which the ethical individual regards his obligation to perfect his own nature, according to the moral law.

But for Kierkegaard to have referred unqualifiedly to the human self as absolute, in an age of absolutist philosophies, would have been misleading to his readers. His own theory of the stages of life required him to distinguish the ethical position from prevailing metaphysical theories of the absolute. Although handicapped in this instance by the use of a pseudonym and by his own hesitation concerning the nature of the individual, he did succeed in setting off the stand of Judge William from three alternative interpretations of the self as an absolute: the Fichtean, the Hegelian and the Romantic.

Fichte's theory of the creative self, which posits both itself and nature, gains a sympathetic hearing from Kierkegaard only because of the moral inspiration which Fichte drew from it. But Kierkegaard rejects any suggestion that man's moral life is a finitized expression of God's own productive freedom. The only kind of creativity which the finite self enjoys is a participated one, which is both received and freely originated, to use the language of Louis Lavelle. Kierkegaard points out that his use of the Fichtean term *Setzung* or *positing* does not imply an original and independent auto-creation, for it supposes a given reality in the choosing agent.[14] What is presupposed is the natural being of the individual, taken as a person of a given physical and psychic sort and with certain social relations. The given self about which ethical choice is concerned also includes the entire range of esthetic development of personality. Yet all these factors are transformed as the consequence of a fundamental moral choice: the individual is responsible for making himself what he is in the order of freedom.

We can best understand Kierkegaard's remarks about the absolute character of the free act by recalling the "spiritual idealism" advocated in our own time by the French philosopher, Léon Brunschvicg, who was also deeply indebted to Fichte. He has written some persuasive pages on man's spiritual life as a secular venture in self-realization of scientific thought and love.[15] He stressed the qualitative difference between human reality as a brute datum and as a free affirmation and aspiration of intelligence and will. Brunschvicg, however, refused to recognize a transcendent, personal God, out of fear that such a being would impede the free development of the individual. In this refusal, he stood apart from the main tradition of French philosophy of the human spirit, with which Kierkegaard is in close affinity. With Pascal and Maine de Biran and Lavelle, Kierkegaard would take up the problem of divine and human freedom precisely at the point where Brunschvicg declares it to be insoluble and eliminates one factor. The mystery of personal rebirth lies in man's situation, as being both a product or given reality and a free center of activity. Man's freedom is a participated power, having as its primary task the conquest of selfhood, no longer regarded as an objective datum but as a self-determining choice.

The moral choice also reveals the absolute difference between good and evil. Were good and evil only designations for limited aspects of the absolute Idea, as Hegel maintained, then man would not be faced with a genuine choice of an unconditional kind. Furthermore, the freedom of the act of choosing would be compromised, were good and evil entangled in a necessary dialectic, which mediates all opposites. What is lacking in idealistic absolutism is an adequate explanation of sin. Judge William is aware that the best way to awaken a sense of the irreconcilability between good and evil and of man's creatureliness is to admit sin. He tries to make a place for sin and evil in his account of ethical existence, but Kierkegaard's verdict is that the ethician attains only to a *malum metaphysicum*, conceived with considerable pathos. This adverse judgment hinges upon the fundamental criticism of the ethical conception of God which is to be analyzed in the following section.

Finally, the Judge takes advantage of another religious conception—repentance—in order to differentiate his teaching from that of the Romantic sort of pantheism. In choosing one's self, the ethical individual must accept this self from God's hands in all its singular reality and also in all its inherited and acquired guilt. This admission of guilt in the use of freedom prevents any confusion of the absolute choice of a finite self with self-creation, and also rules out any identification of this self with God. But when Judge William explains in detail what he means by repentance, it turns out to be more an honest recognition of the individual in his concrete nature than a religious sorrow over sinfulness and a determination to amend. It is a deliberate replacement of the individual in his actual social and historical environment, as a countermeasure to the Romantic tendency to divorce the individual from his real setting and to substitute for it a tissue of idealized possibilities and lineages. Ethical freedom must accept and seek to transform not only the isolated individual but the self as a member of a world and an outcome of history.

Kierkegaard is quick to detect any false employment of religious notions, such as sin and repentance. One of his main arguments against Hegelianism is that it deforms the meaning of distinctively religious notions, by interpreting them in terms of the Speculative dialectic. From his analysis of the ethical stage of existence, he concludes that a similar deformation results when the moralist attempts to bolster his position by an appeal to religious truths. This is certainly the case when such truths are fitted into an independent morality, but Kierkegaard acknowledges that ethical life has a natural ordination to religiousness. When the ethical sphere remains open to a decisive religious influence, these two aspects of existence mutually strengthen each other and work toward the unity of the personality. Because of the strong appeal which an autonomous morality makes in the modern age, however, Kierkegaard was more concerned in his esthetic works to explore the points of conflict between the different spheres, as a preface to establishing the right order on the basis of a good understanding of the issues. In his discourses and religious writings, he exhibits the positive good which follows from the harmonious working of ethical and religious influences.

Ethical Existence as the Absolute End

In the last of the esthetic books, *Stages on Life's Way*, Judge William is again the spokesman for the ethical cause.

Now that the three stages are clearly distinguished, the Judge advocates his own position as a definite alternative to both the esthetic and the religious ways of life. He reveals more clearly than before that the ethical idea is a purely immanent one, aiming at human sufficiency. True to his own character, he equates moral perfection and a happy married life as the goal of existence.

Marriage I regard as the highest telos of the individual human existence, it is so much the highest that the man who goes without it cancels with one stroke the whole of earthly life and retains only eternity and spiritual interests—which at the first glance seems no slight thing but in the long run is very exhausting and also in one way or another is the expression of an unhappy life.[16]

All other considerations are to be subordinated to the requirements of married life, for here man finds his chief end. Even service to God must ultimately minister to ethical existence.

The Judge speaks of marriage in extravagant language and usually with religious overtones. He hails it as the beauteous midpoint and center of human existence which realizes esthetic and religious values, within a primarily ethical context. A man is not genuinely and fully human unless he shares in married life, where he finds his eternity in time. The married man feels secure and steady in existence: he is at home here at the very center of temporal happiness and is troubled by no yearning for any perfection which he has not already brought with him into marriage. Judge William likes to consider himself as a kind of anointed priest; he gives his belief to marriage and worships the miracle of love; it provides him with the wedding garment, which alone enables him to sit undisturbed at the banquet of existence. In his wife he finds a renewal of the principles of esthetic life, apart from its selfishness and despair. Thus the married state alone can resolve the tension between the various aspects of human life.

Kierkegaard places these extreme claims into the mouth of his ethical pseudonym, in order to show concretely the consequences of making ethical motives supreme. His method is persuasive, as long as it is limited to illustrating what *one type* of ethical mind thinks about the problems of practical living. But it is not universal enough to bear the full burden of his argument. The esthetic works provide no satisfactory account of how a married life might be incorporated within the religious sphere of existence. Kierkegaard's personal case impresses him so forcefully, that he is ready to conclude that marriage is the prime factor in directing personality to exclusively immanent and finite ends and in sponsoring an esthetic interpretation of religious concepts. The varieties of ethical experience are not investigated in as much detail as are the varieties of esthetic experience. Insufficient attention is paid to individual self-sufficiency, to dedication of one's life to humanitarian ends, or to other prominent forms of ethical existence which also present themselves as substitutes for the love and service of God. Where marriage is involved, Kierkegaard is more concerned to provide a corrective for his own temptations than to give a balanced account of its ethical function. This is an invidious sense in which it is true that the esthetic books mark first of all his own education in the meaning of existence.

4. THE CONFINES OF THE ETHICAL VIEW

In the critical portions of his treatment of the ethical problem, Kierkegaard tries to overcome the drawbacks of the method of dealing solely with individualized attitudes. He accepts the popular version of Kant's moral philosophy as the typical expression of the moralistic outlook. Without undertaking any direct criticism of Kant himself, he repeats the usual charge of formalism which is brought against the Kantian conception of ethics.[17] But Kierkegaard does not content himself with noting the empirical and pragmatic difficulties of modeling one's conduct according to the Kantian rule. His primary concern is with the moralistic interpretation of existence and with the place God occupies in such an interpretation. Indeed, his objections reduce to the two points that God occupies a subordinate position in this system, and that it cannot account for all the relevant existential evidence.

One of the earliest entries in the *Journals* protests against the rationalists' attempt to depersonalize God and to stress duty above love. They bid us improve ourselves, just because reason says that this is best. Such a motive may be sufficient in a closed system of ethics, but it cannot carry greatest weight for actual individuals, who are moved by persons and personal relations more than by universal commands. The moralists reduce the living God to a mere *deus ex machina*, needed only to lend numinous sanction to the categorical imperative. In *The Concept of Dread*, Kierkegaard explains the bad consequences for the individual, when God is not placed at the center of moral effort.[18] The ethician boasts that his ideal conception is an exacting one, in contradistinction to the merely wishful and dreaming aspirations of the esthete. Yet the ethician completes only one phase of what should be a double movement. He convinces the individual of his unconditional obligation to follow the moral law, but he does not provide the power to carry out the morally good act. Duty is brought down to the individual, but it is only assumed that the individual has all the conditions for freely bringing his life up to the exacting standard. Taken as an independent discipline, ethics is too abstract to reckon with the effects of original sin or with such a concrete attitude as being in dread before the good. It attributes failure to follow the commands of conscience too exclusively to defects of practical reason, overlooking malice, the wounds of sin, the inclinations of the passions and the fascinated impotence of the individual before a perilous exercise of freedom. Only the powerful aid of God can remove such impediments to the good life, for the actual condition of man is qualified by his distinctive, religious relation to God.

That there are other and more decisive considerations than those of rationalistic ethics in the determination of conduct and personal attitudes, is clearly evident in the case of exceptions to the universal ethical precepts. This appeal to exceptional situations is Kierkegaard's main argument against the adequacy of the ethical interpretation of existence. If there are cases which cannot be accounted for by means of ethical categories, then these categories are proved to be of only limited scope in the solution of existential questions. Moreover, Kierkegaard maintains that these exceptions seem to the ethical mind to be anomalies, because this mind cannot grasp the religious reasons which are present. These aspects of existence remain hidden, unless the individual is willing to subordinate his esthetic and ethical concerns to the more comprehensive' demands of a religious view of existence. The latter is the culmination of this concrete dialectic and the only balanced attitude for the individual existent.

Before examining these cases in detail, some comment must be made on the general nature of the proof. Where a claim to universal validity has been made, the citation of contrary instances is an effective way to undermine the original assertion. In this instance, the concrete and personal approach of Kierkegaard is perhaps the best way to cast doubt upon the exclusive competency of ethical principles. He is under no obligation at this point to show that all exceptions are religiously motivated, although this problem arises when religious piety is recommended as the most adequate and inclusive outlook on life. He does choose instances from the field of sacred history and from his own "many-tongued reflections" upon the psychological states of religious individuals. In drawing his conclusions, however, he mentions only one major implication: that *individuals* must attain a wider perspective than that provided by the rationalistic ethicians. There is another positive lesson contained in his investigation: that the prevailing *science* of ethics is too narrow and must be replaced by a more adequate moral philosophy. Kierkegaard is anxious to "dethrone" ethical self-sufficiency, but he is little inclined to undertake the arduous work of rehabilitating ethical science within its proper field. His discourses are certainly aimed at awakening the ethical concern of the individual, an indispensable work, but not the only one called for in our day. Moral philosophy no more stands and falls with Kant than does metaphysics with Hegel. A few indications will be given of how reform must take place not only in our moral life but also in our moral science.

At the end of each of Judge William's essays (in *Either/Or* and in the *Stages*), mention is made of individuals who consider themselves to be exceptions to the moral law.[19] The Judge faces these apparent breaks in the solidarity of his world view, but finally declares them to be explainable for the most part on consistent, ethical grounds. But he is not entirely satisfied with his explanations, which sometimes verge on a beautifully expressed retreat from the difficulties. This is readily apparent in his discussion of that type of exception which is made out of obedience to God, rather than to man or law as humanly conceived. The irreducible character of the religious exception is illustrated quite exactly by the story of Job and his rationalizing comforters.[20] In *Repetition*, Kierkegaard remarks that Job tends to break through all our narrow categories and proclaim his quite singular status, as a man under visitation from God. A predicament of this sort does not fit into either esthetic or ethical categories, indicating that existence has other aspects and other laws. But the full import of the presence of religious exceptions is only brought home in the pages of *Fear and Trembling*, which is a sustained meditation upon the significance of such persons for an existential dialectic.

The Biblical Abraham is the dominant figure in *Fear and Trembling*. Kierkegaard presents his story in several different ways, each time furnishing for reflection a different aspect of his character and predicament. But these accounts teach the same lesson. Abraham is a prototype of the exception, called by God to perform a task which is a scandal to the ethical mind. God singles out the patriarch as an individual under trial, addressing and testing him without the aid of intermediaries. Regardless of the temptation to consider the sacrifice of Isaac as a violation of moral law and paternal feeling, the father is bound to respect the word of God above all else. He must bear his secret alone, even at the cost of appearing to deceive his wife, his servant and even his intended victim. In his isolation before God, Abraham is supported only by his utter faith in God and His promises. It is this faith which leads him forth as a single individual, beyond all the customary limits of human conduct and sympathy. In giving his all to God, the father of nations receives all back in full measure and overflowing. These are the essential lines of Kierkegaard's conception of Abraham.

The pseudonymous "author" of the book, Johannes *de silentio*, is himself an ethically formed individual, but one who recognizes in Abraham the presence of something which surpasses his own standards. Hence he raises three questions in connection with the story of Abraham, the only answer to which is the need to go beyond the ethical point of view.[21] Kierkegaard's indictment of an isolated ethic is presented under these three headings.

Problem One asks: "Is there such a thing as a teleological suspension of the ethical?" This question is sometimes re-

framed by commentators to state that Kierkegaard was inquiring about an absolute suspension of ethical principles in
their own reality, whereas it is in fact a question about their
scientific formulation. As understood by Kierkegaard, Kantian ethics places man's supreme perfection and end in a conformity with universal law. Kierkegaard's rejoinder is that
virtue is not an end in itself and that universal moral laws
must themselves refer back to the author of the law, if there is
any question of diverting the individual from a search for
God Himself. He rightly distinguishes between the actual
inclination of the moral law and man's actual end or beati-
tude on the one hand, and the prevalent theories about law
and moral perfection, on the other. As he is careful to state,
under no circumstances can there be a suspension of man's
final end itself or the force of moral law. But if a moral
philosophy convinces an individual that anything other than
God Himself is his final end, then this conviction must be
revoked, regardless of whether it entails the dethronement of
an entire moral outlook. What Kierkegaard does not remark
is that the Stoic and Kantian teachings on virtue and universal law have been challenged on ethical, as well as religious
and practical, grounds. The hard-won distinction between
man's final end, considered subjectively, and considered objectively, is intended by theistic ethics to correct the excessive immanentism of Kant concerning moral perfection.
Kierkegaard is pointing out that this perfection cannot be
gained by directing the will to any other good than God.

Kierkegaard also exposes the ambiguity surrounding the
Hegelian ethical reverence for the universal aspect of moral
law. The ethical interpretation is that a man's duty is to subordinate himself, under all circumstances, to the universal
imperatives. If the individual feels an impulse to assert himself precisely in his particularity, then he is regarded as undergoing temptation. Should he follow through this inclina-

tion in actual conduct, then he has placed himself outside the universal order and so has sinned. As a result, ethicians are scandalized at the case of Abraham: they consider him a murderer in intent, rather than a pious man who is to perform a religious sacrifice. This line of reasoning would make of God a wicked tempter, and of sin a mere expression of finitude and particularity. Ethical universality itself becomes the divine, and a man is forbidden to enter into any private and direct relation with God.

Kierkegaard considers this view a relapse to a pre-Christian position, which misunderstood sin and forgot that the Sabbath is for the sake of man, not man for the sake of the Sabbath. Christianity has revised our view of the universal and the individual, revealing the personal God as the true universal, and individual reality as the perfection in the order of existence. An opportunity is missed by Kierkegaard, however, to support these observations with a metaphysical explanation of our tendency to the good, the nature of universal law and the meaning of moral perfection in the individual. It is sound instinct and religious prompting, rather than a philosophical view of universality and the act of existing, which lead him to defend the rights of the individual self as such. He senses the profound gap which separates the Kantian and Hegelian notions of law and the universal from the Christian view of natural law and the individual existent act, but his own defense of the latter is sometimes mistaken as a plea for subjectivism and antinomianism.

In *Problem Two*, it is asked: "Is there such a thing as an absolute duty toward God?" Since the accepted ethics is powerless to deal with the problem of Abraham, there is need for a new conception of duty and a new view of God. When the ethical order is treated as a closed totality, God becomes at most a "limit-concept," an abstract force which imposes duty universally and attaches holiness to its observance. The ethical individual approaches to God only in so far as he obeys the law solely out of respect for the law. Practically, this Kantian doctrine means that a personal God and a religion distinct from morality are eliminated. Clausen and other rationalistic theologians in Copenhagen did not see this consequence of the theory of autonomous morality, and Kierkegaard never loses an opportunity to point out that such thinkers are providing a substitute for Christianity, rather than a support. He appeals to the faith of Abraham as an instance of a kind of duty which is directly founded upon God, rather than upon the universal character of law. Abraham's obligation of obedience is a direct and absolute one to God Himself, and not one which carries a divine sanction only because of its universal applicability.

If Kierkegaard had been educated in the Scholastic tradition of moral philosophy, he would have found himself discussing with Kant about the proximate and ultimate norms of morality and foundations of duty. His purpose is not to contrast these norms and to dispense with the proximate one, but only to protest against treating the latter as though it were absolute and ultimate. Whether human reason be taken empirically or transcendentally, it remains a derived rule of conduct and its force of obligation is a participated one. Men do not respect moral law just for its own sake, but because it is a sharing in the wisdom and goodness of God, the foundation of all law. As Kierkegaard puts it, one who has known the living God "determines his relation to the universal by his relation to the absolute, not his relation to the absolute by his relation to the universal." [22] This is the kind of relativizing of moral law which he sought: not a diminution of the unconditional character of duty but an explicit founding of duty upon God's goodness, in opposition to the widespread conviction that the removal of God would make no difference in moral life. By anticipation, this criticism extends also to theories of secular morality, such as became popular at the end of Kierkegaard's century. He divined that the Kantian theory of obeying the law out of sheer respect for the law might well issue in a rejection of God and, ultimately, of the unconditional and divine nature of moral law.

Despairing of any philosophical corrective for this current of thinking, Kierkegaard rests his case on the religious examples of men who scandalize the world or seem to be fools, and yet who perform their duty to God. They are witnesses to the insufficiency of a closed ethical system and the need to organize ethical values around some center other than duty and the universal, taken in isolation. In terms of his existential dialectic, he maintains that ethical reflection can appropriate the entire order of esthetic life but cannot extend by itself to a new sort of immediacy in man: religious faith. This is a dimension of inwardness which is called into being by God Himself. But the nature of faith is only hinted at in *Fear and Trembling* and the other esthetic works. Abraham does not convey the full meaning of faith, since Kierkegaard depicts him as one of God's elect who does not have to wrestle with sin.

As a *Third Problem*, Kierkegaard inquires: "Was Abraham ethically defensible in keeping silent about his purpose before Sarah, before Eleazar, before Isaac?" He reflects that Abraham passed by in silence the three tribunals before which ethics would require him to be open and to divulge his plans. The wife, the servant and the son became symbols of the ethical waystations between the religious soul and God. It is beyond their competence to pass judgment upon actions performed out of direct obedience to God. The Kantian dictum about universality and openness, as well as the Hegelian dictum about the inner and the outer, is placed in jeopardy by the silence of Abraham. He is a type of the responsible individual, who obeys the call of faith without seeking to be justified before anything less than the presence of God. His responsible bond with God is maintained, not by means of the Speculative dialectic or the categorical imperative, but by reason of his personal, inward dedication of self to God.

Here again, Kierkegaard has called attention to a truth which is important not only in a religious and practical moral way but also in a properly philosophical way. Abraham's silence calls to mind several doctrines in the moral philosophy of St. Thomas. It is a Thomistic teaching that the secrets of the heart, especially those associated with the disposition of freedom, remain inviolable. They are open only to God and the individual, for not even the angels can pierce this inscrutably private zone, without the individual's consent. One's personal moral state is strictly beyond the judgment of any other finite mind. It is not only inviolable but also in a way ineffable: the individual cannot, if he would, communicate to another his complete attitude. And not to know the subjective side of a man's actions—his motives and aids and understanding of the issue—is not to know the decisive factor in morality, as found in individual life. Furthermore, the final judgment of prudence, in accord with which the individual act is produced, is an inalienably personal and private operation, which cannot rely solely upon universal principles or a necessary dialectic of objective reasons. Every systematic moral philosophy is inclined to overlook or depreciate the personal element in moral life, out of a keen regard for certainty and universality of statement. Kierkegaard's reflections on Father Abraham are a warning that such neglect is often paid for by a loss of the allegiance of fine minds, which are aware of the infinite complexity and personal risk of actual moral decisions.[23]

Kierkegaard's intent throughout this critique is not to abolish, but to restrain and restore to just proportions, the ethical factor in human nature. Only a religiously orientated outlook can assign to esthetic and ethical interests their proper place in human existence. This conclusion is based both upon his own experience and upon his carefully developed dialectic of the spheres of existence. He would have succeeded better, however, had he elaborated a theory of natural law, in harmony with the metaphysics of creatureliness and participation-in-being which is implicit in his view of God and the individual. Such a philosophical basis would have saved his position from being exposed to the plausible charge of depreciating the lower spheres of life, in order to make room for his religious convictions. It would also have prevented these religious convictions from being swept away or volatilized with such ease by some contemporary existentialists. Actually, Kierkegaard is not a mere special pleader for religious interests. His meditations on ethical life have brought to our notice important but neglected aspects of the personal exercise of freedom. No moral philosophy should consider itself well-founded, until it has survived the tests which Kierkegaard proposes.

Chapter Four

The Attack upon Hegelianism

IN THIS chapter and the following one, an analysis is made of the books which Kierkegaard himself designated as his "philosophical works": *Philosophical Fragments, Concluding Unscientific Postscript to the Philosophical Fragments,* and the Introduction to his psychological study on *The Concept of Dread.* The importance of this group of books lies in its critique of the reigning philosophy of Hegel and its preliminary sketch of a new theory of existence, as religiously orientated. Only the first or negative aspect will be taken now, reserving an analysis of Kierkegaard's theory of existence for the following chapter. These books have occupied the major part of the commentators' attention, because of their apparently straightforward, academic presentation of doctrine. Many writers are satisfied to limit their exposition of Kierkegaard's position to a summary of the *Fragments* and the *Postscript,* but the results have been misleading. There are three chief reasons for the misapprehensions which have arisen. Kierkegaard's thought has been considered without due regard for (a) the general historical situation, (b) his own earlier views on the same subject, and (c) the pseudonymous character of these philosophical works. The first two sections below suggest a way of remedying these defects in the usual approach. In the final section, the main lines of the critique of Hegelianism are set forth.

I. WHAT KIERKEGAARD KNEW ABOUT HEGELIANISM

For the sake of orientation, it is well to recall a few comparative facts in the history of post-Kantian idealism. Before Kierkegaard was born (1813), Hegel had already passed through several important phases in his development. The years of Kierkegaard's youth coincide with the period of Hegel's greatest productivity and his ascendancy in the German academic world. Kierkegaard entered the university in 1830, one year before Hegel's death.[1] During the decade of Kierkegaard's residence at the University of Copenhagen (1830-40), the battle over Hegel was raging in Germany. This was the time which marked the appearance of Hegel's collected works (including the religiously preserved lecture notes of his last years), the initial split in the ranks of his followers into left and right wings, the editing of various Hegelian and anti-Hegelian journals, and the radical application of Hegelian principles to theology, the Bible, and church history. Within the decade following Hegel's death, Schelling sought to recover his old popularity at Berlin; Trendelenburg brought his tremendous erudition in classical philosophy to bear against the prevailing historical views; the great Fichte's son criticized Hegel's religious position. The eighteen-forties witnessed a further defection from Hegel on the part of Feuerbach, Ruge and Stirner, along with the radical social philosophy of Marx and Engels. Kierkegaard's students days and first years as a writer coincided with this time of great ferment and uncertainty among the young Hegelians.

Intellectuals in Denmark were for the most part provincially unconcerned about this unrest. They took Hegel's esthetics and philosophy of religion as a permanent gain, as a secure framework which only needed to be altered in minor ways and filled out in detail. Notwithstanding their critical declarations to the contrary, leaders like the litterateur, Heiberg, and the theologian, Martensen, were completely dependent upon the basic postulates of Hegel's logic and metaphysics. They regarded his philosophy as being capable of assimilating both the latest literary offerings and the Augsburg Confession. In matters of politics and popular culture, they confidently expected a new era of reason and peaceful advance. With the exception of P. M. Møller—whom he celebrated as the friend of Socrates and interpreter of Aristotle—Kierkegaard found no sympathetic Danish support for his attack upon Hegelianism. His was a lonely dissident voice, *vox clamantis in deserto*, which rose in protest against the illusory hopes of his countrymen. That is why his case was not presented with full assurance at the beginning, but was tentative and incompletely thought out. Yet even during his bout of romantic intoxication, he answered with a firm negative the query whether Christianity and Hegelian philosophy can come to terms. For a while, he was attracted toward a "Christian speculation" by the vague aspirations of the Romantic philosopher, Franz von Baader; but Kierkegaard considered it possible and desirable only as a foil to the Hegelian System. He was seeking some way of distinguishing Christianity definitively from Hegel's philosophy, without condemning himself to utter silence.

During the years of his regular enrollment for theological lectures (1831-35), Kierkegaard had a chance to judge for himself about the problem of Christianity and (Hegelian) philosophy. The fact that he did not know any philosophical tradition other than the Hegelian, at this time, led him to become suspicious of all systematic uses of philosophical method and concepts. The only alternatives, from the theological standpoint, were the older rationalism of the eighteenth century and the new attempts to bolster orthodoxy with the aid of Hegel.[2] It is understandable that he should have been thrown into confusion in the face of this situation. The theologian, H. N. Clausen, sought to defend the faith with the aid of the Enlightenment, somewhat in the fashion of the New England divines of the previous century. But his "proofs" of Christian dogmas fell flat in the Copenhagen classrooms. For, in making reason the standard to which dogmas must be accommodated, he was robbing religion of its claim to absoluteness and a unique content of revelation. Kierkegaard never found the relation between faith and credibility clarified in the accepted manuals of apologetics and dogmatic theology. Hence he was led to depreciate the service which reason can legitimately perform for revealed religion. In criticizing him on this account, however, we should be careful not to fall back into the theological rationalism which he rightly deplored.

For a while, Kierkegaard thought that the solution of his difficulties was to be found in Schleiermacher, to whose famous *The Christian Faith* he was introduced in 1834 by his tutor, Martensen. Schleiermacher reintroduced into Protestant theology the sense of wonder and humility, the direct realism and the respect for individual experience, which had been lacking since the time of Kant and the Enlightenment. These factors were also conspicuously absent from the Hegelian philosophy of religion, a fact which Kierkegaard took as a weighty objection against explaining Christian doctrine in terms of this philosophy. Further meditation upon Schleiermacher's stand (especially as expressed in spontaneous, Romantic fashion, in the *Addresses on Religion*) convinced him, however, that its basis in feeling was as insecure as the older reliance upon reason alone. Schleiermacher did not succeed any better in securing the independence of Christian belief and the religious attitude as such. The mere feeling of creaturely dependence is not sufficient to account for religion and prayer, for it does not permit of a distinction between man and the rest of created nature. Schleiermacher's Romanticism has a close affinity with Gnosticism, in regarding man's finiteness as no different in kind from his sinfulness. As a consequence, both God's freedom and holiness and man's freedom are compromised. Kierkegaard did not see how Schleiermacher could avoid either attributing evil to the Author of finite nature or maintaining human determinism under original sin, since a man cannot avoid having the finite nature he does have.

During his years as a theological student, Kierkegaard was sure only of the following points: God cannot predestine a man in such a way as to rob him of his freedom; the act of faith itself is free; the God of the Christians is personal, transcendent, and met with in a personal and morally strenuous encounter, rather than in an obscurely mystical, natural piety. At bottom, Schleiermacher's teaching was not far distant from that of Hegel. A half-hearted pantheism lay at the basis of the former's conception of religion as a kind of fusion of the finite with its infinite, universal source and context. Hence Kierkegaard charged Schleiermacher with mistaking Christian faith for a primitive natural condition, a sort of vital fluid or sentiment of creatureliness, in which we are all originally bathed.[3] He saw that this plays into the hands of the Hegelians, who plausibly argue that faith is only a starting point and that men ought to go beyond our primitive condition, to a higher development of reason and philosophy. Here is another aspect of the young Kierkegaard's significance. He was never content with the religious standpoints of Kant, Schleiermacher, and Hegel which furnished the points of departure for many later developments in Protestant theology. Yet he did not have, as yet, any constructive theological substitute for them. His protests were instinctively sound, without providing a positive way of incorporating both reason and feeling within Christian religion.

Romanticism of a nontheological sort appealed to Kierkegaard, if only because it did not confuse Christianity and philosophy. By 1837, he had a firm enough grasp upon the Romantic conception of life-views to use it in his fight against "philosophy," "logic," "reason," and "metaphysics." [4] One of his literary projects of that year was a work to be entitled "Letters of a Young Doubter." The plan was to have a modern, romantically inclined Faust employ the dialectic of life and the fugitive stream of inner feelings against the ironclad pretensions of Hegelian philosophy. Only a few extant pages can probably be identified as belonging to this projected work.[5] These fragments establish a definite connection between this philosophy and the social and moral malaise of the age. Insight as well as irony led Kierkegaard to lump the professors of philosophy together with the theologians, politicians, social reformers, and journalists, who were responsible for the deterioration of life. But these fragments also show how slim was Kierkegaard's actual knowledge of the philosophical texts. He was relying more upon his keen powers of observation and upon current commonplaces than upon a direct examination of the Hegelian writings.

It is to Kierkegaard's great credit that he took independent steps to acquaint himself with the actual situation in Germany. The years 1837-39 marked the real beginning of his serious study of contemporary German philosophers and theologians, excerpts from whose books and articles were painstakingly copied into his notebooks. His readings were amazingly broad, thorough, and current, bringing him quickly abreast with the best work being done in the eighteen-thirties. He read I. H. Fichte on personality, Rosenkranz on fine points in Hegelian exegesis, Carl Daub on dogma and history (apropos of Strauss' notorious *Life of Jesus*), and J. E. Erdmann's lectures on faith and knowledge. By reading current issues of I. H. Fichte's *Zeitschrift für Philosophie und speku-lative Theologie* and Bruno Bauer's *Zeitschrift für spekulative Theologie*, Kierkegaard kept informed about both sides of the growing controversy over Hegel's meaning, worth, and application. Particularly impressive was the criticism passed by the younger Fichte in the first part of his influential *On the Contrast, Turning Point and Goal of Contemporary Philosophy* (1832-36). Fichte rejected Hegel because of his pantheism, denial of personal immortality, and excessively abstract mode of thinking—points of criticism which Kierkegaard was quick to appropriate for himself. He liked Fichte's new program, based on a personal God, inviolable human individuals who do not suddenly find themselves one with the divine self, divine and human freedom, and a concept of eternity which neither swallows up nor devaluates the temporal order. Equally congenial was the appeal for a return to a philosophical method that would hug closer to what Kant had once called "the fruitful *bathos*, the bottom land, of experience." [6] This implied challenge of the customary identification of Speculative thinking with experience was in line with Kierkegaard's growing conviction that reality must be viewed as individual and non-conceptual. If he had not read so conscientiously in these sources, it is doubtful whether Kierkegaard would have directed his thought in precisely the direction it did eventually take.

One surprising fact emerges from this study of Kierkegaard's readings. He had earlier and wider acquaintance with the mass of Hegelian and anti-Hegelian writings, which followed close upon the master's death, than with the actual text of Hegel himself. The research of Hirsch places his first direct reading of Hegel in the late months of 1837 or the early part of 1838. Even then, he apparently limited himself

to the *Lectures on Esthetics*, which helped him to understand the esthetic views of Heiberg and Hans Christian Andersen and also to gather materials for his master's dissertation. During the next three years, Kierkegaard examined certain relevant sections in Hegel's *History of Philosophy*, *Philosophy of History*, and *Philosophy of Right*. But it was not until some time after 1841 that he gave attention to the *Science
of Logic* and especially to the *Encyclopaedia of the Philosophical Sciences*. The first or logical section of the latter work
was studied more closely than any other Hegelian text; most
of Kierkegaard's polemical discussions take some statement in
the *Encyclopaedia* as a starting point. For the religious consequences of Hegelian logic, Kierkegaard relied more upon
the last section of the *Encyclopaedia* than upon the *Lectures
on the Philosophy of Religion*.

Kierkegaard was not interested in the fine shades of meaning and the purely technical points in Hegel. He studied
Hegel, as one studies the *fons et origo* of a broad intellectual
and social movement. This intent should be kept in mind,
when one reads his treatment of Hegel, for otherwise it will
sometimes appear to be only a caricature. The Dane learned
only too well the Hegelian trick of treating predecessors according to their "world-historical" significance, as representative types of thinking. But he does not deal with Hegel any
more arbitrarily than the latter deals with older philosophers,
like Aristotle or Spinoza. Moreover, Kierkegaard found some
of his exposition and criticism ready-made in the sometimes
unreliable contemporary controversial works. This is not to
say that Kierkegaard's own criticism is historically and the-
oretically worthless. Yet it is evident that he had in mind
Hegelianism, as a widespread attitude, more than Hegel himself, in all his nuances and subtle theorizing. The Kierkegaardian critique must be used with caution, when historical
points are at issue. It is best taken as challenging the popular

understanding of Hegel and its consequences for everyday life and religion.

The two books produced during Kierkegaard's *vita ante acta—From the Papers of One Still Living* and the master's dissertation *On the Concept of Irony*—reflect his growing concern with Hegel's philosophy.[7] The *Papers* is much more than a brilliant but cruel satire upon Hans Christian Andersen, the novelist and self-pitying genius. It is also a tentative public attack upon "Speculation" and the "System," which are the customary ways in which Kierkegaard henceforth refers to Hegel's thought. The book points out that the System theorizes so abstractly about being, that it leaves the actual individual and his subjective life quite unaffected. In order to appreciate what individual existence is like, Kierkegaard advises us to heed the examples of Hamann and Socrates. His master's thesis was composed "with constant reference to Socrates," that is, to the human person's everlasting rebellion against being reduced to systematic concepts. This protest is furthered by the use of irony, for the ironical person assures us that he is unassimilable to the Speculative dialectic and its major assumption that the inner and outer aspects of reality are the same. The import of the ironical attitude consists precisely in revealing their discrepancy, as far as human affairs are concerned.

Kierkegaard saw that total anarchy might result, if the ironical mood were glorified for its own sake. He did not want his opposition to the System to issue in irresponsible action and a disregard for general principles. In the work *On the Concept of Irony*, he tries to avoid this consequence in two ways. First, he admits that there is a valid sphere within which speculative thought holds true: his purpose is only to demarcate this territory and point out instances where the boundary has been overstepped. His quarrel is not with the

System as an itinerary of logical notions, but with it as a total account of being. At least, the human mode of being enjoys a free movement of its own which lies beyond the legitimate sphere of the dialectic. Secondly, he notes that irony is only one among several attitudes which go their own way, uncharted and ungoverned by the System. Socrates was only justified in assuming an ironical stand because he used it to free men from the tyranny of general concepts, claiming to determine all of human life. Irony is only a means, and a means that can never be employed safely, unless a man has attained a certain independence of being. The secret of Socrates—which escaped the notice of Hegel in his *History of Philosophy*—was the direct subjective relation he established with God. In virtue of this relation, he could not permit his actions to be determined merely by the consequences of general definitions. A religiously centered life will not allow itself to dance to the waltz tempo of the speculative dialectic, for it is governed by other music. Kierkegaard is groping in these books toward a conception which will allow a place for life as well as logic, and which will found human life's claim to autonomy upon its relationship to God.

Schelling and Trendelenburg

Of all Hegel's contemporary opponents, Kierkegaard was most deeply influenced by Schelling and Trendelenburg. Their polemic had reached its height just at the time when Kierkegaard was beginning his literary career and was feeling the need of providing a definite answer to the philosophical questions raised in his *Journals*. In Berlin, he attended Schelling's lectures during the winter semester of 1841-42. At the age of sixty-six, Schelling had been called from his comfortable home in Munich to the University of Berlin, at the behest of Frederick William IV. Although his lectures were not successful, they did give Kierkegaard an opportunity to hear

Hegel's old enemy expound the views of his last period. Presumably, Schelling developed the same themes which are found in his final but uncertainly edited masterpiece, the *Introduction to the Philosophy of Mythology*. In the second part, or philosophical introduction to his outlook, he set forth his famous distinction between negative and positive philosophy. Kierkegaard explicitly mentions this distinction and draws heavily upon it, in an attempt to limit Hegel's philosophy without falling into irrationalism.[8]

Schelling taught that the most important example of a purely logical or "negative" approach to reality is Hegel's system. Every genuine philosophy must begin with a negative phase, in which there is a careful analysis of the meaning of concepts and their inferential relations. This logical or rational moment is negative, in the sense that abstraction has been made from real conditions, so that the mind can examine general meanings. Hegel's mistake was to take negative philosophy in a rationalistic way, as the definitive and exhaustive account of being. Schelling proposed, on the contrary, that logic should undertake a program of self-criticism and self-limitation. He distinguished sharply between essence and existence. Although negative philosophy can treat of the "what," or possible essence, it cannot extend to the "that," or concrete existent (*das, was das Seiende selbst ist*—a turn of phrase later appropriated by Heidegger). Although the logical method of Hegel is competent in the sphere of possibilities and general essences, it cannot determine the state of actual existents. Only a "positive" philosophy can explore the latter region.

Kierkegaard concurred with Schelling's "break-through to actuality," only in so far as it supported his own contention that Hegel's method was out of place in dealing comprehensively with the world of fact, real movement, and freedom. But he could not follow Schelling in his theosophical talk about the primitive sadness of God and the unfolding of the universe from the divine bosom. Kierkegaard regarded these "positive" speculations as a typical instance of the spoiling of both metaphysics and dogma, by treating metaphysics dogmatically and dogma metaphysically. He was ultimately disillusioned about both I. H. Fichte and Schelling, because of their efforts to reconstitute a systematic, speculative idealism, albeit an absolute idealism of an anti-Hegelian tenor.[9] Kierkegaard did not want to take back with his left hand what he had already rejected with his right. There is *no* valid idealistic system of existence, Hegelian or otherwise.

In his *Journals*, Kierkegaard records with chagrin his failure to attend the lectures which Trendelenburg gave in Berlin during that same season, 1841-42. Kierkegaard avoided him because of his reputed Kantianism, and hence never made personal acquaintance with this great Greek scholar and opponent of Hegel. But from 1844 onwards, Kierkegaard made up for this lost opportunity by reading most of Trendelenburg's books. What first attracted him to Trendelenburg was his sound philological training, combined with his interest in Plato and Aristotle. He shared this interest with Hegel and the whole generation of thinkers affected by the Romantic love for Hellas and Greek philosophy. Hegel himself saluted Aristotle as "the teacher of the human race." So great was his respect for the Stagyrite that one Hegelian scholar has declared that the best introduction to Hegel's philosophy is a reading of the *Metaphysics* and *De Anima* of Aristotle. Anyone who has read Hegel's lectures on the history of philosophy is impressed by his treatment of the peerless Greek minds and by his own project of making a new synthesis of Plato and Aristotle. Now, Kierkegaard himself began reading these Greek masters during the eighteen-forties, in order to form an independent judgment about the Greek outlook. His conclusion was that Hegel stood in direct contradiction to the Greek spirit, which was characterized by its realism, its finite good sense, and its recognition of the limitations of logical tools. It seemed to Kierkegaard that Hegel extended the Greek categories to cases they were not intended to cover, and at the same time failed to grasp the meaning of their valid application.

What surprised and heartened Kierkegaard at this point in his Greek studies was the confirmation of his appraisal of Hegel contained in Trendelenburg's notable series of polemical writings: *Elements of Aristotelian Logic* (1836), *Logical Investigations* (1840), and *The Logical Question in Hegel's System* (1843).[10] While he was composing the *Postscript*, Kierkegaard relied heavily upon these Aristotelian studies. In 1847, he acknowledged that there was no philosopher from whom he had learned so much as Trendelenburg. The latter's well-known study on the categories prompted Kierkegaard to search for "a new category," which would express what is unique in Christian existence. He found it, later on, in the notion of "the individual," which enabled him to get beyond the standpoint of Trendelenburg himself, without relapsing into Hegel's notion of the concrete universal.

Trendelenburg sets out to test the Hegelian System logically, by means of a number of careful investigations. His criticism centers upon Hegel's basic postulates concerning an absolute beginning, the power of negation, and the law of immanent identity. None of these postulates can be supported either by an appeal to the Greeks or by logical analysis. (a) A logical doctrine cannot make a presuppositionless beginning, since the initial step in the logical order supposes at least the act of abstraction on the part of the thinker whereby he prescinds from the physically real mode of being. This precondition is overlooked, when a logical way is found to derive the *concept* of reality, which is confused with that which it signifies: *existent* reality. (b) Hegel's appeal to the dynamic power of negativity is equally sterile. He mistakes the movement of thought, as it clarifies its notions by means of contrasts and comparisons in the conceptual order, for existential movement. Hegel's famous derivation of becoming from being and nonbeing is seen to be a failure, when the distinction between conceptual and existential movement is kept in mind. The abstract notions of being and nonbeing simply blunt and cancel each other out, if taken by themselves, rather than interpenetrate and give rise to physical becoming. Hegel's pure categories lack the one essential factor required for obtaining knowledge of real movement: sensuous intuition of a body in space and time. What Hegel called sensuous intuition, is only a disguised moment of dialectical thought. (c) Finally, no tracing out of the systematic interconnections between logical categories can yield an adequate understanding of God's nature and his plan for the world. Trendelenburg affirms "an infinite specific difference" between God and the world, a difference such that no pure logic of dialectical identity can determine the concrete, providential relation between them.

All of these points reappear in Kierkegaard with, of course, his own further development. Trendelenburg encouraged the native strain of realism and empiricism in Kierkegaard. From Kierkegaard to Lenin, the historical and critical studies of Trendelenburg have served as forces of liberation from formalistic idealism in logic and metaphysics.[11] Whether realism is to be religiously existential or materialistic depends, however, upon the service to which the realistic dialectic is put. Kierkegaard's Romantic and Christian tendencies led in an opposite direction to that of dialectical materialism, despite a common return to epistemological realism.

2. THE ANTI-HEGELIAN STRAIN IN THE ESTHETIC WORKS

Kierkegaard did not remain silent about Hegel in the interval between the publication of his master's dissertation and the philosophical writings. During this time, his esthetic works were written. Their main concern was, necessarily, with problems associated with poetic existence and the levels of awareness. Because of his strong attraction toward the Romantic view of life, Kierkegaard was urgently moved to determine his own position on this matter very carefully. He never felt drawn toward the System with equal force, despite his love for dialectic and polemics. To him it always appeared as something alien, dishonest, and corrupting in its unqualified state. Yet he discovered that the System stood in ambiguous relation to the various spheres of life and hence required some treatment, even in the books devoted to these spheres. In the present section, some brief indications will be given of the continuity in Kïerkegaard's criticism of Hegel, even during his examination of Romanticism.

Kierkegaard is sometimes criticized for fighting fire with fire, for attacking Hegel with Hegelian methods and concepts. He was not alone in this predicament, for it faced Marx and the whole generation of thinker\, who began writing in the decades immediately following Hegel's death.[12] Original impulses in philosophy are often generated by situations of this sort. The measure of Kierkegaard's technical achievement is the extent to which he criticized Hegel, by placing dialectical reflection upon a nonidealistic basis. What made his task the more difficult was precisely his sense of technical dependence upon Hegel and his desire to be fair toward him. Kierkegaard's readings in the Greeks and moderns were intended to aid his independent thinking, and yet, within definite limits, he expressed his admiration for Hegel. He prized especially the following traits: the use of a dialectical method, the organization of historical materials, the brilliant esthetic criticism, the great erudition, the study of the categories, and above all the use of the Greek thinkers.[18] Kierkegaard hoped to use these same instruments in a nonidealistic and nonabsolutist way. In his own estimate, there was only a hairsbreadth of difference between himself and Hegel: the difference between reality and a concept of reality. He was willing to admit that Hegel was the world's greatest thinker, on condition that he did not pretend to be more than an experimenter in thoughts. But since, in point of fact, Hegel did try to equate reality with his own systematic articulations, he appeared to Kierkegaard as a comical figure, whose pretensions are belied by life in its existential richness.

(a) *Either/Or.* Except for one long aside, only indirect attention is paid to the problem of Speculation in *Either/Or.* The reader is liable to overlook the anti-Hegelian significance of certain points of agreement between the esthetic and the ethical spokesmen. They both oppose the Hegelian assumption that everything immediate is destined only to be torn down and rebuilt in a higher synthesis. They jointly satirize the marvelous objectivity of systematizers, who are so concerned with the plight of others that they forget their own, who can dismiss "unhappy consciousness" in a couple of disinterested paragraphs and then pass on, just as unconcernedly, to a disquisition on other equally impersonal topics. The poetic youth clings closely to chance, "the occasion," the category of the interesting, and the discrepancy between one's inner conviction and outer manifestation, in a desperate effort to defend individuality against systematic generalizations. Similarly, his ethical counterpart, the Judge, maintains that such passions as resolution and repentance cannot be explained in terms of a natural necessity.

Yet there is a definite parting of the ways between the

principals in this grand-scale dialogue. In marking the difference between his own moral standpoint and estheticism, the Judge explicitly pairs off the latter with the Speculative outlook.[14] They share in common the presumption that all extremes can be mediated. What makes this claim plausible, is the admitted fact that the abstract method of generalization through necessary laws does hold true in regard to logic, natural science, and so-called world history. Kierkegaard is willing to admit the competence of general concepts and systematic inferences within these disciplines, with the proviso that they do not embrace all of human life and its interests. But Hegel's universal extension of this method prevents him from constructing a true ethics, for this method admits no distinction between an interplay of concepts and a free choice between the good and the evil. In such a choice, there is no possibility of watering down both extremes to a neuter factor or of synthesizing them in a "higher morality." Moral requirements thus present a scandalous instance of nonmediation, a sign that in the realm of freedom some other approach than the Hegelian must be taken.

(b) *Repetition.* Kierkegaard's studies in Aristotle are put to good use in *Repetition.* Here Constantine Constantius, the amateur psychologist, commends a re-reading of what the Greek thinkers taught about being, nonbeing, and the instant. He advises that special attention be paid to the Greek concept of *kinesis* or motion, which stands in contrast with the Hegelian notion of transition.[15] What the Hegelians fail to tell us is how movement comes about, in the first place. Is it already contained in the thesis and antithesis, or does it spring forth as a novel element? On the first explanation, there would be no genuine change or realization of that which previously was not actual. But the second alternative would commit one to a completely irrational explanation, since no sufficient cause is present. The only escape for Hegel would be to confess that the movement for which his dialectic accounts is not real movement. In this case, progress need not involve further actualization or a real cause in operation. But such an admission would also restrict the System to the conceptual order, which is the end at which Kierkegaard is aiming. Like Aristotle, he is suggesting that illegitimate profit is being made from an unanalyzed situation. The requirements of real motion cannot be satisfied within Systematic confines, since human existence and action require real "passion," as well as thought.

Kierkegaard's references to real motion are sometimes puzzling to students, because of his custom of passing insensibly from motion in general to human free action. His attitude seems to be that, for a general analysis of motion, we have the text of Aristotle to consult. This general solution is sufficient to dispel the belief that Hegel has given an adequate cosmological treatment of change. Aristotle stresses the need for a physical cause in actual operation and for the production of new actual being. It is enough for Kierkegaard to note that the Hegelian dialectic can supply neither of these factors of change. His own interest lies chiefly in the direction of human actions and their freedom. Kierkegaard remarks that, in human action, something over and above thought must enter as a motive principle. He refers to this plus factor as "passion," and it is similar to Pascal's emphasis upon the heart and Rousseau's upon the emotions. Its importance for the history of philosophy lies in its repudiation of a centuries-old tendency to obliterate the real distinction between the cognitive and the appetitive orders, between the knowing and the desiring-and-willing powers. Spinoza and Hegel were most consistent in drawing out the consequences of a reduction of desire to knowledge. It rules out ordinary empirical freedom on man's part, and prevents a reasonable explanation of the transcendence of God. Along that way lie determinism, pantheism, and monism; and therefore Kierkegaard will have nothing to do with this reduction. Hence his insistence, at every opportunity, upon the passional element in human action, the need for resolution and an intervention of will, as well as for the calculation of intellect. By disregarding the unique role of the desiring powers, Hegel is unable to explain how motion transpires at the human level. His dialectic accounts only for the conception of a plan of action, not for the physical occurrence of the action as a novel and free event in the world.

(c) *Fear and Trembling*. The open and detailed assault upon Systematic pretensions begins in *Fear and Trembling*. Irony is deliberately used by Johannes *de silentio*, the pseudonymous author, against the popular manifestations of the new philosophical mentality. Nowadays, he satirically observes, "every crofter and cottar in philosophy" brags about the ease with which everything can be doubted and new certainties established. What once constituted the genius of a Descartes and the holiness of an Abraham—the ability to doubt and to remain faithful throughout a lifetime of trial—is today the commonplace possession of all and the starting point for far greater triumphs. One has only to criticize great men and think about great things, in order to be considered great in one's own right. What matters is only the visible result: the speculative tome, the social order, or the public reputation. To belong to the *avant-garde* is not to be in the spearhead of attack and danger, but to be in conformity with the spirit of the age and protected from the shocks and discrepancies of existence.

In this book, Kierkegaard continues his discussion of motion, as it applies to human affairs. One of the mighty passions, which have moved men to perform great deeds, is faith. A contrast is established between the religious view of faith and Hegel's teaching on conscience. The point of departure is found in Hegel's section on "Good and Conscience," in his *Philosophy of Right*.[16] Here, it is argued that both universal objective good and moral conscience, or subjective will, are abstract. Conscience belongs to the intermediate sphere of morality (*Moralität*), and hence is a transitional moment, destined to be sublated in the higher ethical life (*Sittlichkeit*). This latter state is the concrete universal, the dialectical union of the objective factor of universal norms and the subjective factor of conscience. It is a typical instance of Hegel's dialectical resolution of problems, by the application of the principle of mediation. The conscientious individual calls into question the accepted norms, and thereby his will becomes at least potentially evil. This evil condition can only be overcome by bringing one's moral subjectivity, or conscience, into conformity with universal principles. The norms which were once "vaporized" in individual conscience, must again be "condensed" in concrete ethical, institutional life. Thereby, the concrete universal *Sittlichkeit*, the ethical absolute, descends from heaven to earth.

Our concern here is not with the general antipathy of the religious mind toward this conception of ethical life, but with the specifically anti-Hegelian contrast between faith and the view that conscience is an intermediate step. Johannes *de silentio* does not himself have the strength to make the movement of faith, but from a distance he sees that faith is a judgment passed upon the Speculative theory of conscience. For, the faith of Abraham is a vindication of the righteousness of the individual, taken precisely in his particularity. This "gigantic passion" throws light upon both the nature of human subjectivity and that of the absolute. Faith would be senseless, unless it were a free dedication of the human person, in his individual reality, to a God who is personal, loving, and transcendent. There is no mediation of God and man in a higher unity. God does not turn out to be the innermost essence of man, and the individual believer is not asked to volatilize his personal relation of creaturely devotion and obedience to a personal God. There is nothing higher or more concrete, for the aim of human life and its goodness are attained, once the individual learns to exist as such before God.

Faith is an extreme instance of the inability of the Systematic dialectic to generate a real movement. The reflection upon which this dialectic is based may be of aid in passing from an uninformed and naive state of mind to a more enlightened one. But the change which faith brings about in a man's life is more than a clarification of mind and extension of thought. It is capable of altering the entire course of a man's existence, redirecting all of his powers and interests, in virtue of a new, personal relation to God. Faith moves a man precisely in so far as he is this individual existent, not as a subordinate moment in the absolute concept. It is an existential, rather than a conceptual, determinant. Hegel went astray in confusing religious and moral faith with natural confidence and warm inner feeling, which men like Jacobi and Schleiermacher called faith. *Their* state of faith can pass away into philosophical knowledge, but the latter still falls short of producing the kind of passion which moved the Biblical men of faith.[17] Faith, in the existential sense, is a *new* sort of immediacy, which philosophy is powerless to give. For, one does not pass to it by a process of reflection alone but by the engagement of one's whole being and loyalty. The Greek sense of awe before what cannot be comprehended through philosophical categories, is preferable to the Hegelians' claim to sublate conscience and faith in scientific knowledge.

No special consideration need be given to the treatment of the Hegelian problem contained in *Stages on Life's Way*. Kierkegaard sums up his previous criticisms in the statement that Hegel's fundamental shortcoming is his suppression or misinterpretation of the passional features of human subjectivity. When they are given a place in the System, they are there as "buccaneer riches," stolen from the richness of life and denigrated by the Speculative method. Even after this method has introduced the finite mind into the state of *das absolute Wissen* or absolute knowledge, existence persists in asking its quiet question: How did this individual suddenly become the absolute, metaphysical selfhood? In a word, Kierkegaard is saying to the Hegelians: "Come, let us stop playing at being gods and get to work at the serious task of becoming worthy men." His metaphysical inquiries are made with the aim of clearing the atmosphere, so that his counsel will be heard and heeded.

3. SPURIOUS PILLARS OF WISDOM

Kierkegaard did not analyze Hegelian philosophy for its own sake, but only as a principal cause of the watered-down version of moral life and Christianity to which his age was exposed. He traced the misunderstanding between true Christian existence and this philosophy to Hegel's failure to grasp the meaning of existence, in the human mode of inwardness. As a consequence of its mishandling of existence, the System also mistakes the nature of the individual and his ethical requirements. Some of the arguments advanced by Johannes Climacus (the pseudonymous "author" of the *Fragments* and the *Postscript*) are of little more than historical interest today, as proof of Kierkegaard's close acquaintance with the fine points of the post-Hegelian controversy. But his major contentions retain their theoretical value, and can even be applied to more recent versions of absolute idealism. By reducing them to three main theses, their worth can be determined more exactly than in the diffuse form of their original presentation. (a) Hegel does not see that the very act of existence as such can never be subsumed within a system of finite thought, no matter how broad and inclusive its principles and method.

(b) In the metaphysical order, Hegel is inept in dealing with the basic notions of being and becoming; this is due to his failure to distinguish between these concepts in their logical status and as representative of objects, which are themselves nonconceptual. (c) Hegel's theory of world history is inimical to man's ethical life as a responsible individual.

These charges are found, in substance, in the Introduction to *The Concept of Dread*.[18] Here, Kierkegaard singles out some leading Hegelian concepts which he believes to be inadequately explained: actuality, contingency, faith, the beginning, immediacy, reconciliation of thought and being, mediation, ethics, the negative principle, movement, immanence, and evil. Only the briefest mention is given to each concept, so that this Introduction provides only a concentrated program of attack. The actual, detailed reasoning is supplied in the *Fragments* and the *Postscript*. In the latter work, the shrewd remark is passed that no one should attempt to criticize Hegel who is not equipped with sound common sense, a share of humor, and a dose of Greek ataraxy.[19] Not only is this a sharp observation, but it explains how Kierkegaard could achieve such considerable success in his campaign against Hegel, without the formal aid of a realist philosophy of being.

Kierkegaard's common sense told him that all would be lost, if he were once lured into conducting the discussion on the idealistic terrain. He saw that, were the Speculative labyrinth entered even for a moment, the Ariadne thread connecting him with the real world would be snipped, beyond repair. Hence his analyses are directed at the presuppositions and the initial steps in the Hegelian dialectic. This is a sound tactical policy, which might be followed by any critical student of idealism. At the same time, the problems cannot be dismissed; and hence Kierkegaard recommended a kind of mitigated skepticism. To keep one's assent free, and yet be concerned about the issues, is the only alternative to dodging the challenge of Hegel. Calmness of mind and suspension of judgment can be maintained, provided that one always keeps in mind the comical aspect of the System. All Systematic arguments are carried on within a huge parenthesis, which is no longer adverted to by the Systematic adepts themselves. There is no danger of being swept into the dialectical vortex, once it is observed that the whole discussion leaves existence and real being out of consideration, even while discoursing about the concepts of *Existenz* and *Sein*. No one should approach the study of idealism or the critical problem, without profiting by Kierkegaard's advice about the proper personal attitude to be maintained. There is no purely objective and impersonal formula to be followed in this matter, unless one wishes to ignore the question entirely.

The Inhuman Comedy: A System of Existence

The first charge against Hegel can be stated in two simple propositions: a logical system is possible; an existential system is impossible.[20] Kierkegaard's mind is not fairly described unless due weight is placed upon the first, and often neglected, proposition. His is not an antilogical and irrational standpoint, but rather one which would insist upon the difference between logic and metaphysics.[21] Had he known the texts, he would have agreed with Aquinas that the former discipline is concerned with the universe of being, precisely in its logical status as conceived by the mind, whereas metaphysics is directed primarily and properly toward being in its physical reality and act of existing. As it was, however, Kierkegaard had no acquaintance with a metaphysics which is clearly distinguished from logic; and hence his positive contention was that the act of existence is beyond the reach of every philosophical discipline. This is due, not so much to a bias against metaphysics, as to despair of man's ability to recapture philosophically the realist spirit of the Greeks. Hence his own efforts were concentrated upon keeping at least the Christian view of existence free from Hegel's logicizing metaphysics, the Speculative System. Following Trendelenburg, Kierkegaard held that logical categories can yield some knowledge, but only on condition that they never pretend to finality of explanation and are constantly ready to submit deductive results to the test of fresh experience and novel process. Moreover, logic prescinds from, and is indifferent to, real existence and existential determinants of real movement. It should not attempt to explain these realities exhaustively, through its own postulates. But its indifference toward existence and real motion should be taken as a confession of its own limitations, rather than as a depreciation of the philosophical significance of these aspects of being.

Kierkegaard admits that the greater part of our thinking is carried on in terms of objective, abstract reasoning. The natural, mathematical, and social sciences deal with objects through their essential natures, abstract relations, and inductively necessary natural laws. Such sciences give genuine knowledge within these methodic limits, but they are not competent beyond the sphere of essence and possibility. Scientific laws do not determine the condition of the individual as such, nor do scientifically constructed concepts give formal insight into existence and the actual order. The sort of scientific understanding that recognizes and acknowledges these limits upon its competence, is usually termed by Kierkegaard *abstract thought*. Abstract thought is the theoretical counterpart of the esthetic life. They are both carried on in the medium of possibility: poetizing and imagining transpire in the possibility of moods and sentiments, whereas abstract reasoning and induction transpire in the possibility of general categories. The latter prescind from existence, without repudiating an existential and experiential point of origin. Scientific thought can deal not only with nonhuman nature, but also with man himself, to the extent that the self can be grasped abstractly, generally, and statistically, as one among other naturally determined objects.

In contrast with the position of abstract thought is what Kierkegaard calls *pure thought*. This term—*das reine Denken* —has a precise technical sense in Hegel, signifying the state of Systematic philosophical knowledge, as it is formally aware of its own nature as absolute science or wisdom. Kierkegaard appropriates the same term to connote the radical difference between the valid meaning of science and the idealistic transformation of this meaning. Kierkegaard is no enemy of abstract thinking for its own sake, but he protests rightly against any attempt to disguise the fact of abstractness and so to deny the limitations of scientific thinking. Pure thought denies its original dependence upon a nonconceptual source, and claims to include existence and actuality within itself, in such an absolute way that they are generated in and by the dialectical movement of thought. Hence, there is a great chasm separating abstract from pure thought, one which Kierkegaard feels called upon to emphasize rather than bridge.

Readers trained in the tradition of realistic philosophy would add that there is a third position, which Kierkegaard has overlooked. While admitting the restricted scope of abstract scientific thought and joining in the opposition to absolute idealism, Thomistic realism would yet propose a view of metaphysics in which the formal object is being as existent, rather than a "pure" concept of being, correlative to a concept of nonbeing. A nonidealistic metaphysics is based upon an original judgment of existence, which gives some knowledge about the act of concrete existent being. An existentially orientated metaphysics does not pretend to be able to give a complete conceptual formulation about the existent subject, but returns to it again and again, as to an independent and inexhaustible source. A metaphysics so considered has a wider and deeper range than the particular sciences and the more abstract parts of philosophy, but it makes no pretense to engulf being within itself, as an originative dialectical principle. It deals by means of concepts and judgments with that which is more than, and other than, concepts and judgments. It is the perfection of *human* scientific thinking.

Such an alternative did not present itself to Kierkegaard, except in so far as Aristotle was on the track of such a notion of first philosophy. Kierkegaard's historical situation should never be forgotten; if we give heed to his remarks on his great philosophical predecessors, it will *not* be forgotten. He read Aristotle only informally and as presented by Trendelenburg, who had idealistic preoccupations of his own; his interest in Plato was largely confined to extracting from him a picture of Socrates; Kierkegaard's philosophical thinking was determined, for the rest, by the modern writers. Concerning Descartes, he observed that he embarked on an impossible task, when he attempted to base surety about his own existence upon the act of abstract, theoretical thinking. From such an act and the resultant determination of an essence, it is impossible to arrive at the real human self, the existent subject. Existence cannot be deduced from essence alone, and the Cartesian *Cogito* always remains at some distance from both the self and the world as existent things. Hence, in Kierkegaard's eyes, Kant was justified in stressing the cleft between thought and being, phenomenal object and noumenon, provided that abstract thought is in question.

Kierkegaard consistently referred to Kant's position in regard to pure reason as a form of skepticism. This position would be admissible, if the abstract thought of the sciences were our only form of knowledge, but Kant has no right to generalize the scientific method. Against a view that the existent thing, or noumenon, is unknowable and perhaps unknowing, Kierkegaard pointed to the fact that the individual man both exists and thinks as a single personal entity, and to the further fact that there can be some knowledge of the self in its personal being. Now, unfortunately, Hegel is prevented by his dialectical monism from accepting the condition of the finite human individual as decisive, and from regarding God as really transcendent to a finite reality which He knows and loves as distinct from Himself. Hence he cannot offer any genuine certitude against the arguments of Kant. Kierkegaard did not lust after certainty at any price, and hence he did not grasp eagerly at Hegel's new dogmatism. His verdict was that Hegel became so alarmed by Kant's skepticism, that he decreed an arbitrary solution of the problem, one just as sterile and groundless as the "new beginning" made by Schelling.[22] Hegel simply stipulated that, in his System, thought and being must be regarded as fundamentally identical. Thus, he developed his notion of pure thought, so as to beguile himself into believing that philosophical reasoning is productive of actual being.

Historically considered, Kierkegaard was ripe for reception of a realistic metaphysics. Having repudiated the Hegelian postulate, he was unwilling to relapse into Kant's concealed skepticism. For him, it was no sufficient proof of the unknowableness of existence that it finds no place in abstract thinking, and is denatured in the context of pure thought. He hoped to show that existence is indeed accessible to an ethico-religious dialectic, but he placed such knowledge beyond philosophical science. We cannot expect guidance from him in solving the question of existence *philosophically,* and that is why many existentialists have returned covertly to idealism. Yet we do not need to follow their example, in order to profit philosophically by Kierkegaard's sound conviction that "pure thought" violates the nature of existent being.

Kierkegaard traces the Hegelian conception of the System directly to the "one lunatic postulate" about pure thought.[23]

Only in the fantastic medium of pure thought can being be regarded as (in principle) completely understood and finished, for only in this medium is existence—with its uncertainties, contingencies, and fresh processes—revoked. The Speculative System is persuaded of its own sufficiency, not only in regard to the complete content of knowledge, but also in regard to its beginning, which is conceived of as a self-priming start. It purports to make a presuppositionless beginning in philosophy, to start immediately with the immediate. In this way it produces its own objects, as the dialectic moves along. The result is a comprehensive explanation, every link of which is necessary and necessarily connected with the next step. The System is the organic totality of philosophical science, and ultimately is the divine Idea, which has arrived at articulate self-consciousness. Hegelian philosophy views itself not only as a doctrine about the absolute but also as an absolute doctrine, in the strictest sense.

In Trendelenburg's path, Kierkegaard challenges the two cardinal, Hegelian notions of making an immediate beginning and philosophizing without any presuppositions.[24] Consulting the opening pages of Hegel's *Logic*, he finds that by "the immediate" is meant the most abstract content, like "being," which remains after a quite exhaustive reflection upon our various concepts. He submits that, with *this* sort of immediate principle, one can never make an immediate beginning, since it supposes the entire process of abstraction and reflective analysis. It is not the initial point of thought, but a term which has been arrived at through a process, which is both psychologically and logically prior to the supposed starting point. The so-called primitive concept of being, with which the *Logic* begins, is already shot through with dialectical suppositions, including the reference of being to nonbeing, as its antithesis. Similarly, the opening sections on sense certainty and perception, in the *Phenomenology of Spirit*, describe a situation which is far more sophisticated and laden with ideal-istic prejudices than are actual empirical cases of sense per-ception. Now, if so much is presupposed, both on the part of the subject and on the part of an already functioning dialectic, before Hegel's "initial" steps are reached, then there is no more foundation for the claim to make a presuppositionless beginning than to make an immediate one.

Attempts at founding an entirely presuppositionless philos-ophy have always ended—from Hegel to Husserl—in the dis-appearance of the empirical human self. A reading of Kierke-gaard should place us on guard against any such attempt, and should enlighten us about its consequences. For us men, think-ing must retain its reciprocity with being and its dependence upon existence. Kierkegaard sees that our knowing begins not with a dialectical concept of pure being, which passes over necessarily into its antithesis, but with existence as the prior factor. As he puts it, thinking is our human response to the irruption of existence into our subjectivity. An absolute beginning is indeed made by our minds. It is made, however, not from nothing, nor from our own dialectical machinery, but from the forcible entrance of existence, as it is met by a passionate and decisive response on our part.[25]

It is not too difficult to translate this conviction into the language of the Thomist theory of existential judgment and the first affirmation that something exists. Kierkegaard is stress-ing the giveness of being and man's immanent response to this gift. He speaks about beginning our speculation with a resolu-tion of will. It would be farfetched to see in this a return to the Cartesian view of judgment as the act of will, although Kierkegaard lacks any clear notion of judgment. By this re-mark, he seems to convey something of his assurance that thought is not self-sufficient and self-priming, but is first impregnated by that which is existentially prior to, and other than, our thought. Furthermore, he asks that men confess this dependence of their speculations upon a given principle, which is not generated by our mind. Equivalently, he is asking that the first judgment be an affirmation of that which *is*, considered precisely as exercising its own act of being in its own otherness or self-reality. And he sees the need for rectitude of will, throughout the long process of translating the original situation into an accurate and honest philosophical statement.

Behind the polemic against the System lies Kierkegaard's concern for the threatened reality of God and man. One question is never far from his lips: how does the finite, empirical, human self stand in relation to the absolute and divine self? Hegel makes an easy transition from the standpoint of the individual mind to that of the absolute mind, considered as a process of thinking its own development and self-explication.[26] Kierkegaard admits that the transition could be made, if it could be shown that, for the finite human self, *to be* means *to-be-a-moment-of-pure-thought*. Now, this equivalence can be demonstrated only in the imagination, by abstracting from, and then forgetting about, the existing reality of the individual. This can be done in a fit of absentmindedness, perhaps, but the pose cannot be maintained for long, under normal conditions and under the gaze of the comic spirit. Kierkegaard maintains that the Hegelian interplay of opposites does not provide the deepest form of comedy. The latter arises from a comparison between systematic conclusions and the individual systematizer, who draws them. *Hic homo intelligit*, this individual man does the knowing, as Aquinas curtly reminded the Averroists. After Hegel has had his majestic laugh about the dialectical identity of all apparently hard-and-fast contrasts, there remains the last mirthful and tragic moment, when existence settles its accounts with this individual man, as being responsible to his God.

A truly systemic view of reality belongs only to God, for

only He can embrace within His eternal vision the breadth, temporal span, and secrets of existence and becoming. To achieve this systemic viewpoint in an actual way, one must either be the eternal and infinite being or forget that one is a temporal and limited being. Hence Kierkegaard's final verdict about the System is that it is valid only for God or for some fantastic *quodlibet,* a philosophical will-o'-the-wisp. Since the Hegelians betray occasional signs of being something less than divine and eternal, it is likely that they have been led into their position by a trick of imagination. Hegel, the metaphysician, and Goethe, the esthete, are so enamored of the notion of a "pure humanity," that they seem to forget the empirical and quite individual being that each one is. This places their thought in comical contradiction with their life, and forces the rest of us to face the one question left unasked and unanswered by the System. What does it mean for each one of us singly to be a human being, existing in an individual, finite way, and with a unique ethical and religious task to perform?

Two Metaphysical Problems: Being and Becoming

From certain texts in the *Postscript,* the reader who is unfamiliar with the preceding discussion about the presuppositionless beginning may conclude that Kierkegaard is definitely antimetaphysical, in his repudiation of the concept of being. What is true is that he opposes Hegel's notion of being, because of its excessively "pure" and Systematic character. He was not unfamiliar with Hegel's assertions about the concrete universal, but he denied that concreteness is ever attained in the System. When Hegel says that thought becomes concrete, he forgets to add that it does so, only within the general determination of pure thought. To Kierkegaard, this meant that only a representation and loose analogy of concreteness is attained, since pure thought is stranger to the particularity of individual existence which constitutes, for him, the authentic concrete order. This is a basic criticism, one that is applicable also to the views of Croce and other contemporary idealists. Kierkegaard had too much regard for the existent subject— for what he called the self, and Thomists, the supposit—to agree to its inclusion within the Systematic dialectic. Hegel is prevented, in principle, from developing a metaphysic of concrete reality. His fatal identification of being with pure thought cuts him off from insight into the finite mode of concrete being. Being in general cannot be one with pure thought, for then there is no way to distinguish the general notion of being from the divine being or to distinguish the absolute being from concrete, finite beings, which are not just moments in the expansion of this absolute being.

Kierkegaard never solved the question of the nature of the concept of being as such. He warned against dialectical monism and its pseudo-concrete universal concept, but he did not provide a positive alternative, which might found a valid science of metaphysics. Yet he made valuable observations about the *modes* of being, which is the only sense in which he attached a meaning to "being."

The two genuinely real modes of being are: that of God and that of existing individuals. Kierkegaard's language in the *Postscript* and *Fragments* is more technically exact than is sometimes suspected. He seldom speaks about *being* in an unqualified way, except when dealing with Hegel. He prefers to refer to the divine being as God's *eternity*, and to finite being as *existence*.[27] God's being is His eternal actuality, and eternity belongs to Him alone. This eternal mode of being is neither cut off from, nor identified with, the being of finite existents. The latter share in being, by receiving existence from God. Because of this relation of participation, and because the innermost secrets of individual existing beings are known to God, He can be said to "include" the order of existence within Himself. This enclosure is by way of God's free, creative causality and knowledge, rather than by way of a dialectical identity and necessary emanation. What is peculiar to finite existents is that they *come to be* what they are. Their being is the being of process; the law of reality for them is to persevere in becoming, throughout time. This is the being of finite, temporal existence, rather than of eternity; yet it is also a being filled with the powerful and providential presence of eternity. There is an Augustinian note about this explanation of the eternal and existential modes of being. Newman has transcribed this analysis into the language of devotion, when he declares: "My unchangeableness here below is perseverance in changing."

An additional reason can now be cited for Kierkegaard's concentration upon real movement: it is the qualifying mark of finite reality. Hegel's failure to understand real change, is one with his general failure to grasp the meaning of finite being. In the *Postscript*, Kierkegaard synthesizes his criticisms on this score which were scattered throughout the esthetic works.[28] With the aid of Aristotle and Trendelenburg, he also offers some further objections, which are brought into conformity with his technical remarks about pure thought and existence. Kierkegaard states his case so aphoristically and poetically, however, that it is sometimes difficult to grasp the details of his reasoning. Yet the main lines of the argument stand out clearly, against the background of his anti-Hegelian aims.

God's being is the only locus for real necessity, eternity, and immutability. On the other hand, real contingency, temporality, and change, are found only in the world of finite existence. This world is known by men only with the aid of sensuous intuition; motion is grasped within the context of space and time. Existential thinking must have this empirical basis, and must adhere to it in humility before God. What place is left for scientific propositions? They can be validly enunciated, owing to the abstractive power of the human mind. It can consider the things of the spatiotemporal world in an abstract way, according to their essential meanings and relations, as well as their statistical frequencies. Mathematical and physical statements have necessity, because of an abstraction from the original existential conditions and a formal restriction to the essential order alone.

Pure Speculative thought eliminates the empirical, existential origin of our concepts, since such an origin would contradict the boast of the System to embody the absolute Idea itself, in its complete autonomy. The outcome is a misconception of both eternity and temporal existence. The abstract necessity of our concepts of essences is mistaken for the real necessity and eternity of the divine being, thus encouraging the confusion between God's self-knowledge and the Systematic idea of God. The consequences for the question of change are equally unacceptable. Becoming, along with the principles of act and potency which are involved in becoming, is withdrawn from the existential sphere. The ideas of becoming, act, and potency, are taken by themselves and hypostatized. Their reference to empirically real conditions is rejected, in favor of a "pure" treatment in terms of separate essences, which are no longer referred either to real eternity or to real existence. The result is to endow the dialectical method with a pseudo sort of necessity and to view things under a specious form of eternity, which refuses to acknowledge itself as dependent upon an empirical, abstractive act of the human mind. Pure thought views changing things in the light of a false notion of being and eternity, replacing real change by a dialectical play upon the idea of becoming. Systematic thought is in complete antithesis to God's way of knowing and including the world of temporal existence. He gives to existents their *to be*, which is a becoming, whereas the

System revokes the very conditions which alone permit of real becoming.

Hegel's theory of becoming is based upon "pure" necessity and the absence of physical causality, diverging on both counts from Aristotle's explanation. After repeating Aristotle's celebrated definition of motion, Hegel adds that both potency and act unite in the higher synthesis of necessity. Kierkegaard agrees that this is consequential enough, since the whole process of Hegelian becoming takes place in the ideal region of essences.[29] But this abstract kind of necessity cannot be attributed to any real mode of being. For, God's mode of being is not abstract and dialectical, whereas the being of temporal existents is contingent through-and-through. In the real order, what is necessary cannot undergo change, and what does undergo change cannot be unconditionally necessary and cannot become unconditionally necessary. The fact that something has acquired its being through a process of becoming, indicates that it belongs completely and irrevocably to the contingent, existent mode of being. For this reason, the ultimate reference of the potential and the actual principles is to existence and hence to contingency. They are principles of real temporal being, rather than of logical structures and relations. Hence nothing which comes to be, does so merely in virtue of a logical ground. Along with Kant and Schelling, Kierkegaard holds that the adequate principle of change is not a logical premise but a real cause, and that the ultimate cause of becoming is a free cause. Causation remains radically contingent, no matter how carefully one can plot the statistical course of events or specify the determining conditions and essential pattern of action.

World History vs. Ethical Life

Finally, brief mention must be made of Kierkegaard's criticism of the "world-historical outlook," cultivated by the

Hegelians.[30] His reason for stressing this point is that any true wisdom ought to bear the stamp of the ethical upon it, whereas the world-historical attitude is antagonistic to everything of an ethical nature. He supports this conclusion by a phenomenological analysis of the kind of standpoint which is fostered by Hegelian philosophy.

The attempt to fulfill the moral law by becoming an observer of world history is demoralizing. For, one becomes entangled in a set of categories and a dialectic that have no proper place in ethics. One's concern is centered upon what men regard as historically significant, and this need not coincide with ethical obligation. Historical stature is reckoned in terms of greatness, public recognition, and the magnitude of one's effect upon subsequent events. These criteria depend, not upon the purpose and rectitude of individual will, but upon what is for the most part fortuitous and beyond the power and responsibility of the individual. The historically centered man is caught in the web of destiny. No matter how noble his intention or how obdurate his will to evil, he cannot assure himself a place of importance in history. In the end, he becomes unable to distinguish between an ethical line of action and one determined according to morally neutral, metaphysical categories, like cause-and-effect and world-greatness-and-insignificance. The incalculable play of forces takes the place of deliberation of conscience, in his soul. He comes to consider himself as being beyond the law of good and evil, as it applies to ordinary single individuals; the cosmic wave of past-becoming-future moves him, where moral exhortation leaves him cold.

Both God and man are degraded, when this view of world history is proposed as a substitute or equivalent for ethical life. Kierkegaard does not underrate the preponderant role of accidental circumstances, the nonhuman environment and amoral considerations, in shaping human history. But these factors do not tell the whole story of human action, and not even the most important part. For they fall short of explaining the ethical situation, in which the individual is concerned mainly about how he himself stands in relation to the infinite, personal God. To do all that lies in one's power to further the good, and then to leave the outcome and the wider result confidently in the hands of providence—this is an attitude which escapes the devotees of world history and its movement. They are forced to make a claim to see the process of history from the vantage point of eternity; but it is only a sham kind of eternity to which they have access. There is a similar artificiality about the necessity which they ascribe to historical processes. It is a "pure" necessity, based upon an undue abbreviation of concrete, subjective factors, such as conscience, personal intention, and inward freedom. It leaves out the secrets of the human heart and the free play of providence.

Kierkegaard does not deny a meaning and purpose to history, but only the claim that this meaning is laid bare in the Hegelian, or any other, philosophy of history. He reserves such knowledge to God alone, and to men only after they have attained to the vision of eternity. The idealistic theory of historical contemplation is a premature accession to the beatific vision, and hence is quite alien to the requirements of ethical existence of real men, still en route to eternity. The Hegelians would like to arrogate to themselves the role which belongs exclusively to God, in regard to human history. What John Dewey has so often castigated as the Aristotelian spectator-theory of knowledge and the Christian theory of contemplation, is in fact this world-historical viewpoint of the Hegelians. It severs the individual from his empirical relations, robs him of personal freedom and responsibility, and saps the initiative from human planning under genuinely contingent circumstances. This is the consequence of converting the Christian theology of history into a philosophical doctrine.

Throughout his attack upon Hegel, Kierkegaard intends to protect what he likes to call the "possibility-relationship" between man and God.[31] This relationship is one of freedom on both sides, and without it ethical and religious life would be impossible. The final import of his polemic is that Hegelian philosophy strikes at the heart of this relationship and, consequently, at the structure of human existence. Existence builds upon the personal bond of freedom, which men can establish with God and each other. Hegelian philosophy suffers from the perspectival illusion of viewing history as the freedom of necessity, simply because it is the region of what has already come to pass. From our previous study of becoming, however, it is clear that the historical process, like every other instance of becoming, remains contingent, and offers further opportunity for the growth of human freedom and the working of divine providence. These are considerations which lie beyond the System, which has systematically removed the traits of existence and true eternity from its account. Kierkegaard sees his positive task to be the restoration of a sense of the possibility-relationship between God and man. This is the only way open to a deepening of human existence.

Chapter Five

The Meaning of Existence

I. TRUTH AND EXISTENCE

BOTH sound instinct and the turn of Hegelian philosophy incline Kierkegaard to make a close association between existence and truth. He takes as his point of departure the classical definition of truth as *adaequatio mentis et rei*, the conformity between mind and thing.[1] The standard of conformity can be either thought or being. But whereas classical philosophy distinguishes in this way between ontological and logical truth, Kierkegaard holds that the distinction is between an idealistic view of truth (conformity of thing to mind) and an empirical view (conformity of mind to thing). His opposition to Hegel leads him to criticize the former conception of truth. Absolute idealism rests upon the postulated identity of thought and being in "pure thought." Kierkegaard observes that the definition of truth as the conformity of being with thought is a concealed tautology, a mere restatement of the view that the truth *is*, and that the status of being is attained only on the ground of *das reine Denken*. This can be taken as the proper truth for man and his philosophical activity, only if being is a concept in the System. It rests upon an artificial interpretation of both the knowing subject and the knowable object. Kierkegaard firmly rejects both the pseudo-subject and the pseudo-object, which the Hegelian dialectic brings into conformity. Their distinction is epistemological rather than ontological, and even epistemologically it is only a provisional one. For, Hegel admits the distinction between mind and thing only from the standpoint of the dialectically undeveloped understanding, and with an eye toward demonstrating their fundamental oneness.[2]

Kierkegaard does not deny this identity in an unqualified way, although this has been done by atheistic existentialists. The latter see no other way of combating apriorism in philosophy than to eliminate all traces of divine exemplar-ideas, divine providence, and a transcendental relation between the true and being.[3] Although he had no technical knowledge of these basic doctrines in theistic philosophy, Kierkegaard sought a way to safeguard the religious conception of God's omniscience and providence, along with the intelligibility of being which it implies. Hence, he admits that, in the eternal reality of God, there is a oneness of thought and being, mind and thing. He would allow, then, that there is such a thing as ontological truth, provided that it find realization in the *divine* mind alone. This kind of truth is an actual perfection of God, but Hegel would also make it the sole kind of truth which holds for *human* philosophizing as well. The whole trend of post-Kantian idealism is to wipe out any lasting and real distinction between the divine intellect and the philosophically well-informed human mind. As a counter-balance to this tendency, Kierkegaard insists on the real distinction between knower and thing known, when it is a question of human cognition. In this respect, he favors the empirical theory of truth and often refers to the empirical strain in his own outlook. The mind of man retains its finite and humane character by submitting to things which exercise an independent act of being.

Unfortunately for the development of his own thought and for subsequent speculation which has depended upon him, Kierkegaard did not investigate the problem of logical truth

beyond a general affirmation of "empiricism" or epistemological realism. Our philosophical debt to him would have been
very great, indeed, had he further investigated the meaning
of "thing" and "object" and the nature of the mind's conformity with them. But as a moralist and religious writer, he
turned away from this task in favor of one more closely connected with his own interests. He sensed a danger in the empiricist stress upon objectivity and the discipline of experience.
To him, it seemed that a dehumanized and anti-religious attitude could result just as directly from excessive concern about
the world of non-human nature as from a Systematic doctrine
about divine and human mind. The amoral and deterministic
view of world-history fostered by idealism has its counterpart in the naturalistic preoccupation with the process and
structure of objective nature. The various natural sciences
cover a valid field and give truth within their own limits, and
to this extent they are set off from the Hegelian System. But
the subjective effect of such studies upon the scientists and
those influenced by the scientific viewpoint, must also be
weighed. In this respect, Kierkegaard felt that his age needed
to be warned about the shortcomings of naturalism, as well as
idealism, in the human sphere.

There is a point beyond which we should not rely exclusively upon the scientific method or what Kierkegaard
called "abstract thought" and "objective reflection." The
movement of this method is away from the personal, interested
subject, in the direction of impersonal laws and statements of
determined fact.[4] If one's life is completely governed by the requirements of such research, the significance of the individual
man is liable to be reduced to nothing more than that of a ma-
nipulator of scientific instruments, a point of departure in the
exploration of the material world. When man is studied by
means of this objective reflection, he is treated in terms of the
same laws, traits, and determining conditions that prevail in

the rest of nature. This is reasonable enough, until it is declared to be the *only* valid way of regarding man, a claim which has been made by naturalism in every form. Kierkegaard realized that such a claim involves an overthrow of human values and a destruction of the right order upon which morality and religion build. The rule of prudence is destroyed, when exclusive rights are given to the method and categories of the natural sciences.

For this reason, Kierkegaard seeks to delimit the scientific method in the case of man, and so to make room for another kind of truth. He customarily refers to the truths obtained by means of objectively orientated research as "hypothetical" and "approximate." [5] This is no anticipation of later developments in the statistical theory of scientific law, for it does not concern either the nature of the material thing or the exactness of our knowledge of it. Rather, it calls attention to certain aspects of the situation which are overlooked by the scientist as such. His knowledge is "hypothetical" in its purely objective state, in the sense that it does not take full account of the human knower, who must affirm the theory, read the registrations of the instruments, and bring to bear the primitive distinction between what can be and what does in fact exist. This same knowledge is "approximate," in that it never reaches to an understanding of the thing after its own mode of being, as a subject exercising existence in its own right. The cognitive needs of man are wider than is the ability of the scientific method to satisfy them. Men cannot help asking questions about the meaning of existence, the nature of the human person, and the uses of freedom. These questions fall within the region of what Kierkegaard terms "subjective reflection" or "existential thinking." The most important human issues lie in this latter field, rather than in that of objective reflection.

Kierkegaard's thesis that existential thinking is subjective,

is open to misconception, unless it be interpreted in the light
of his preoccupation with idealism and naturalism. His opposition to idealism is sufficient indication that by "subjective"
is not meant a priority of thought over being, in any absolutist
sense, let alone a glorification of personal whim or private
fancy. In attempting to go beyond the epistemological dilemma between idealism and empiricism, he gave a moral and
religious meaning to subjectivity. His thought should rather
be assigned to the Augustinian tradition, for he would approve
the custom of addressing God as *magister interior* and of declaring that, in all that matters most to men: *in interiore homine
habitat veritas*, truth dwells in the inner man. For Kierkegaard, subjectivity means inwardness or the existential attitude of the individual soul. His youthful resolve to dedicate
himself to a discovery and propagation of "edifying truths"
is in conformity with this defense of a kind of truth which
does indeed build up *homo interior*. Since he also believed,
with Augustine, that man is most truly man when considered
in relation to God, Kierkegaard concluded that humanly significant truth is primarily ethico-religious truth. A man's subjectivity is his personal, inward condition in respect to the
moral law and religious life, a phase of human reality which
is not open to scientific inspection. In this sense, existential
knowledge must be both subjective and edifying.[6]

Before passing on to a discussion of the characteristics of
existential truth, as described by Kierkegaard, it is well to
observe that his solution of the truth-problem cannot be a
complete one. He recognized the inadequacy of the report
of the particular sciences, without being able to provide a
full supplementary explanation. While it is true that there are
aspects of reality not accessible to the scientific method, it
does not follow that all of these aspects lie in a subjective and
human direction. There are truths about the realm of nature
and quantity which can be reached philosophically, without

calling upon idealism, but Kierkegaard does not discuss philosophical truth of the cosmological and mathematical orders. Moreover, there is a way of regarding man and nature together, metaphysically, without falling into either idealistic monism or naturalism. What is missing from Kierkegaard, is a treatment of existential truth along speculative and metaphysical lines. He has not supplied a metaphysical analysis of truth and existence, and this failure has forced later thinkers in the existentialist line to choose between an idealistic and a naturalistic metaphysics. For this same reason, his insistence upon practical considerations of a religious and moral sort appears to be as narrow, in its own way, as the pragmatic concentration upon practical results of scientific research. It would be misleading to accept his teaching as a rounded, theoretical study of truth.

In Kierkegaard's estimation, existential truth is practical, always unfinished, and essentially paradoxical.[7] It is practical, in the pregnant sense in which practical doing and self-development are distinguished from making and transformation of the external object. Its concern is with the state of the individual human existent, rather than with general laws and impersonal natures. Subjective reflection is ordained to a moral operation: to the cultivation of the self, in its free relations with God and other human selves. Perhaps without knowing it, Kierkegaard has supplied an acceptable sense in which thought is capable of measuring being, even on the human plane. Although he does not allow any idealistic identification of mind and thing, he sees the need for a rational standard or ideal governing human moral and religious activities. The office of subjective reflection is to make a constant comparison between a man's actual condition and the requirements of God and the moral law, not in order to reach a speculative conclusion but as a guide and spur to further growth in character and devotion. Without such a practical intent, Kierkegaard does not admit that thinking can be termed existential. His fear of a purely "disinterested" attitude toward practical issues prevents him from distinguishing clearly between the speculative judgment of existence and the moral judgment of obligation and conscience. His existential judgment is not one which affirms something to be exercising the supreme act of being, but one which lays down what someone ought to do here and now, as before God.

Kierkegaard makes some interesting remarks about why practical truth must always concern unfinished business. These observations show that he places existential thinking, not in the speculativo-practical order, but in the intensively practical order of concrete moral judgment and action. Subjective reflection is concerned with human existence and hence with that which is temporal and free. The human subject, in its inward dispositions, is not a completed reality but one involved in a constant process of becoming and free striving. Because human existence and its potentialities are regarded in relation to the infinite God, they can never be treated as being in a state of equilibrium and rounded-off completion. Existential truth does not merely state what the right relation of men in general to God should be: it tries to specify the actual condition of some particular individual and the steps he should take, in the present situation. It is not so much a general body of ethical doctrine as a manner in which the individual applies this doctrine to himself, with heartfelt concern about the consequences for his inner life. As long as a man remains in existence, he can only make an approach to his proper perfection. Not only must our ultimately practical judgments face a continual change in circumstances, but our lives themselves are a constant striving, *immer strebend*. In the final analysis, existential truth is a progressive realization of the human measure in an individual life, so that a man can be said to live the truth and be made free in and by it.

Speaking aphoristically, Kierkegaard asserts that what matters in existential truth is not so much the *what* as the *how* of knowing.[8] This statement is sometimes construed as favoring a separation between doctrine and action, and hence as approving of any "well-intentioned" belief or "earnest" deed. Kierkegaard cannot be said to have guarded sufficiently against such an interpretation, so vehement was he against a purely speculative attitude in practical affairs. The maxim has relevance primarily for ethical and religious life. From Kierkegaard's comparison between a merely nominal Christian and a genuinely devout pagan, it is evident that by existential truth is meant both a practical kind of knowledge and actual practice itself. It presupposes, however, that one can determine, in a general theoretical way, the morality of living up to one's professed belief, and can also estimate the respective merits of paganism and Christianity. In the speculative order, the *what* of knowledge must specify the *how* of our cognitive act. In this instance, Kierkegaard fails to underline sufficiently the coercion which the thing rightfully exercises over the mind, in the formation of the speculatively true judgment. But he has seen the importance of establishing the right order in our conduct, in conformity with what we think ought to be done. In the practical sphere, insight is often withheld from him who gives only lip-service, and is given to him who tries to pattern his life upon his belief. The latter individual benefits from a kind of connatural knowledge and also from the rectitude of his will, which classical morality takes to be the standard of conformity and truth in moral knowledge.

There is some ambiguity in Kierkegaard's position, since the notion of truth as inwardness refers to a moral condition, as well as to a state of practical knowledge. In regard to morality and the order of love, the agent's intent is the decisive, specifying principle, as compared with the object or material content of the act. Here, the primacy of the subjective *how* of the individual's purpose is maintained over the *what* of the deed accomplished in the objective realm. A favorite observation of Kierkegaard's is that existing is an art rather than a science.[9] His views on inwardness and existential truth apply most aptly to a Platonic art of human life or an Augustinian *ars bene recteque vivendi*, for they are intended to promote a closer union between sound thinking and upright living, on the part of a moral and religious person. This agrees with his demand that truth make a difference, not only in one's thought but also in one's manner of existing. Yet Kierkegaard himself tries to avoid endorsing sincere fanaticism by noting that wholehearted attachment to a thesis does not guarantee its truth, even though such attachment may receive a due moral reward, in spite of the error. Mere fanaticism arises, when a man bestows infinite concern upon a finite object or when he approaches the infinite reality in a completely objective, disinterested way. Existential truth is not only inward but also dialectical, since it is a personal concern about God and His ways, a juxtaposition of one's own existence and the divine majesty. Hence, this kind of truth tries to synthesize the highest *what* of knowledge with the deepest *how* of creaturely response, both cognitive and volitional.

2. EXISTENTIAL KNOWLEDGE OF GOD

What Kierkegaard calls "the supreme passion of reason" is its tendency to learn all it can about another reality, which remains irreducibly itself. Every case of human cognition which considers the existence of the thing known, partakes of this paradoxical quality and helps to develop an awareness of the knower's own subjective being. But Kierkegaard locates the highest paradox of existential thinking in the mind's effort to know God. His thoughts on this problem are set down in the *Fragments*, in a section entitled "A Metaphysical Crochet." [10] The treatment is very compressed and is made more difficult by a quite special use of terms. Many students of Kierkegaard fail to make sense out of the section or to give an exact rendering of the argument. It deserves to be explained and criticized in some detail, because of its importance for the whole problem of Kierkegaard. Historically, the task is lightened by attending to the fact that Kierkegaard was deeply engrossed, at this time, in the philosophical works and letters of Jacobi. These he had consulted both for their own sake and for the vivid picture they convey of Lessing's personality. [11] Kierkegaard liked the humor, resilience, and personal independence of Lessing, hailing him (in the *Postscript*) as a prototype of the subjective, existential thinker. But he found attractive qualities in the philosophy of Jacobi also, especially his defense of the role of intuition in existential and historical questions, as against purely deductive procedures. Kierkegaard's conception of faith as a synthesis of paradox and belief combines the best features of these two thinkers. His actual discussion of the problem of demonstrating God's existence has three phases: (a) repudiation of the ontological argument in its modern form; (b) distinction between the eternal reality and the existence of God; (c) acceptance of Kant's paradox concerning a finite mind and an infinite being.

The Ontological Argument

The use of this argument by Spinoza and Hegel is no mere revival of the Anselmian proof but is bound up with the special aims of their own systems. Kierkegaard's contention is that the monistic and idealistic version of the proof depends upon the postulate of "pure thought," for once this postulate is granted, the entailment of being from autonomous thought must also be conceded. From the standpoint of human understanding, however, the hypothesis of pure thought must be rejected in favor of a realistic and humane recognition of the independence of the thing known by us. The only kind of existence which we can reach in an *a priori* way is an ideal mode of being, which lies wholly within the order of essence and does not determine any factual, concrete existence, including that of God.[12] Men can argue *from* factual existence, once it is given, but not *to* it, on the basis of the conceived essence alone. Once the existence of the thing has been apprehended in some other way, conceptual analysis and deductive reasoning can then extend our knowledge of the thing's nature and attributes. Kierkegaard maintains that this explication of the divine essence is the only sense in which demonstration applies to God. His existence itself is not subject to demonstration. Whence, then, comes our assurance of His existence?

God's Existence and Eternal Reality

It is Kierkegaard's contention that God's existence can be grasped only by being believed. His existence is assured to us, only when we "let the proof go" and execute the leap of belief, what William James spoke of as the *salto mortale*. Is this a case of fideism? It seems likely that the answer must be in the negative. By existence, Kierkegaard means exclusively a finite, temporal mode of being, which is essentially subject to becoming. Hence, he is prevented from applying the term "existence" to God, considered in His own eternal mode of being. In speaking of God's existence, he means the paradoxical fact or mystery of God's becoming man in a temporal instant, the Incarnation.[13] The truth of the Incarnation is a strictly existential truth, one which has reference to an historical instance of existence as a temporal event. In the final section of this chapter, the connection between historical existence and belief will be considered for its own sake, with special emphasis upon the historical fact of the Incarnation and the corresponding act of religious faith. But it is clear even now that, in the Kierkegaardian sense of "existence," God's existence means the truth about Christ, the God-man. This is a matter of faith, rather than of demonstration. The truth of the Incarnation is reserved for the eyes of faith.

But most philosophers are intent upon proving what Kierkegaard terms the eternal reality of God. When he himself is asked for an answer to this question, the reply is lacking. He does not have the metaphysical foundation for a demonstration which will avoid the ontological argument. Again, he shifts the discussion to religious grounds, instead of providing a positive solution in speculative terms. He admits, without pressing the point, that a man like Socrates had genuine knowledge of God, entirely apart from faith. Due to his anti-Hegelian bias, however, he is compelled to limit such knowledge (as distinct from faith and existential apprehension) to the essential sphere. This natural knowledge is not a result of "pure thought," but its validity does not seem to reach beyond the essential order. Is this the same as a knowledge of God's eternal reality? No answer can be forthcoming from Kierkegaard, since he does not specify the sense in which being and essence apply to God's eternal reality. This reality is distinct from abstract and ideal essences, but we are not told how it differs from them or how it is known. Apparently, Kant had convinced Kierkegaard that this problem is insoluble, on theoretical grounds.

The Kantian Paradox

Internal evidence in the text of the *Fragments* seems to indicate that Kierkegaard was a close student of Kant's criticism of the theological idea (God), especially as presented in the *Prolegomena*. Kant maintained that reason becomes involved in a self-ironizing predicament, when it affirms that the infinite God is or exists, according to the eternal mode of being. For, this kind of being is absolutely different from temporal being and the existential truth of the human mind. The mind expresses this complete unlikeness by designating God as the Unknown, the "totally heterogeneous." Kant took this Unknown in the theoretical order to be a positive limit or boundary (*Grenze*), which refers beyond itself to a region of unknowability, rather than merely a hindering fetter or restraint (*Schranke*) upon the mind. By a natural tendency, reason leads us "to the objective boundary [*Grenze*] of experience, viz., to the reference to something which is not itself an object of experience, but is the ground of all experience." [14] Kant held, further, that our application of analogical predicates to the Unknown gives us no knowledge of it, as it is in itself, but only of our reference to this boundary. Hence, the conclusion is reached that the only valid use of the theological idea, in the theoretical order, is to urge the understanding onward to more complete and systematic unity of explanation. By some miraculous correspondence, this regulative function of the theological idea is in harmony with the moral need for God, and clears the way for a practical belief in His goodness and holiness.

Kierkegaard was not equipped with a theory of being and of essence-and-existence adequate enough to deal constructively with this Kantian argument. Concerned as he was to distinguish between whatness and factual existence, in opposition to any idealistic merger of the two, he was led to take a univocal view of their relation as being one of real distinction, wherever they are present. This prevented him from developing any *a posteriori* demonstration of the truth about God's actual being or any analogical predication of essence and existence to Him. Progress in this direction could be made by distinguishing between God's own mode of being and our manner of knowing this being. It need not follow that, because essence and existence are one in God, therefore our reason can argue "ontologically" from an idea of His essence to His existence. Hence essence and existence might be attributed to Him, without thereby lending support to the ontological argument and the idealistic theory of pure thought. This would suppose, of course, that some reasonable account can be given of the application of the common term "being" to both God and creature. This could be done, if Kierkegaard would allow that existence, as well as essence, can be found in a temporal mode of being but need not be confined to this mode. Such a negative or separative judgment about existence would allow for some analogical apprehension of the divine reality which would be both natural knowledge (rather than faith) and existential knowledge in the speculative order (rather than in the order of practice, appetite and connaturality).

Finally, such a metaphysical theory of essence and existence would supply the key to a problem which Kierkegaard uncovered, without explaining. He divined that, in some way, God and man are both like and unlike each other. God and man are akin, in respect to what man derives from God. This admission led Karl Barth, who advocates a rigorous view of God as totally other than the creature, to repudiate Kierkegaard as being infected by the Thomistic theory of the analogy of being. After admitting a certain likeness between man and God, however, Kierkegaard is faced with the need to explain their difference. Unfortunately, he locates this difference in something other than the very perfection which founds their likeness. He designates sin as the principle of difference, since man derives sin from himself and his own activity.[15] This leaves two things unexplained: how the rest of the created universe is distinguished from God, and how the divine mode of being is set off from that aspect of human being which is perfect, in a natural or supernatural way. A metaphysical theory of participated being would begin by pointing out that, by *deriving* its being from God, the temporal existent is unlike God, even in that respect in which they are alike: *tanta similitudo, maior dissimilitudo*.

Yet, if Kierkegaard did not settle the metaphysical problem, at least he had the courage to cast suspicion upon the Kantian and Hegelian settlements of the paradoxical situation outlined by Kant. He refused to grant either that the eternal reality of God is a Kantian limit-concept of reason or that like and unlike are ultimately identical, in accord with the Speculative dialectic. Instead of resolving the paradox, Kierkegaard let it stand and even sought to intensify it. He went out of his way to insist that Christianity is no easy escape from the problem. Rather, it heightens the paradox of existential truth to the uttermost, by proclaiming at once the utter unlikeness between God and sinful man and their absolute likeness in the God-Man, Christ.

3. EXISTENCE AND THE SUBJECTIVE THINKER

Another way of illuminating the meaning of existence is to contrast the attitudes of the subjective thinker and the Hegelian systematist.[16] Kierkegaard's purpose in making this comparison is both polemical and constructive. The boast of Hegelians is to have surpassed the Greeks, and to have uncovered the "deeper" philosophical meaning of Christianity. In reply, Kierkegaard contends that Hegelianism not only misunderstands and perverts the Christian doctrine but also falls far behind the high point of Greek development. He places Socrates at the apex of Greek speculation, declaring that he has the advantage of being an existential thinker, rather than a Speculative philosopher, even though Socrates falls short of the Christian understanding of existence. In the *Postscript*, Kierkegaard revises the portrait of Socrates which he had drawn in his master's dissertation. Instead of stressing the Romantic and ironic traits in his Socrates, he now underlines the positive, existential features of his personality and thought. Despite his voluminous writings, Hegel forgot "the subtle little Socratic secret" that truth is inwardness and transformation into the individual existing subject.

Like most thinkers in the German tradition, Kierkegaard gives a quite personal and polemical account of Greek philosophy and its exponents.[17] The deepest intuition of Greek philosophy is embodied in the proposition that knowledge is recollection. This means that truth is an immanent and eternal possession which *can* be made actual, if a man will but shed his temporal conditions and return to an original state of being and knowledge, outside of time and the existent order. Whether a man *ought* to divest himself of his finite state, is the question over which the Kierkegaardian Socrates and Plato part company. Kierkegaard's Plato is a kind of classical model for the Hegelian systematist, since he follows the lure of recollection back to an unparadoxical eternity, which turns out to be the true being and essence of man. But Socrates never forgets that he is an existing individual and, therefore, never chooses to follow up the possibility of recollecting himself back to eternity. The possibility is admitted but is not permitted to prevail over the fact that God intends a man to be an integer, to exist as a human whole, rather than divide himself and betake one part of his person to the clouds. Socrates also agrees with Plato that time has no decisive significance, in comparison with eternity. Still, he adds that one is bound to use one's time in accentuating one's human existence and inwardness, rather than in identifying oneself with the timeless paragraphs of Systematic philosophy.

Kierkegaard had great admiration for Aristotle, especially for his keen speculations about the life of God and the nature of human happiness. He recognized in the Aristotelian teaching that happiness consists primarily in *theoria*, in the theoretical and contemplative exercise of intellect, a very noble pagan conception. But he considered that Socrates came still closer to the Christian view, when he expressed his passionate and humble personal concern for happiness. He would rather stake his life unreservedly and courageously upon the *if* of human immortality, than confuse immortality with eternity, human with divine being. He was a subjective thinker in being aware of the *insecuritas humana*, the infinite uncertainty of human existence, and the need to hold fast to what Kierkegaard referred to as militant certainties and what William James called truths with a fighting chance. For Socrates, immortality was not just an essential state of being, which a man cannot but retain, but rather a chance to win or lose one's soul in God's sight. Kierkegaard agreed with the early Fathers of the Church that Socrates gave an inspiring example and a point of continuity with sound humanity everywhere. Behind his irony and maieutic method lay a personal regard for the truth, not only as an objective thesis, but also as a moving practical principle, which should make a difference in one's life. His paramount concern was for the manner in which his auditors related themselves to the truth and were modified by it, in their mode of existence. Hence, the subjective thinker is led to communicate truth in an indirect way, so as to provoke personal reflection and appropriation on the part of the would-be learner.

A subjective thinker like Socrates is not content with the movement of thought among analytic meanings and inferences, in the order of essence and possibility. He is constantly putting his theories to the test of actual existence, as the ultimate referent and touchstone. In the informed and literary manner which befits the personality of the pseudonymous "author," Johannes Climacus, Kierkegaard attacks the central Hegelian notion of *Wirklichkeit* or "actuality," from several angles. The argument is not entirely free from confusion, however, due to the fact that Kierkegaard uses the correlative term "possibility" in two different senses.[18] When he wishes to demonstrate the incompatibility between ethics and the Speculative System, he maintains that the latter is deterministic and does not preserve man's possibility-relationship with God. In this context, possibility is equivalent to moral freedom: the choice between good and evil must be left open for men. But in regard to cognition, possibility refers to essence alone, apart from actual existence. A knowledge of possibilities is not as perfect as an apprehension of what has actual and concrete being. Now, in the human sphere, Kierkegaard teaches, actuality is found in contingent existence and concrete individual subjects, rather than in essential moments of the dialectical progress of the absolute concept. Hence, only the existential thinker can bring thought to perfection.

In this respect, the subjective thinker is differentiated from both the esthetic and the Speculative minds. Estheticism and Speculation agree in seeking to reduce every *esse* to a *posse*, whereas a thinker like Socrates would preserve the reference of *posse* to personal *esse* and moral action. At this point, we notice the drawback of modeling the existential thinker too closely after a Socrates. As Kierkegaard envisages him, Socrates finds the world of essences and possibilities worthwhile, only in so far as it ministers to his own moral perfection. He is concerned about his self-actuality rather than that of others, justifying this preoccupation by observing that he can know only himself, as an actuality. Other selves are known primarily as possibilities, and as actual only in reference to his own existence and designs. Kierkegaard is dissatisfied with this limitation, declaring that it is characteristic only of existential thinkers in the ethical sphere. Religiously existential thinkers can gain some insight into the actuality of other selves in their own right, whereas Christian faith impels a man to regard the actual state of others as of equal importance with one's own.

This amendment of the "Socratic" position is by no means

satisfactory. Kierkegaard has stumbled upon a real difficulty, which philosophers do not often face as honestly as he does. He puts it in this way: I can know myself as I actually am, but how can I know others as they actually are, since I must approach them by means of abstract thinking? An answer to this question would place one at the very heart of the existential conception, but Kierkegaard only supplies a few hints. In the first place, he does not clarify what he means by self-knowledge transpiring "in the medium of actuality." The point is assumed rather than explained. Even in knowing oneself, concepts, along with a certain amount of reasoning, are usually employed. There is no mention of an intuition of self or even of a feeling of self, in moments of activity. The epistemological aspects of the problem do not interest Kierkegaard. His argument is, rather, that an ethically serious thinker always relates his thoughts about himself to some plan of action and self-development. They are existential thoughts, in that they always retain this orientation to a free plan about one's personal existence and moral condition. But if this accounts sufficiently for existential thinking, then the latter does not differ *in the cognitive order* from other sorts of thinking. Only the use and personal reference of the thinking are different. The conclusion is inescapable that only a non-cognitive shift of attitude is needed to convert abstract thinking (not, however, Hegelian "pure thought") into existential thinking.

Kierkegaard would probably not accept this conclusion, pointing out that some distinction is required, in the order of truth and knowledge proper. This is quite true, since the existential thinker *refers* his abstract concepts to existence, only because he *knows* the existence of a thing in some way. But no explanation is advanced about the exact manner of such existential cognition. Kierkegaard likes to express the difference between his position and Hegel's as one between existence and the concept of existence, but he does not tell us how the former can be known speculatively, without the assistance of the Speculative System. In order to justify his design to grasp the truth "existentially and in existence," he would have to work out a theory of existential judgment and intentional being.[19] Only with their aid can the human mind apprehend the act of existence of another, without presupposing either an impossible physical identity of the two or an equally impossible conflation of the two in an idealistic dialectic. Kierkegaard thinks that no theoretical way can be found to make the thinker one with some other reality, and hence he turns to practical and connatural ways of knowing and even to ties of concern and sympathy, which are not strictly cognitive. In his religious writings, he exhibits marvelous perception concerning the close sympathy which religious bonds establish and which can *result* in mutual understanding. But he has no basic philosophical explanation of the existential way of knowing the other—whether a thing or another self—precisely as another subject, *in quantum aliud*. Despite his own intentions, this weakness has led to theoretical solipsism and practical egoism, on the part of some later existentialists.

Socrates, the prototype of existential thinkers, would remind us that no matter how indispensable the speculative judgment of existence may be, it is not sufficient to assure a good character. Even practical knowledge is inadequate to this end, unless it overflows in concrete action. This requires the co-operation of the will and the passions, for one must ultimately aim to be a good, existing man and not merely a thinker about existential problems. Kierkegaard's final counsel is that the existential thinker should strive after personal integrity, through the harmonious workings of his cognitive and conative factors. The result will be a synthesis in the order of existence itself, not as signified in thought but as exercised in actual fact. Thus, his analysis of the subjective thinker coincides finally with his doctrine on existential truth: both are brought to perfection in an actual embodiment of human values in personal existence.

4. EXISTENCE AND RELIGIOUS TRANSCENDENCE

The admonition against attributing unqualifiedly to Kierkegaard opinions expressed through his pseudonyms, applies with special force to the views on religiousness advanced in the "philosophical writings." Johannes Climacus is a pagan thinker, who is reporting on the natural religious spirit, as he himself may have experienced it, and on Christian faith as seen from the outside. He is not interested in the doctrines of Christianity nor its truth-claim, but only in the religious traits of soul displayed by sincere Christians. His approach to religiousness is descriptive, rather than dogmatic or apologetic. Certain aspects of his religious phenomenology cannot be omitted from a study on existence. Kierkegaard is convinced that existence has a definite religious import, and some suggestion of his own standpoint is conveyed through the medium of Johannes Climacus, although the latter does not share Kierkegaard's own Christian faith.

All contemporary existentialists agree that human existence is set off from nonhuman reality by the note of transcendence. Man is not content with the given situation in which he finds himself, and in which he is but one thing along with innumerable others. He seeks to assert his own selfhood over against the solid reality of things and to assure his dominance over his natural environment. His cultural and technological achievements attest to this uneasiness and constant need for self-affirmation, on the part of the human spirit. Sartre holds that the human self is, by definition, a search for a reality which will be at once solidly actual and self-conscious. This is only another way of stating that the human self, the *pour-soi*, is by nature placed on the track of God. Thus, Sartre gives an essentially religious interpretation to human transcendence: human aspirations reach out for God and are specified by a hunger for him.

Yet Sartre's metaphysical principles and phenomenological method lead him to regard the concept of God as contradictory. He cannot see how the perfection of being and that of intelligence can coincide in a supreme intelligent actuality. Hence, he concludes that the transcending activity is futile and doomed to failure, if man hopes thereby to enter into communion with a responsive reality other than himself.[20] This sort of existentialism admits transcendence but not the transcendent: man remains enclosed within himself, no matter how urgent and ineradicable his desire for the transcendent. It is this stultifying conclusion which is attacked by Gabriel Marcel, who admits the reality of God and the possibility of human communion with Him. For Marcel, the tendency of transcendence is man's inborn response to God's call. God takes the initiative in giving man the power to make this response, although it must be made freely and generously. It is not as though we first chose Him and determined Him to this relation, but rather that we have come to recognize ourselves as indeed His children and to desire to reach our fatherland again. Our free movement of transcendence is the measure of the depth of our existence and personal maturity.

Which of these contemporary existentialist accounts of transcendence can claim to follow the mind of Kierkegaard? As far as the philosophical writings now under consideration are concerned, the reply must be that Kierkegaard is partially responsible for the atheistic view, although his own positive thought lies in a religious direction. The failure to prepare a metaphysical basis for our knowledge of God's existence and nature lends some weight to Sartre's contention that our desire for God can never be satisfied by a real being and a real religious union. But there can be no doubt that Kierkegaard tries to compensate for this lack of speculative demonstration, by the carefulness and persuasiveness of his descriptions of religious traits in man. One entire dimension of human existence is overlooked, if the question of transcendence is not raised. And that transcendence is fundamentally religious and genuinely founded in being, is Kierkegaard's firmest belief. His analysis of religious consciousness is intended to evoke a similar belief in others. It is at this descriptive level that we must accept his statements.

Kierkegaard's own study of transcendence starts from man's search for an eternal happiness.[21] Without probing into questions concerning the nature of desire and the good, he takes it as empirically undeniable that man naturally seeks happiness. He would agree with Aristotle's classical survey of the various goods in which men claim to find their happiness, with Charles Peirce's discussion of the disappointment which attends the willing of a finite end in an absolute way, and with St. Augustine's report on the inquietude of the human heart until it comes to rest in God. There is a remarkable unanimity of testimony on the problem of happiness among thinkers of all ages and cultural origins. Kierkegaard is only setting down the common conviction, when he states that serious and reflective men seek their abiding happiness in some eternal reality. His original contribution lies in his restatement of this view within an existential framework, and in his determination of the unique element in the Christian solution of the problem of happiness. For the latter purpose, he is careful to distinguish between transcendence, as understood by religiousness generally, and as found in a specifically Christian religious attitude.

The general principle is laid down that whatever increases the factors of pathos and paradox in human subjectivity, also contributes to the enrichment of human existence. That happiness is an existential problem, is evident from the fact that some temporal process is required in making the search for, and passage to, a state of enduring happiness. In general, the pathetic factor is aroused by the contrast and distance which the individual perceives to lie between himself and such an absolute good as could give him permanent and complete satisfaction. This discrepancy arouses his yearning, his striving, his ever increasing sense of unlikeness to the object of his heart's desire, and his feeling of uncleanness before it. The eternal reality of God appears to him as a *mysterium tremendum*, an overawing and holy power. Were only this pathos of the holy present, however, yearning might turn into dreaming, and striving into a hopelessness. For genuine transcendence, a dialectical challenge and spur are also required. To retain the language of Rudolf Otto, the mystery of God must be *fascinans* as well as *tremendum*. The awareness of, and desire for, eternal happiness are rendered dialectical by reflecting upon the decisiveness of one's temporal actions for eternal issues. No matter where his happiness is to be found, a man can reach it only by a free, individual act, which is also an historical event. To become aware of the paradoxical tension between the temporal act and the eternal outcome is to enter into one's inheritance of transcendence. At the same time, it is to grow in religious inwardness and responsible existence as a man.

Having established this proportion between transcendence and the religious mode of existence, Kierkegaard then faced the problem of distinguishing between religious transcendence in general and the peculiarly Christian form of religious transcendence.[22] He was in conscious reaction against the tendency of two centuries of deism to wipe out the differences between religions, as well as between faith and philosophical reason. He did not regard Christian spiritual life as just one among many equal varieties of religious experience, but rather as the supreme form of religious existence. He felt that this could be shown in terms of existential truth, which is the common perfection of religious life and yet is not realized everywhere in equal measure. It is only for the light it may shed upon Kierkegaard's conception of existence, that the comparative religious question is introduced here. But the important place which it occupies in his "philosophical writings" is ample proof that these books are not ordinary philosophical treatises and that their ultimate concern is a religious one.

The basic difference concerns the meaning of immanence and transcendence. Pagan religious consciousness has developed the pathetic factor to a high degree. In the light of the eternal good, it is prepared to resign the finite goods of this world, to confess the guilt of its own manner of being, and to seek release from these earthly bonds of existence. Paradox is admitted, not in the nature of man and God taken separately, but only in their mutual relation. It is only the process of appropriating the highest good which holds a sense of mystery for such religiousness. The tendency is to regard the conditions of individual, temporal existence as hindrances to the attainment of the absolute good—and yet there is no other way to approach it than to remain oneself and perform acts of devotion and obedience which transpire in time. A Socrates will resist the temptation to seek release from time and human existence by means of some dialectical retreat to the purely eternal mode of being. But the possibility of such escape still remains open to him, with the implication that genuine transcendence involves a flight from existence. Permanent values may be present in this life, but they reveal themselves to man as eternal and essentially separated from the temporal sphere.

Christianity is a vindication of the dignity of human existence, but it achieves this goal in a paradoxical way. Like every other religious attitude, it supposes the passional factors of resignation and suffering which set off religious realism from the dreaming inactivity of the esthetic and Speculative outlooks. But it places emphasis upon the dialectical factor in religiousness to such an extent, that it cannot be deemed a mere continuation of the natural religious life. This dialectical tension is achieved by asking men to have faith in the mysteries of Original Sin and the Incarnation. The effect of this faith is to introduce paradox into the reality of man and God taken in themselves and not merely in their mutual relation. Original Sin closes the possibility of an escape hatch, which would allow the individual to slip away to eternity through the process of recollection or some other acosmic device. Existence, as it were, has man twice within its power: he not only has a temporal mode of being but lives in time as a sinner. This twofold stamp of existence upon his being hems him in, blocks the road back to a Golden Age, sets him in a definitely forward direction.[23] Temporal existence is now regarded, not as an external and provisional mark placed upon an eternal essence, but as the concrete and proper mode of human being. Yet a man would despair, were this the entire message of Christianity. In bidding men be loyal to their creaturely condition, it also announces that the hope of eternal life is to be found in time itself. The Incarnation means that the eternal has subjected itself to the law of becoming, that the All-Holy has taken upon itself the conditions of sinful existence, that God has become Man.

So great are the mystery and paradox of Christ that Kierkegaard's pseudonymous spokesman is willing to speak of the Incarnation as an absurdity, and of faith in it as a crucifixion of the intellect. This extreme and inexact language should not deflect attention from the main purpose of emphasizing the fact that, in the Christian economy, all things are made new, above all, man himself, who becomes *nova creatura*. The individual no longer seeks to exchange his finitude for a merger with the absolute, but gains a new sense of the worth and human value of creatureliness. Time is not to be fled, and neither is it merely to be endured strongly but without hope of fulfillment. The eternal is now found to be immanent in the temporal order, in such a way as to give time significance in itself and for eternal happiness. Transcendence is also revalued. The eternal good is confronted in time and on the human plane. One need not pretend to become something other than human, and yet more is asked of the individual man. The *more* is the act of faith, not only *as* a temporal event but also *in* an historical event. Human inwardness and existence are brought to their highest pitch in Christian faith, but only because God Himself first came among us and gave us the power to hold fast to Him.

Kierkegaard's treatment of religious transcendence is not entirely free from difficulties, from the standpoint of his theory of existence. To the contemporary reader, who no longer finds Hegelianism a natural atmosphere for philosophical discussion, the analysis seems too formalistic. Kierkegaard was in search of an appropriate mode of speech to convey his existential insights, but he was too close to Hegel not to pattern his "existential dialectic" closely upon the Speculative model, even as he attacked the latter. The formalism is evident in his handling of pathos and paradox, as constituents of existence, and in his restriction of non-Christian religiousness to the quite arbitrary and "Systematic" figure he drew of Socrates. The comparative question in religion is by no means settled so easily, for considerably less than justice is done to both the non-Christian and the Christian religious life by this schematization.

Moreover, the differentiating feature assigned to Christianity backfires upon the previous study of existential truth. Kierkegaard warns the reader that he is discussing "religiousness," one's personal attitude, rather than "religion," a body of objective doctrines. This follows from the existential accentuation of the manner of appropriating a truth. But Kierkegaard's explanation of the paradoxicality of Christianity is unintelligible, unless due prominence is given to the content of belief in Original Sin and the Incarnation. Here the *what* and *Who* of truth are primary and, indeed, regulative of the *how* of one's individual acceptance or refusal.[24] This is implicitly acknowledged by Kierkegaard, when he teaches that the individual's act of faith supposes God's initiative in regard to the actual situation of sinfulness and the coming of Christ, as well as in regard to the power to believe in them.

Kierkegaard opposed, by anticipation, the Nietzschean doctrine of the atheistic revaluation of all values. This is the main philosophical significance of his theory of transcendence. He could have accepted Nietzsche's call for a revaluation, but not his banishment of God and his cultivation of the myth of an eternal recurrence of the same round of affairs. Nietzsche was afraid that belief in an absolute good, distinct from the cosmic plenum, would entail a depreciation of the natural world and an abandonment of the effort toward attaining heights beyond man. Kierkegaard could have told him that this fear is groundless, and that he need not take refuge in the myth of absolutized nature. Nietzsche judged Christianity by the low points of nineteenth-century spirituality and by the idealistic philosophies of religion; Kierkegaard was also opposed to these, but precisely on existential and Christian grounds.[25] Nietzsche was a witness to man's unquenchable search for both transcendence and a justification of the human conditions of existence, but he could not bear the paradox of these apparently antagonistic aims. Kierkegaard's point was that transcendence is a characteristic of existence itself, and that the deepening of existence depends upon the manner and degree of transcendence. He did not offer any philosophical explanation of this proportion in terms of participation in being, but he did show that the religious task is to grapple with this paradox rather than to explain it away in a poetic and acosmic fashion. The genuinely religious elements in Nietzsche's image of the superman are rescued and given a basis in actuality in Kierkegaard's man of faith.

Kierkegaard's final word about the question of actuality is that it is found in a plenary way in ethical and religious existence. Transcendence does not lead away from actuality in its human mode but gives new meaning to what is concrete, temporal, and contingent. It does this, not by confusing the existent world with the eternal mode of being, nor by finding its "inner essence" to be eternity, but by confessing the presence of the eternal being in the fullness of time, the *pleroma*. The Incarnation respects the proper reality of both eternity and temporal existence, transcendence and immanence. Yet it also removes from the absolute its aloofness and impersonality, and from the finite its incapacity to present man with the substance of enduring happiness. This substance is given to us in faith, which is man's supreme inward act of free dedication to the good and the holy. The subject matter of faith is nothing other than the most pregnant form of actuality: the temporal coming of the Son of God in the flesh. Kierkegaard is led to refer to Christ unqualifiedly as "the existential," meaning thereby that, in His person, time and eternity are freely joined in all their strong contrasts and their demands upon human intelligence and will.[26] This is his final answer to Hegel, in whose system Christ is explained by a process of conceptual mediation. Were the divine and human natures subject to a sublation into something higher, the need for faith and personal service would pass away.

In refuting Hegel, however, Kierkegaard exposes himself to a certain criticism, on the basis of his own explanation. An orthodox account of the natures present in Christ attributes the full perfection of actuality to the divine nature, as well as to the human. Consequently, there is no ground for restricting existence to the temporal order. Both time and eternity are modes of *existent* actuality, a conclusion which is strengthened in the Christian mind by faith in the divine person of Christ. Christian faith emboldens one to regard God as an existent, as well as an actual being, because His eternal perfection is revealed in Christ to be loving, merciful, and mindful of our salvation.

5. FAITH AND THE HISTORICITY OF EXISTENCE

Kierkegaard's conception of existence as intimately bound up with becoming and time led him to examine the nature of history and historical apprehension. His conclusion that existence is by nature historical and grasped by faith has been widely influential. Heidegger and Barth are representative of the several tendencies to which his thoughts have given rise.

Since he had rejected the Hegelian theory of "world-history," he felt obliged to offer in its stead an existential treatment of historical process and understanding.[27] This obligation was all the more imperative, because his repudiation of the "world-historical outlook" also meant a repudiation of current attempts to bolster faith by means of biblical criticism and ecclesiastical history. Whatever the legitimate place these disciplines might hold among the historical sciences, Kierkegaard felt that some basic confusion about the relation between faith and history was responsible for employing these sciences as positive props of Christian faith. The attempt to treat the historical factor in Christianity Systematically meant a regression to a point lower than the Greek religious view. Along with Augustine and other Christian writers who have reflected upon the meaning of history, Kierkegaard held that the Greeks were lacking in historical sense and that men owe their appreciation of historical values mainly to Christianity. The Greek theory of recollection tended to empty time of all significance. Every teacher or point of departure in time is accidental and indifferent, a mere occasion in the backward march to eternity. Now, on this score, Hegelian philosophy did not succeed in transforming the pagan mentality, despite great efforts to link the Dialectic with history. Kierkegaard wanted to show that the reason for this failure is to be found in the barrier which "pure thought" erects between itself and the natural medium of history: real becoming and freedom. Hence, the folly and disaster of submitting sacred history to the procedures of idealistic philosophy of "history." This philosophy is, in principle, impotent before the cornerstone of Christian faith: the coming into temporal existence of the eternal truth, the Word of God, as a unique, individual teacher and savior. Yet it is this belief in the Incarnation which enables men to appreciate the proper dignity and decisiveness of history and historical efforts.

Kierkegaard justly acknowledges a debt to Schelling and other idealists, for having stressed the difference between natural duration and human history. The broadest and least important meaning of the historical is that something has its being by reason of having come to be. Nature is subject to the rule of becoming, and hence has a kind of past and an intimation of history. Apart from man, however, there is no case in nature where the immediate passage from future to past is grasped as such and made the subject of reflection. Everything transpires as though there were only the present, and even in higher animals equipped with memory, there is no sign of an appreciation of temporal process as such. Human history is not non-natural, in the sense of occurring outside the flow of natural events, for it must maintain this natural foundation of becoming. But man is not merely a being to which something happens. He is capable of reflecting upon his situation in time, and hence of recalling the past to his

present service and of estimating the requirements of an un-
certain but determinable future. At the heart of natural history, human history takes its rise. Intelligence and freedom
make the difference between being merely a point in the
temporal flow and being a point in this flow which is aware
of its predicament and capable of filling the present with the
actuality of what has been and the possibility of what is yet
to be.

When he cares to make use of metaphysical principles,
Kierkegaard does not hesitate to employ such reasoning to
strengthen his own view. Against Hegelian historical determinism, he makes a quite rigorous application of his general
analysis of the conditions of becoming to the case of historical
becoming. There is a certain immutability here, in that what
has come to be *has* indeed come to be and cannot be undone.
But at no moment does this factual immutability pass over into
the immutability of strict necessity or of what could not be
otherwise than as it is. Strict necessity positively excludes
every change and possibility of change, remaining in a constant relation of identity with itself. But an historical happening always involves some becoming, and hence remains forever
contingent and radically mutable. It could have either not
come to be or come to be in another way than it actually did.
Historical reality thus unites the stability of a given course
of actualization with the contingency which attaches to every
such process. The contingent factor is based on a twofold
possibility, which is actualized but not with strict necessity:
that an event should occur rather than not occur, and that it
should occur thus rather than otherwise. That it has happened
is not necessary; that in happening in this way it has canceled
out other possible ways of emergence, does not confer any
real necessity upon the process. Because existence is temporal,
it is historical and contingent.

The significance of this metaphysical analysis is that it helps to determine the kind of apprehension which is appropriate for historical or existential truth. Kierkegaard supposes that there must be an exact correspondence between historical reality itself and the human ways of apprehending historical reality. The factual immutability and contingency of historical process are paralleled by a combination of dependability and uncertainty in our knowledge of history. As a consequence, Kierkegaard rules out three claimants to historical knowledge. Two of these claimants are indeed valid sorts of knowledge but do not give knowledge of history, whereas the third class does not give knowledge of any kind. These three possibilities which he eliminates are: sensation, immediate intellectual understanding, and Speculative Dialectic.

This classification corresponds to the three prevailing views on existence and history with which Kierkegaard was acquainted: the empiricist (higher criticism and positivism), the idealist-intuitionist (Schelling and Jacobi), and the idealist-dialectical (Hegel). (1) Sense experience gives us knowledge about existing things but not precisely as existential and historical. For, the senses are limited to what is immediately present or bound up with the present. Hence, they do not grasp the formal meaning of becoming and, consequently, of the historical. Sense perception is also confined to the phenomenal order and the surface expression of events. But existence and historical development involve the entire being of the individual. (2) The theory of a pure intellectual intuition goes to the opposite extreme. It would attempt to place us in possession of the essence, but of the essence as deprived of its empirical context. This approach would eliminate the very conditions for the occurrence and apprehension of actual events. The intuitive method leads only to an essential understanding of what has happened: it cannot inform us about the happening itself, in its historical mode. Both empiricism and intuitionism suffer from too immediate a consideration of the object, taking it in its given appearance or in its essence. They are not dialectical enough to illumine the mystery of becoming, as a synthesis of non-being and being. (3) The Hegelian doctrine on history certainly remedies this latter defect, by reason of its thoroughly dialectical standpoint. But it is dialectical at the expense of both the real essence and the empirical situation. Kierkegaard's general criticism of the Speculative postulate of the identity of thought and being is also applied in this case. This postulate prevents any understanding of becoming and existence in their physical reality. Hegel's philosophy of history regards its subject matter in terms of necessity, whereas it can be appreciated only within a framework of contingency and freedom. Hence, the artificiality of the resultant view of history is not accidental but the inevitable outcome of applying the Speculative method to historical data.[28]

Kierkegaard's conclusion is that historical existence, by its very nature, evades philosophical analysis. In holding that there can be no strict philosophy of history, he would probably agree with the description of historical study as "a calculus whose asymptotic term is science." Because of the contingency of historical circumstances and the freedom of human agents in history, this domain is knowable only in a probable and approximative way. Not science but belief is the means of gaining historical insight. Historical becoming and belief are exactly proportioned to each other: the former is the physical way, and the latter the cognitive way, of reducing possibility to actuality. Such actualization demands an intervention of the will. A will-act is required in historical becoming, in order to realize the event and realize it in this way; it is required in belief, in order to assent to a process of becoming upon its own terms. In historical apprehension, one may not expect to deduce particular happenings or to arrive at any necessary conclusions. At most, one may hope to grasp the meaning of events through an act of free belief, on the basis of presently available evidence. But this conviction never becomes a comprehensive knowledge or a scientifically compelling law. This is all to its honor rather than its discredit, for it is respecting its subject matter. The attitude of belief is the only honest way of dealing with the multitude of circumstances and decisions which form the woof of history.

There is a final aspect of Kierkegaard's notion of historicity. In addition to natural becoming and ordinary historical events, he distinguishes a third sort of historical principle: the paradoxical event. This is his customary way of referring to the Incarnation, the advent of the eternal and immutable God in time and the flesh. Since the Incarnation is an historical event, it cannot be known formally by any philosophical means, but only through belief. Philosophy may discuss the possibility of an incarnation and the dialectical problem involved, but assent to the actual fact must be reserved for an act of belief. This is Kierkegaard's reply to the theologians of the Hegelian Right and Left, who thought that philosophy's office is to prove or disprove the basis of Christian religion. Biblical critics on both sides are on the wrong trail, in expecting to achieve more than approximate results by treating the Incarnation as just another historical event.

The entrance of God into history is a unique event, and so can be apprehended only by a unique sort of historical belief: *faith*, in the strict sense of religious and supernatural assent to the God-Man. Kierkegaard calls faith man's supreme passion and his highest act of existence. This act occurs in the *Instant*, a kind of synthesis of time and eternity, in which the believer is rendered contemporaneous with Christ.[29] God Himself must give the power to believe, and the individual must freely commit his understanding and will into God's hands, as he makes the act of faith. It is no mere speculative assent but the culmination of existential truth.[30] In the Instant or situation of believing, the man of faith engages his entire self in a temporal, historical act, which has an eternal import for him. Thus the problems of human happiness and historical existence receive a common answer in Kierkegaard's account of Christian faith. All of Kierkegaard's inquiries into the meaning and deepening of existence come to focus in his reflections on the Incarnation, our act of faith, and its influence over our way of living. But he allows "Johannes Climacus" merely to suggest that our existence is radically modified by faith, rather than witness personally to what it means to live in a Christian way. His "philosophical writings" bring us to the portals, but do not carry us across the threshold, of authentic Christian existing.

Perhaps because his conclusion about existence and historicity is broadly sketched rather than established in detail, Kierkegaard's position is open to criticism on several counts. Only two unsatisfactory issues will be mentioned here, a philosophical point and a theological one. His identification of existence with the historical is too narrow for the philosopher, and too equivocal for the theologian. By restricting existence to the historical order, Kierkegaard *eo ipso* restricts our understanding of existence to belief. But even if existence were found only in historical modes, this would not be sufficient ground for limiting our grasp of it to an act of belief. He never examines critically the principle that there must be a strict correspondence between the manner of being and the manner of knowing. Certainly, some proportion needs to be established between the knowing power and the object, yet the act of knowing need not be exactly parallel to the object's own act of existing. Hence belief need not be the only way of grasping existential becoming. Nor is there any need to restrict the scope of existential truth to the historicity of existence, since other aspects are clearly in sight.

If Kierkegaard binds existence down too closely to history

to achieve philosophical breadth, still in another sense he fails to include all of history itself somehow within his religious purview. Granted that a comprehensive and rigorous philosophy of history is beyond our power to construct, there remains the possibility of a theological interpretation of history. By distinguishing so sharply between ordinary historical events and the unique paradoxical event, Kierkegaard establishes a cleavage at the heart of history which he does not attempt to bridge and which, perhaps, he thinks neither can nor ought to be bridged. The Instant or medium of faith has some temporal duration, as well as an eternal significance, for the individual believer. But, on Kierkegaard's reckoning, this meaningful duration does not extend to the historical continuity and relations between individuals and peoples. The contemporaneity of each individual believer with Christ tends to cancel out the ordinary historical process and abandon to meaningless triviality the secular generations and their travail. The Incarnation does not become for Kierkegaard, as it did for Augustine, the central reality *in and for all* history, lending it sense and direction and a motive principle. Opposition to Hegel's grandiose perspectives on the historical epochs and the march of the Spirit prevents Kierkegaard from developing his own positive insights into an inclusive theory of historical existence.

Yet these shortcomings do not lessen the value of Kierkegaard's real achievement, what Gilson has called his chief contribution to the common good of philosophy and its progress. He has made it impossible for subsequent philosophers to dream of logicizing existence and hence of making a successful deduction of it from some more primary principle of essence. The Kierkegaardian dilemma is not complete, but it is challenging: either you must choose a complete System of pure thought, which falsifies existence, or you must choose the existent being of things, grasped in a non-philosophical way. Confronted with such an either/or, a man is naturally inclined to side with the concretely real, no matter how uneasy the philosopher within him may be about the commitment. Kierkegaard wins the support of our intelligence to his two basic theses: the meaning of history cannot be comprised within any philosophical science, and existence is not subsumed within the idealistic dialectic. We need not go along with him in the further inference that the apprehension of existence is one with the apprehension of the historical Incarnation of the Son of God. Faith is indeed an existential kind of cognition, but it is not the only way in which men can know existing being, just as the Incarnation is the highest but not the only mode of temporal existence. Kierkegaard is driven to equate faith and the existential sort of truth because of the failure of philosophy, as he knew it, to respect the real principles of being. His difficulties compel us, in turn, to rethink the philosophical meaning of existence and the conditions which being and its ultimate act impose upon philosophy. If Kierkegaard is not a philosopher, still he is one of the grand inquisitors of the human spirit, before whose tribunal it is well for a philosopher to allow himself to be summoned. For, questions will surely be asked, which every philosopher ought to be prepared to answer.

Chapter Six

The Nature of the Human Individual

1. THE PLACE OF THE INDIVIDUAL IN KIERKEGAARD'S THOUGHT

KIERKEGAARD'S position concerning the individual person won him bitter notoriety in his own day, furnished a model for Ibsen's Dr. Stockmann—the protagonist in *An Enemy of the People*—and has continued until now to provide a basis for the customary charge of excessive individualism. It is one of the two most important stands of his mature years, the other being his critique of the ecclesiastical establishment in Denmark. The controversy which the doctrine of the individual has aroused, often prevents rather than aids an understanding and fair appraisal of his mind. This is particularly unfortunate, because of its crucial role in the formation of his thought. Without any exaggeration, Kierkegaard could refer to the notion of the individual as "his own category," and could define his mission in modern Europe as the reinstatement of respect for what it means to be an individual man. He regarded his entire viewpoint as resting on the foundation of "the individual before God," all of his dialectical genius being concentrated upon the explanation and defense of this bedrock foundation.

By a characteristically dramatic and defiant gesture, Kierkegaard called attention to his conviction toward the end of 1845, in his article attacking P. L. Møller. In commenting upon the ensuing campaign waged against him by *The Corsair*, he made it clear that irresponsible journalism was a potent instrument for the general demoralization of public life.[1] He then extended his attention to the wider political and social upheavals which marked the troubled years 1847-48. The revolutions which swept over Europe during the latter year touched Denmark only lightly. But repercussions were felt in the change to a constitutional monarchy, with an assembly elected in part by the people, and in the agitation which led to the loss of the duchies of Schleswig and Holstein to Prussia. These events confirmed and further specified the theories which Kierkegaard was forming about the trends of his age. The dislocation and weakness evidenced on a small scale in the *Corsair* incident were symptomatic of a widespread social malaise, which he sought to diagnose and cure in principle, through his teaching on the individual.

Most of the books and articles written during the 1846-48 period reflect this orientation of Kierkegaard's thought to the problems of public life.[2] But this was not an entirely new preoccupation with him—a point which cuts the ground from under a psychiatric attempt to explain away his defense of the individual as being only a product of wounded pride, overcompensation and inability to make the required social adjustments. For one thing, such an explanation overlooks the unvaried dedication of the *Edifying Discourses* to "his reader, the single individual." This significant formula is found in the earliest *Discourses* (1843), which are contemporaneous with the first of the esthetic works. The trend of these religious addresses is to detach the individual from the crowd and make him aware of himself precisely as a personal center of responsibility, selfhood and equality. They are attempts to deal homiletically with problems of individual living, even before the difficulties are given open, theoretical formulation. Yet even in the esthetic and other pseudonymous books, which parallel the *Discourses* both in time and theme, Kierkegaard shows a special concern for the fate of the individual in modern society. Indeed, in the *Stages* and the *Postscript*, this question threatens to crowd out other matters and upset the careful plans of the pseudonymous "authors." A careful informal exploration of the subject was thus made, before Kierkegaard finally set down his mature conclusions on the matter.

Yet the journalistic lampooning did give "a new string to his instrument," and the actual course of European affairs did convey a specific lesson to him. These events confirmed his suspicions about the rottenness of the aristocracy and middle classes, the danger of the mass-man, and the urgent need to generate a sense of personal worth and accountability in each of his readers. Nevertheless, he qualified his remarks about these points in a way unmatched elsewhere in his writings, asking that allowance be made for the peculiar circumstances under which the views were elaborated.[3] He warned that, to some extent, his position is the outcome of his characteristic ways of thinking and feeling, which stand in need of correction and supplementing. The early *Journals* contain frequent references to the danger of self-isolation and to his own unjustified withdrawal from God and human society. Still, he was also convinced that God had made good use of this failing, in order to educate him in the special ways of his vocation, which required an unusual degree of self-discipline, reflection and private risk. He regarded his own calling as being similar to that of the spy or the lonely sentry, occupations which tend to exaggerate the independence and importance of the single individual. Furthermore, his work was largely specified in a negative way by the viewpoints which had already been promulgated and which he felt obliged to counteract. Because his contemporaries looked to public opinion and mass movements for *their* criterion of truth, he was inclined polemically to support the cause of the private person, even to the point of rupturing familiar social ties. Kierkegaard was right in warning us against the one-sided individualistic developments, which are certainly entailed by such a strong reaction against the idols of the day.

Having alerted critical intelligence to these exaggerated features in his own thesis, Kierkegaard is also convinced of the soundness of the central conception. He refers to the notion of the individual as a sufficient basis for an entire philosophy of life and the world. It bears a definite relation to his previous investigation of the spheres of existence and of Hegelianism, and is his nearest approach to a philosophical synthesis. The esthetic essays are so thoroughly dialectical and indirect, that they place us in touch with *possible* outlooks, without providing the decisive capstone of insight into the *actual* condition of the world. In his account of the individual, however, Kierkegaard supplies this lack in as forthright a way as his theory of truth and communication will permit. Moreover, he is no longer reticent about the positive content of the highest sphere of existence, the religious view of man, but offers a frankly religious interpretation. The various loose ends in his theory of the stages of life find, in the category of the individual, a principle of integration. His rounded view of the concrete self does not emerge, until these strands are united in a consistent account of individual existence.

This is also the conclusion reached in the "philosophical" works, especially the *Postscript*. For there is no way to deal critically with absolute idealism, except by assuming a position outside of the System itself. Hegelianism having made a claim to be all-inclusive of reality, Kierkegaard looked for this extra-Systematic basis in an existential direction, since existence alone is able to resist and refute this claim. In the individual existent he found his long-sought Archimedean or "spermatic" point, which breaks through the limits of dialectical idealism in the finite order, in a way similar to God's own independence of the System. "Existence corresponds to the individual thing." [4] What was formerly established about the traits of existence is now used to support his theory of the individual: the subjective view of the truth *for me*, the nature of concrete actuality and of the finite, temporal self, and the emphasis upon a truly human way of knowing and doing. Above all, Kierkegaard wished to support, in his own way, the first principles of thought and being. Hence his insistence upon the irreducible character of the individual existent and his actions. Against both estheticism and Hegelianism—and, by foresight, against some phases of recent existentialism—he urged that the distinction between being and non-being be firmly maintained, on pain of losing the human proportion and perspective. His defense is not as metaphysical as that of Aristotle, but it is just as radical. For, if the principle of contradiction is surrendered, it is even more futile to try to exist as a definite individual being than to try to make a statement or undertake a journey.

A final service which the teaching on the individual can render us today, should be mentioned. We are confronted with several rival interpretations of Kierkegaard's viewpoint, each one representing itself as the authentic version. Is his contribution to thought primarily esthetic or psychological, metaphysical or theological? Thinkers in all these fields have profited by his far-flung inquiries, but we should not overlook his own attempt to cast his thought in a distinctive mold. God and the human individual are the organizing principles which give unity and hierarchy to his various findings. The religious orientation subordinates, and provides a single context for, the many outlying developments. Kierkegaard remarks rather cryptically that as a thinker, but not as a person, the question of the individual is most important for him. [5] This probably means that his work as a polemical writer, ethically concerned about his own contemporaries, forces him to pay more attention to temporal problems of human individuality than he might otherwise have accorded them. For this, we are grateful. But when he speaks, not according to a professional plan, but out of the fullness of his heart as a lover of God, he invariably places the emphasis upon God, by reason of Whom and before Whom alone finite beings exist and men are individuals.

2. POLITICAL AND SOCIAL CRITICISM

Along with most of the important nineteenth-century thinkers, Kierkegaard was highly critical of the prejudices and institutions of his day. His approach shows significant points of affinity with the views of the Romantics and with the Hegelians of the Left, but he had the advantage of being located one remove from Germany, with its special problems and prejudices. Although not attracted very strongly to the ideal of the Holy Roman Empire, he did have a respect for hereditary monarchy, for the beneficent effect of an authoritative religious principle and, withal, for the solvent power of individual endeavor. Kierkegaard sometimes described himself as a man of conservative disposition, but he did not permit unchecked temperament to decide his mature social thinking. For, he saw that conservatism is an ambiguous attitude: it may signify either a sensible resolve to hold fast to proven truths and generally workable arrangements or merely a hedonic regard for the perpetuation and comfort of the fortunate groups, now in possession of the world's goods. Part of Kierkegaard's own social education was his disillusionment with the so-called better classes and the esthetic circles, which deliberately turn away from the oppressive conditions affecting the majority of people, in order to take refuge in the diversions of "fine society" or in ineffectual dreams about revolt and return to a golden age. These dreams could not be converted into constructive programs, until the defects in the Romantic idea of man were removed.

Apart from Feuerbach and some obscure representatives of "utopian" Socialism, Kierkegaard was not familiar with the radical social thinkers who followed in the wake of Hegel.[6] The many similarities which exist between his criticisms of the bourgeois order and those made by Ruge, Stirner, Hess and Marx, can be traced to the common historical situation and common philosophical training, rather than to any direct dependence. His method was not as rigidly academic as that of the Young Hegelians and in no way approached the technical economic studies of Marx and Engels, during their later years. He drew his data from the streets of Copenhagen rather than from reports in the library, while his positive suggestions involved not a "radicalization" of Hegel but an attempted clean break with him. While Karl Marx was penning his Communist Manifesto to the workers of the world, Kierkegaard was quietly correcting the proofs of his *Christian Discourses*, addressed to every man as an individual. Both men were aroused by the revolutions of 1848, seeing in them fulfillment of their own predictions and a good auspice for the future. Kierkegaard allowed himself a rare moment of complacency and exultation, referring to the events as the "one triumph" which was granted him in this world. This appraisal is unexpected, in view of his well-known repudiation of violence and mass movements.

The explanation is to be found in the theory of social change, which is outlined in the *Journals* and in the writings of 1846-48.[7] According to this interpretation of history, there are three stages in the growth of the European political consciousness. In Greek antiquity, the principle of leadership by great men was accepted and led to a sharp distinction between the few exceptional men at the helm of government and the multitude, which was either without franchise or without effective means to initiate policy. The gap was lessened somewhat, during the high period of Christendom, by means of the principle of representation. The distinguished individual not only supplied direction for the community but also embodied its highest ideal, in which all members of society participated in various degrees, through their representatives. In the modern era, however, largely under the influence of Cartesian doubt and Protestant separatism, this representative bond has gradually lost its cohesive power. We have become too "reflective," too much aware of our personal being and its depth of possibility and freedom, to be satisfied with the previous social and political agencies, which still linger on into the present.

Hence our time is a revolutionary one. Kierkegaard regarded the first half of the nineteenth century as one of the great turning-points in history. He felt that nothing around him was stable, that the old gods had fled the temples and that a great creative activity was called for, and perhaps being initiated, during his own lifetime. The contrast between the enthusiastic Revolutionary stirrings during the previous generation and the relentless inroads of the industrial revolution and of the absolutist philosophies of the state in his own generation, struck him forcefully as an instance of the fatal separation, in modern culture, between passion and reflection. This antithesis was not overcome by the Hegelian method of reducing the order of praxis to that of creative reason. Consequently, Kierkegaard found fault with any social philosophy —whether a dialectic of spirit or one of matter—which does not take issue with Hegel on this crucial point. He could agree with Marx's charge that Feuerbach is too exclusively theoretical, but Kierkegaard's own attitude toward action was much more than a "putting of theory into practice." Concerning the post-Hegelian appeal to action, he remarked that such reform movements are too hastily and narrowly conceived, in that they fail to include what is sound in the Revolutionary and Romantic experiments, namely, respect for personal conviction, human dignity and individual effort. Romanticism, in its political aspect, represents the protest of individuals and organic corporate groups against the total and uniform mechanization of human relations. An explosive situation or revolution results when such aspirations are thwarted either by middle-class industrialists and bureaucrats or by the masses, whipped into retaliation by demagogues.

Kierkegaard was not in sympathy with the liberal steps toward reform made in Denmark from 1830 onwards, but the reason for his opposition was not merely a sentimental fondness for the monarchy or a conservative fear of change. He regarded the parliamentary movement as futile in its assumptions and dangerous in its alliances and consequences. In proof of the pointlessness of mere political change, he suggested that the day of sweeping, constructive progress in the political sphere had passed and that European countries would, for the most part, remain content with some modified form of the monarchy. Instead, the truly revolutionary processes may be expected in the social order, internal to the state. What Kierkegaard feared would happen, is an ever-intensified "combining" of group against group or class warfare.[8] People whose thinking runs customarily in political channels only, would not be prepared for this crucial shift in vital interests from politics to social structure, and would lend themselves unknowingly to one or another side in this internecine strife. Through his social writings, Kierkegaard tried to make these new conditions apparent and inform men about the underlying issues.

Analysis of the situation convinced him that "the dialectic of the present age tends towards equality, and its most logical —though mistaken—fulfilment is levelling."[9] Equality is the social ideal which corresponds, in our time, to the principles of leadership and representation in past ages. Equality itself is a legitimate human value, and its attainment would mark a step of progress toward a more equitable order. But Kierkegaard objected to the abstract and quantitative way in which the notion was being conceived and applied. Because equality is sought apart from other goods, such as liberty and personal integrity, its actual pursuit leads to the breakdown of the unity and order of human life. Instead of furthering the individual's integral development, the partisans of equality offer a one-sided, tyrannical program, which subordinates actual persons to the abstract requirements of number and mass pressure. Qualitative diversity or social pluralism is feared, whereas soulless uniformity is substituted for unanimity among free men. A depressive social leveling is the logical issue of this inhumane sort of equality.

Like Nietzsche, Kierkegaard is troubled by the spread of the herd mentality, as the end-product of modern egalitarian trends.[10] They agree that the individual is being emptied of all value and engulfed in some dominant totality: the majority, the race, the class, the nation or humanity itself. Kierkegaard calls the typical contemporary self a cipher-man or a fractional man, having importance and purpose not in himself but only as an element in a quantitative social whole. What counts is not the quality of individual judgment and character but the weight of public opinion. The public is an anonymous but all-powerful presence, whose ends are advanced by the press and other means of impersonal communication. Kierkegaard drew upon his own experience for the observation that decent men seem to be corrupted and transformed into something inhumane and demoralizing, when they sink corporately into the crowd. They lose the human norms and evade responsibility, when they try to decide problems of eternal import by numbers and impersonal pressures.

Against the uncritical, popular opinion that truth lies with the masses, Kierkegaard advanced the existential counter-proposition that the crowd is untruth. He agreed with Nietzsche on the additional point that we are coming back to the predicament of the ancient world, in which the problem of the masses was foremost. But the similarity ends here, since Kierkegaard did not allow the possibility of a complete return to the same situation as faced the Greeks. Neither the Greek Dionysos nor the Nietzschean Superman is a feasible solution, for in both cases there is a depreciation of, and flight from, ordinary mortal men, from the "common or garden humanity," which Kierkegaard tried to defend and edify. His religious principles prevented him from converting his hostility toward the crowd into a discriminatory distinction between citizen and slave, ruler and herd. His only possible stand was that, although the mass-man is a danger to life's seriousness and integrity, every man in the crowd has the power to liberate himself from it, with God's help, and to become an individual self, an "uncommon man." This is the new hope of human equality, undreamed of in older civilizations and only clumsily formulated in our own time.

At this point in his social analysis, Kierkegaard abandons political and secular problems for an ethico-religious approach. He reasons with Augustine that all social forms are determined by a radical "love" or orientation, based upon one's relation to God. Yet this shift from secular to religious evaluation is disappointing in some respects, for there remain numerous difficulties of a more proximate sort, which Kierkegaard has failed to settle. Two of these problems are of outstanding importance for those who are concerned about the future of democracy: what is the eventual fate of politics and the state, and what is a reliable guide in temporal action?

Kierkegaard approximates, without ever duplicating, the Marxian theory of the withering of the state. His contention is, more precisely, that political questions are of secondary importance at the present stage of history. This does not mean that the state and civil order are bound to disappear eventually, but rather that the major decisions and movements of our era are occurring on another plane. The particular forms of government, the political ruling of society and the international question, do not seem to Kierkegaard to be as close to the heart of modern life as the struggle for the individual's basic "love" or allegiance. This conflict is transpiring within the state and independently of the particular disposition of political power. But although he explicitly mentions and repudiates class warfare, incited by economic issues, he passes over this area in favor of cultural analysis. While Marx is interested in the statistics of wealth and labor, Kierkegaard devotes himself to a study of such cultural phenomena as *ressentiment*, talkativeness, facile reasoning, publicity-seeking and anonymity. These are more revealing of the condition of the individual soul. His outlook remains that of the phenomenologist and moralist—but with the intent of calling men back to a way of existing which is animated by religious motives.

Marx and Kierkegaard are both opposed to Hegel's view that the state is the supreme temporal and ethical embodiment of the universal Idea. Taken in this way, the state would be identical with what Kierkegaard calls the theocentric crowd or public, and ought to be done away with. But Marxists add two further statements, with which Kierkegaard would not agree. They hold that the welfare of the social economy is man's absolute consideration and that the state, which will eventually wither away, must meanwhile be used as an instrument for securing the triumph of the classless society. From Kierkegaard's standpoint, neither proposition is acceptable. The social economy cannot be erected into an absolute end, without leading men once more to a form of idolatry of the finite order of things. No aspect of man's life in the world can be given unconditioned allegiance. Furthermore, the state is not simply going to disappear from the face of the earth. Despite the fact that political issues are not paramount today, the state and political problems will always remain with us. But the state is a power that needs to be tamed: it is all too powerful a tool of egalitarian or aristocratic oppression. Kierkegaard does not propose to give a direct solution of the question of political power, but rather to attack it indirectly, by stressing personal worth and man's religious vocation. He foresees a restoration of the state and political life and a corresponding decline of Romantic individualism, once human individuals become aware of their proper dignity and responsibilities. In the meanwhile, there is no justification for contending that the state *ought* to be (in Lenin's words) a bludgeon in the hands of the ruling class, even though this is the actual case.

The fact remains, however, that men are still implicated in political life and its forced options, no matter how we rate this phase of our existence. Political and, generally, secular situations call for enlightened decisions, made not only on the basis of "technical" evidence but also with an eye to the moral and religious bearings of our conduct. Here, Kierkegaard disappoints us by failing to point out, at least in principle, the nexus between his religious dialectic and a moral philosophy which seeks to regulate the wide range of secular interests. He discourages investigation into methods of adapting moral and religious teaching in a proportionate and relevant way to social and political problems. This sep-

aratist attitude stands in bold contrast to Hegel's softening
of the transcendent, paradoxical and anti-worldly aspects of
revealed religion. But it is inadequate as a positive statement
of ethical doctrine, developed according to its own requirements and its responsibility to actual individuals.

The one danger point to which Kierkegaard is sensitive is
the encroachment of human opinion—whether in the form
of philosophical reasoning or of majority political opinion—
on the unconditional right of God's revealed word to exact
the obedience of faith from us. Once it is allowed that, in
religious matters, God's truth and power cannot be over-
awed by any sort of public pressure, he is all too willing
to let the more particular principles of a just social order
go unspecified. His dictum that the crowd is untruth, is
applied mainly to questions of eternal import and ethico-
religious concern. As for material interests and temporal
problems, Kierkegaard concedes that here the public is fully
competent to reach its own decisions. Admittedly, he does
not want to abandon this realm entirely to the powers of
the world. "Christianity is not indifferent to anything secular, on the contrary, it is solely spiritually concerned for
everything." [11] Granted, however, that it is necessary to
specify the formal aspect under which things are of spiritual concern, still in practice Kierkegaard isolates ethical
and religious norms and makes an uncritical identification
between the temporal world and the spirit of worldliness.

Such a restricted view of the relevance of religious and
moral principles paves the way for a surrender to amoral
power politics. It accords neither with Kierkegaard's general notion of existence—which is firmly grounded in temporal and empirical conditions—nor with the radical implications of his attack upon the featureless crowd. He once
defined worldliness as the positing of temporal conditions
and differences as decisive between man and man. If this

definition is taken in its full rigor, it applies to *every* project of the mass-man, whether economic or social or political, and not merely to his formally religious relationship. Consequently, ethics cannot side-step the specific problems which arise in these other areas, since there are moral issues involved in every reduction of the individual to a quantitative unit and instrument of mass policy. More positively expressed, one's opposition to worldliness stems not only from solicitude for the primacy of the spiritual but also from solicitude for the right use of material goods, temporal opportunities and human associations.

From Kierkegaard's jeremiad against liberalism, the press and modern inventions, it might be concluded that his social criticism is sterile and escapist in its ultimate import. This impression needs to be corrected by a reading of other texts, in which a more positive account is given of the good use of modern instrumentalities. He believed that, even in the present time, the divine plan will not be mocked but will fashion available materials to its own purpose.[12] It is true that the terrible leveling tendency has destroyed *das geistige Band*, the organic lifestream of society, and has reduced all intermediate organizations to empty hulls or frivolous aims. Providence can, however, turn this atomization to good account, by making direct contact once again with individuals. When men are no longer able to lose themselves in the affairs of secondary groups and when they find themselves alone before Leviathan, then the opportunity for calling upon God is almost forced upon them. And since it is necessary to approach God not *en masse* but singly, as individuals, the principle of individuality and existence can be seen at work behind and within the modern search for equality. The very frustrations and divisions which are provoked by the this-worldly attitude, can lead to a complete reversal of mind and a finding of one's individual self. This hopeful view has more in common with Hegel's statement on the cunning of reason than with Marx's thesis on the deliberate worsening of conditions. It helps to confirm Kierkegaard's enheartening verdict that everything in the world's development, including the tides of revolution, tends to establish the importance of the individual. It could also be made the point of insertion of a moral philosophy, concerned with regulating man's temporal activity.

3. EQUALITY AND THE INDIVIDUAL

The doctrine on the individual is intended to supply, not what the present age openly demands, but what it needs. Kierkegaard proposed it explicitly as a religious response to "the literary, social and political conditions" prevailing in modern Europe. These conditions are reducible to two correlative traits: dissolution of the order of existence and contempt for the individual man. What Gabriel Marcel refers to as "the stifling sadness of the contemporary world" is almost a literal transcription of Kierkegaard's description of the oppressive weight of worldliness, in a period when temporal values alone are pursued. Vision and expectancy, as well as stability, are lacking in a society which no longer gives heed to God's eternal law. Unless God, the constant friend of order, is recognized as the ground and goal of our temporal life, we have no principle of integration and cannot strike a balance between anarchy and totalitarianism. These extreme positions are enemies to human personality, and yet the attempted compromises are essentially unstable, because they run counter to man's natural hunger after eternal life. The more the transcendent God is excluded from our civilization, the more violent become the revolutionary shocks of existence, rising up in protest against this thinning of personal goals.

In his social writings, Kierkegaard does not give much attention to anarchist tendencies. Formless individualism is treated by him primarily in connection with Romanticism and the esthetic outlook. As far as contemporary life and institutions are concerned, the weightier problems lie in the opposite quarter: in placing all our trust in social efforts and the security of the collectivity. Because Kierkegaard directed most of his arguments against those who advance the interests of society, his position is often mistaken for an individualistic, anti-societal plea. In fact, he saw that social illusions are the stronger today and must be dispelled, as a condition for the renaissance both of the individual and of humane social life. He speaks out against the anti-humanistic and anti-theistic forms which society has actually taken, rather than against the social aspect itself of human nature. But he adheres so closely to his mission as a corrective, in a particular time and situation, that he gives plausible grounds for the charge of excessive individualism. Invariably, he contents himself with exposing the weakness of existing associations and with advocating personal initiative. He does not give constructive counsel about the regeneration of private and social life together.

Kierkegaard has a keener eye for the weaknesses of communal existence than for its healthy state, and yet his pathological analysis is pertinent and advances some of his abiding themes. He asks, first, why men today cannot join together in a sound social union, and then, why they do in fact constitute some kind of society. In answer to the first question, he traces back our social troubles to the prevalence of Hegelian philosophy and the "theocentric" outlook which it instills into people. Because of this "theocentric" or pantheistic bias, the distinctive conditions of temporal existence are revoked, in an eagerness to view everything contemplatively and self-forgetfully in the light of eternity. Thereby, the basis of human communication and joint endeavor is also destroyed. If the eternal truth is immanent in each of us, then we stand in no essential need of our fellow men and sustain only accidental and instrumental relations with others. In the Hegelian universe, there is no footing for genuine co-operation, since every end is already attained in essence and dialectically imposed upon our efforts. Communication and co-operation are only possible when men are taken as genuinely finite individuals, dependent upon God and present in a common situation of temporal becoming and choice.[13]

The conditions of contemporary life are more apt to arouse in the individual a sense of futility and personal insignificance than a spark of divinity. It is to the common persuasion about the individual's worthlessness that Kierkegaard attributes the urge to combine with others, in every sort of organization. This gregarian tendency of "joiners" fits in with the Hegelian stress upon objectivity and its criticism of whatever is particular and subjective about men. The only way to realize the ideal of a "concrete universal" seems to be through an aggregation of individuals, whose majority opinion is held to be true and divine, by the mere fact of expressing the will of the many. There is an unseemly horror of remaining a single person, unsupported by the public. Kierkegaard calls the uncritical desire to join the group a form of mass hysteria, and traces it to a wish to be stimulated by others and to be drawn out of one's own emptiness into at least a quantitative fullness and stability.[14] He also detects here a fear of personal solitude, self-scrutiny and personal responsibility for choices, thus anticipating the findings of later psychological and sociological research into the mass mind and the lonely crowd.

These metaphysical and psychological reasons convinced Kierkegaard that the existing modes of social being are only pseudo-communities, since they are substitutes for personal worth rather than its complement. He felt that it would be better to break these social ties, where possible, than to base agreement upon a common declaration of personal bankruptcy. This is the decisive reason why Kierkegaard was willing to neglect the problem of what constitutes an authentic mundane community, in favor of a further inquiry into what makes for individual sanity. The current practice of submerging the individual in the social "organism," out of despair over the value of the single self, can be checked only by emphasizing the primary value of individual integrity. Strength rather than weakness, honest humility rather than self-deception, should be the motives prompting men to band together in society. But the preparatory work must be done in the soul of the individual, where all decisive battles are fought and permanent foundations laid. This is Kierkegaard's reason for proposing the category of the individual as the answer to the modern dilemma.

Kierkegaard did not employ the terms "crowd" and "public" in an invidious sense, as connoting the poorer or less intelligent groups of people. Any association of men is marked as a crowd or herd, if the component individuals become impenitent and irresponsible in regard to corporate actions. Whereas Hegel made a sharp distinction between naive minds and philosophers, Kierkegaard called for simple men of wisdom and, furthermore, maintained that everyone is capable of acquiring the basic wisdom of human living. This equality of opportunity is predicated upon neither the special favors of nature nor a favored economic position (whether that of the bourgeoisie or of the proletariat). After reading Schopenhauer, Kierkegaard concluded that he was not a serious moral philosopher, for the fact that he made moral well-being a matter of taste and genius.[15] The esthetic view of the good will, as being dependent upon some special endowment or fortune, makes nonsense out of human dignity and duty, for it places moral perfection outside the reach of the ordinary individual. The only kind of moral talent would be will itself, and if this were lacking in certain men, then for them there could be *no* question of a responsible formation of character and of moral obligation.

From what he knew about early socialism and communism, Kierkegaard also rejected any one-sided proletarian interpretation of human equality. He remarked that the rich and the powerful are not the only ones who are tempted by material goods and inequalities, as though the poor are justified in employing every means to equalize their lot.[16] Indeed, rich and poor alike stand in danger of losing their souls, through a failure to rise above the worldly idea that such differences are of ultimate importance. Both groups are inclined to rely upon the accident of birth, the fictitious innocence of a special economic class, or some other device which splits mankind into the innately good and those who are of good only as instruments and sacrifices. Even the most benevolent capitalist and the most far-seeing leader of the proletariat perpetuate discriminations in the actual world, because of their common ideological position that problems of human equality and justice find ultimate settlement in terms of material goods. Hence leaders of both parties in class warfare tend to deny the primacy of the political order and its ordination to human welfare, broadly conceived. Kierkegaard at least leaves the way open for a subsequent vindication of the proper role of the state, and for a penetration of social life as a whole by the religious view of human existence. But his own mission is to show the relative status of economic interests, by establishing the integral betterment of the individual man as the measure and end of all social organization and resources.

At times, Kierkegaard comes close to the moral equivalent for the economic doctrine of laissez-faire. Although he is sure that material concerns have no absolute importance, he hesitates about whether, even within their own relative order, they come under a positive moral regulation. His conception of "eternal truth" has nothing to do with the world's inequalities, which not only obtain but ought to persist more or less as they are. This statement is subject, however, to an important qualification in view of his express "spiritual concern" for all kinds of differences. These must be impenetrated and hence transformed by the thought that, whatever their weight, they cannot ultimately decide a man's character and destiny. The function of the idea of religious equality is to relativize, to the very bottom, all the differences between men which spring from fortune, natural disposition or the competitive activities of others. However large they loom in the world's reckoning, they are as nothing in the incorruptible judgment of eternity. This belief was Kierkegaard's personal consolation and joy, throughout his own struggle with worldly power and privilege. In his *Edifying Discourses*, he repays his debt by speaking persuasively about the "blessed equality" of men before God, wherein both giver and receiver return thanks for the gift itself in its divine origin.[17]

Kierkegaard's thought runs counter to the naturalistic effort to dissociate the doctrine of equality from its basis in religion and to support it solely by scientific and utilitarian arguments. The latter cannot stand alone, because they cannot supply a normative reason for respecting every man or a sufficient foundation for equality, in view of the obvious and important inequalities between men. It is a question of acknowledging the distinctively *human* conditions under which a moral obligation is laid upon us to treat every man as a brother and neighbor, despite the barriers and points of conflict. Common citizenship in a common world is not enough, since this is too abstract a relation and leaves undefined the extent of the individual's rights and the basis for respecting them, in cases where interests based on divisive material aims lead to a clash. In such a predicament, the concrete and transcendent relationship of every individual to God needs to be brought home. God is at once the well-spring of individuality and the source of human community. Our common situation is not only that of belonging to an encompassing natural environment, but also that of existing together before God and with equal opportunity to enter into personal union with Him.

This leads to a new sort of leveling of differences, a paradoxical fulfillment of the liberal politician's dreams and of the logic of modern history as a whole. The religious basis of equality is paradoxical in two ways. First, it levels by accentuating the eternal significance of each single individual, rather than by sweeping it away; second, it affirms our equality without destroying our freedom. Ours is an equality of essential relationship to God, and of freedom to will the good and perfect our interior existence. Kierkegaard uses Hegelian terms to characterize this as a union of necessity and possibility, in each actual human existent.[18] The individual's nature as a created person is the indestructible and common foundation of human dignity. But man is a being enjoying freedom and acknowledging a correlative duty of self-realization. Individual richness of personality is not only something which each is given, but also something which each must win for himself.

Unconditionally every man *can* realize his own end in freedom, and unconditionally every man *must* submit to a rigorous test, which is proportioned to his ability. God is not just another name for an objective sum of mediocrity and compromise. He is the "compelling subjectivity," the "austere man" of the Biblical parable, Who sows His seed among men in such a way that the integrity of everyone is respected and the capacity of everyone is expected to yield a maximum harvest. Hence Kierkegaard sometimes refers to his teaching as one of strict inequality. There can be truly decisive differences between men, differences which count in the scales of eternity. If a man fails to meditate, in a concerned and grateful way, upon the treasure he has been given or fails to return God love for love, then his mode of existing is a relatively impoverished one. Instead of leveling downwards, after the manner of the mathematical view of social equality, the religious outlook seeks to level in an upward direction.[19] Its conception of human personality is an aristocratic one, based not on the aristocracy of privilege but on the aristocracy of the actual exercise of freedom in everyman's search for the good life.

During his prolonged engagement with Hegelianism, Kierkegaard worked out the metaphysical basis for this doctrine of a demanding equality. Human existence is not a mode of necessity, resulting from a combination of possibility and actuality; it is rather a synthesis of possibility and necessity, leading to a novel and inviolable actuality. A sharp clash of anthropologies is concealed behind this technical jargon. Kierkegaard found a way of eliminating absolute idealism, without at the same time eliminating a similar human nature, present essentially in all man. His view of the individual steers a middle course between idealism and pragmatism, since he allows both an essential nature, commonly present in all men, and genuine freedom in the individual development of human powers. The element of necessity in human life means that a man cannot dream himself into an identity with the divine nature, either by denying his own essential finitude or by denying God's infinity. He remains a finite existent *before* God. But the factor of possibility is a reminder that a man is no mere spectator or passive effect of the causal sequence. He is actively and freely engaged in an effort to share more richly in existence, as a search *after* God.

In conformity with his notion of existence, Kierkegaard declares that the category of the individual is catastrophic and orientated to the future. For him, "the future" refers both to the range of temporal possibilities, open to human freedom, and to the special relation which eternity bears toward temporal freedom. The theory of man proposed by absolute idealism makes no allowance for the future, in either sense of the word. It misconceives the nature of our freedom by confounding it with divine necessity; and at the same time it misconceives the relation between man and eternity by placing man—or at least the philosopher—in an immanent and premature possession of eternal being. Kierkegaard defends the place of novelty and genuine progress-and-regress in human life, thus differing from those existentialists who dwell exclusively upon the despairing and compressed face of things.[20] He traces back the historical oscillation between an exaggerated cult of progress and an unreasonable failure of nerve to a false relationship between eternity and human existence. For existing human individuals, eternity holds the place of the future: it can be gained only through a process of temporal becoming or free effort. In his initial state, a man embodies not eternity but a *pondus* or loving desire for eternity. Individual existence is perfected in proportion to a man's unique perspective on, and progressive sharing in, God's eternal being. But this being must be sought after, and this participation must be gained through free acts, having temporal duration and subject to temporal risks and temptations. Time and eternity conspire to give to human freedom its mystery and depth, what John Donne calls its sense of God's great *Venite.*

Existentialists who deny a transcendent God are forced either to ascribe a fictional eternity to temporal deeds or to cut these projects loose entirely from ordination to an actual eternity. The latter alternative, followed by Sartre, interprets human freedom as our doom, as the futile uneasiness of pure becoming, which can make no real progress, attain no goals and reach no permanence in being. Because of its atheistic premise, its denial of the principle of contradiction and its denigration of freedom and hope, this philosophy of man is irreconcilable with that of Kierkegaard. The so-called absolute freedom of this variety of existentialism turns out, upon inspection, to be an exasperated despair over man's plight. It is an unwilling testimony to the need for an eternal reality, which can provide a reliable future and a measure of action. Similarly, the Sartrean self fails to achieve a distinctive individual nature, because it lacks the foundation of individuality: the essential relation of every human act to God as the transcendent and actual source of personal vocation. Sartre sees that the attainment of selfhood should be a joint affair, but he is forced by his atheism to reduce every kind of human social relation to one of self-aggrandizement and hate of the other.

An answer to this despairing view is found in Kierkegaard's dialectic of "Thou and I," which has been further developed by Buber, Berdyaev and other personalists. The pioneer text is found in *Works of Love*, where Kierkegaard is meditating upon the reason why "love seeks not its own." [21] Love of one's neighbor is the dynamic expression for the equality between men, since it works a cleansing of the partiality which worldly conditions induce in us. In the love of neighbor, I no longer treat him as a distant third party or as a mere means to my own happiness, but as a fellow person—a "thou"—to whom I must respond with all that is most intimate and personal in me. Such an attitude cultivates and reveals the best in our individual selves. We are led to exchange the egoistic and ruthless "mine and thine" for a "mine and thine" based upon common sharing and helping. This is the foundation of true fellowship in a moral and religious "our," the only kind of human community which Kierkegaard is concerned to establish. Until the individual is able to say "we" along with his neighbor, he has not developed all his potentialities. Above all, he has not realized that the spiritual life—the willing of the good and the love of God and neighbor—is something to be realized together. The exclusiveness and differences of the material order need to be regulated by individual outlooks, in which the primacy of the spiritual is the governing principle.

During Kierkegaard's lifetime, the Danish Church was shaken by the reforms and revival initiated by N. F. Grundt-vig. One of Grundtvig's main theses was that the Holy Spirit dwells in the religious congregation, constituting a living, visible community of men. Kierkegaard was suspicious of the entire Grundtvigian movement, including its sentimental praise of the community. This accounts, in part at least, for his reserve and hedging on the question of whether men ever do break through their individual solitude, so as to establish earthly associations enlivened by the "we"-relationship. He was only sure that, apart from the religious basis, social enter-prises only help to deplete the individual selves. Enthusiastic and self-sacrificing people can find the "mine and thine" of mutual understanding and concord, only by first dedicating themselves individually to God, from Whose hands each one receives his personality purified of its overreaching partiality. Kierkegaard spoke of our solidarity and kinship with God and with each other in God; he also stressed the fellowship of solitary individuals in the goods of the spirit. He would assent to Franz Kafka's statement that our relation to others is the relation of prayer. But he hesitated to affirm that human isolation is ever overcome at the human level: each individual remains an island, no matter what distant shores may touch on the common sea. He found no psychological evidence of any lasting and sufficient removal of the barriers, and he feared that a sentimental view would result in the elimination of

God as the indispensable "third party" or "middle term" in all human communication.[22] Only faith is able to overcome the loneliness in principle and to encourage our human attempts to achieve communion with each other. The catastrophic effect of the category of the individual is to reveal the futility of all social efforts which are entered upon without mutual faith in God and humility before our actual condition.

4. HUMANISM AND CHRISTIANITY

Another policy of Grundtvig was to establish Folk High Schools, which would provide Danish children with a general cultural education, as the first step in a return to religion. His idea was that the cultivation of the humanities and national mythology is the most effective way of preparing men for the good news of Christianity. Martensen expressed a similar hope for a synthesis of Christianity and modern national culture. Kierkegaard dealt lightly with this plan, as being only a Nordic variation on a much more serious theme: the vindication of pure humanity, *die reine Menschheit*, attempted esthetically by Goethe and philosophically by Hegel and Feuerbach.[23] In the hands of these German thinkers, "pure humanity" is a weapon for wiping out the transcendent and supernatural principle in Christianity and for reducing its teaching to that of esthetics, Systematic idealism or anthropology. Understood in this sense, humanism is as scornfully rejected by Kierkegaard as it is by Marx, and on the same grounds that it is antithetic to human nature. They agree that this sort of humanism is a weak residue of Christianity, but whereas it is the Christian character of the residue which disqualifies the standpoint for Marx, it is the denaturing of both Christianity and philosophy which is objectionable to Kierkegaard. If it meant the same thing to be cultured and to be a Christian, then the latter would be a problem of cleverness and sensibility alone, and would fall subject to fate and the reign of inequalities.

Other collectivities, like the race or class or nation, have some determinate content and concreteness, by comparison with the ideal of pure humanity. Kierkegaard regarded the latter as the culmination of the trend to place equality on a purely secular basis and to apotheosize the public. It is a hindrance to man's creaturely recognition of God's sovereignty and of the worth of each single individual. Taken in himself and in his relation of sonship to God, each human individual transcends in importance every aggregation and every universal notion, including that of pure humanity itself. There is no existent being which can be designated as "pure man," although existence is certainly a matter of "making individual men pure." This is a paradoxical way of stating the unusual nature of the category of the individual. Like every other "category," it signifies a definite universal trait of being and hence is applicable everywhere. But it can be applied everywhere, precisely because all finite existents are individuals, not because there is any universal entity, "*the* individual," corresponding to this category. Hence Kierkegaard's teaching escapes the charge of hypostasization which can rightly be lodged against the proponents of "pure humanity."

Kierkegaard sees not only that there is something ineffable about being an individual, but also something of an art about communicating in a lively way the sense of being a human individual. For this reason, he presents a good deal of his insight in the form of ethico-religious discourses, in which the individual is asked to ponder the question for himself and in a practical way. His special problem is how to save as many universal human characteristics as possible, within the highly accentuated individual existence which he advocates. This he could not do by appealing to the hypostasized notion of humanity, in which these traits are supposed to inhere and to which individuals are subordinated. The difficulty is the same as that which faced him in the case of secularist morality. In both instances, he was obliged to propose a new meaning of "universal," and to support the cause of the universal only in the amended, theistic sense. Universal human nature does not enjoy a separate existence, and does not intervene as a *tertium quid* between the individual and God. The universal traits are based upon the essential nature or "necessity," which makes us all to be men, and upon the equal, though proportionate, demands made on our freedom.[24] Our duty does not lie in becoming universal, for the universal traits belong to what we already are. The individual is required to make a concrete and unique application of these principles in his own existence; he is asked to realize these common possibilities, in accord with his own special call as an individual participant in being.

Kierkegaard recognized here a region of mystery, concerning how God can call an individual from nothingness and how the inter-working of grace and freedom can perfect the individual. The spread of stereotyped, "sample men," raised under the sign of quantitative equality, can be brought to a halt only by the appearance of "original men," who are in contact with the creative source of their existence. The need of our times is, however, not for a few outstanding political, intellectual and artistic geniuses (as the Greeks and Romantics thought) but for the reintroduction of every individual to his real nature and vocation as *imago Dei*—man the image of God. Religious thought in East and West believes this to be the most radical significance of human nature, the one which makes the most demands upon man and brings him closest to the divine foundation of his existence. Kierkegaard centered his reflections on a Christian humanism around this leading notion. He sought to clarify the common tradition by showing, first, that the image of God is present in men only as individuals and in proportion to their spiritual awareness of their individual existence and, second, that this highest form of individuality is fully attained only in Christian religious existence. The first proposition led him to review the meaning of the human self as spirit, whereas the second one led to an appreciation of the specifically Christian contribution to individual perfection.

There is an Augustinian stamp upon Kierkegaard's reflections on man as *imago Dei*.[25] He recalls the sublime remarks of Plato and the Platonists concerning the dignity of man, but his own approach emphasizes the personalist and Christian aspect. Other creatures have a faint impress or *vestigium* of God's shaping hand in their nature, and render silent witness to His power and presence. Man alone is termed the proper image of God, and he alone can render glory to his maker in a free, intelligent way. Man's superiority over the non-human world is not based primarily upon his bodily makeup or his ability to explore and exploit nature. The essence of human dignity is spirit and the capacity to worship, for in virtue of these traits we not only dominate, but rise above, the rest of creation. Man is a maker of things and symbols, as Dewey and Cassirer recognize, but above all he is a worshiper, whether of false gods or of the living God. It is a paradoxical consideration that this supreme testimony to man's creaturely dependence is also the measure of his nearness to God: his need of God is at the same time his highest perfection, the seal of God's likeness upon him.

There is, however, the sobering fact that men can refuse to worship God and can offer worship, instead, to idols of their own making. Freedom reaches down to the originary decision whether to honor the image of God in oneself or to becloud and pervert it. This is an affair of the spirit, for God can be approached or abandoned only through an act of spiritual freedom. In Kierkegaard's analysis of the nature of the human spirit, two different influences are felt: one stems from Augustine, Luther and other devotional authors, the other from Hegel and Hegelians like Rosenkranz. His own religious-existential position draws most heavily upon the former sources. From this standpoint, to become spiritual means to acquire a depth of personal inwardness. This is an individual task, for only the individual can appropriate truth existentially, as being important above all for oneself. A man is not deemed spiritual, until the belief to which his under-standing assents is also the principle of his actions. Hence spirit also involves the free and inalienably personal commit-ment of the will, in acts of moral resolution. The category of the individual completes Kierkegaard's earlier investigations concerning moral life and subjective truth. The "moral sub-ject" and the "subjective thinker" are aspects of the indi-vidual which signalize his precarious spiritual state and the challenge to his freedom and inwardness.

The entire first section of *The Sickness unto Death*, to-gether with passages in *The Concept of Dread*, deals with the philosophical meaning of spirit. There is a remarkable at-tempt to convert familiar Hegelian terms and concepts to a new purpose, but the outcome is not so much an original theory of man as a sometimes obscure manipulation of the original, ungainly doctrine. Kierkegaard does point out that "spirit" is not merely the third moment in the dialectic of soul-consciousness-spirit, such as Hegel proposed. Instead of positing three stages in the necessary unfolding of the same subject, Kierkegaard advances a tripartite theory of three simultaneous factors in man: body, soul and spirit. Man is defined as "a synthesis of soul and body supported by spirit," but the emphasis is laid upon the synthesis itself, which is sup-plied by spirit.[26] Before a man attains to personal maturity, the decisive spiritual principle remains implicit or childish in him: he has not yet dedicated his bodily and psychic powers to either a good or an evil purpose. His ultimate moral character is the work of spirit, taken as the considered use of intelligence and freedom. This is a psychologico-moral conception of spirit, rather than a metaphysical one. Hence, not too much should be inferred from Kierkegaard's dictum that a man is nothing other than his spiritual selfhood. This is not intended to rule out the essential presence of soul and body in the given nature of man. But it does stress the important distinction between what a man *is*, as a natural thing, and what he *makes of himself* as a responsible agent, having a character. A man does not find himself in a spiritual way, until he has placed his powers in the service of God or mammon.

More important than this dialectical exegesis is Kierkegaard's observation that the finite, derived spirit cannot extricate itself from despair or disequilibrium in existence, solely through its own power. It must not only relate itself to God, but receive from God the conditions of liberation and balance. An individual cannot reach his complete stature without God's help, in a special way. Kierkegaard's usual term for the individual in his plenary perfection, as a man of God, is "the theological self." [27] God provides the infinite measure which gives scope and dignity to human freedom, even when the latter falls short of the standard or opposes it with a defiant will. Pantheism can never account for sin, which is a category of the finite individual existing before God in defiant relation or disrelation.[28] Sin is also a scandal to those who deify the crowd. For, the sinner is neither anonymous nor corporate nor fractional: he is an individual with a kind of integrity and courage to disperse the crowd, think and act in his own right, and accept the consequences of his actions. He is closer to the secret of existence than is the so-called neutral man or amoral social unit. Yet no matter how heroic the personality of Lucifer and no matter how powerful the evil principle in history, the rebel against God is less truly a man than the humble person who daily tries to follow God's will and who asks His aid through prayer.

The most sharply defined individuals are also the most utterly opposed: the sinner and the man of grace. The contrasts of existence culminate in these two antagonistic modes of individuality. The saint is the richer individual, for having realized to the utmost the possibilities of existence. He has remained faithful to God and so has received strength and consolation in Christ. What it means to be a man, is exhaustively revealed only in the person and mission of Christ.[29] Becoming an individual is interchangeable, in Kierkegaard's mind, with becoming a Christian in spirit and truth. Far from reducing religion to a theory of pure humanity (to what Julian Huxley calls "socialization"), Kierkegaard's study of the human individual leads to Christ as the model and source of the power to become fully an individual self. Thus the age in which we live poses an inescapable either/or. *Either* one must be loyal to man and the earth, as Nietzsche counseled, in such a way that one is traitor to God, *or* one must learn to love God above all things earthly and human and thus to love men and the earth the better in Him. Kierkegaard's hope was that the inhumane consequences of following the first alternative will dispose us to choose the other path, so as to build up a Christian humanity, a fellowship of individuals united by faith and charity in Christ.

Chapter Seven

Becoming a Christian in Christendom

1. CONVERGENCE ON THE PROBLEM OF CHRISTIANITY

A LL roads in Kierkegaard lead to the tableland of religious existence. After following his investigations in various fields of secular concern, we are brought to a standstill, unless we are willing to probe into the religious implications of his previous findings. His thought derives whatever cohesion and texture it possesses from this persistent orientation. It justifies his lifelong study of Hegelianism, Romanticism, moralism, and socialism; for all these can be viewed as the prevalent misinterpretations of, or substitutes for, religion and the life of the spirit.

Kierkegaard listened attentively to the replies formulated by his contemporaries, in answer to Kant's most fundamental question, *What is man?* He shared with them the conviction that we are undergoing a revolution in our anthropological notions, and that all the accepted ways of regarding man must be critically revised. But he was left unsatisfied by the proposed revisions as well, for they did not seem to rest on an integral understanding of human nature. Reconstruction along the lines of estheticism, for instance, would take account of our sensibilities, our thirst for beauty, and the insistent pressure of the passional drives, which so profoundly affect our conscious attitudes. Yet a one-sided and disjointed personality would result, if due allowance were not also made for practical reason and the ideal of self-discipline for the sake of the moral good. The desired synthesis of moral and esthetic interests is not to be made, however, on any basis furnished by one or the other outlook.

As worked out in German philosophy, the impasse between Fichte's moral idealism and the estheticism of the early Schelling called forth Hegel's magnificent attempt at synthesizing all human values in a dialectical System. The various phases of this dialectic were identified by Hegel with the pulsations of the divine life and substantial being itself, introducing into God a principle of unrest, self-estrangement, and tragedy. In philosophical self-consciousness, this entire process is assimilated and overcome, by being understood in all its contradictory richness. Man, as the agent who realizes the law of reason and history, is the ground and manifestation of divinity. The act of worship and the act of plenary philosophical speculation tend to coincide, and both in turn can be interpreted as terminal operations in the self-explication of the absolute spirit.[1]

Among Hegel's first critics, Feuerbach saw most clearly that absolute idealism transforms the traditional notions of God and man beyond recognition, and hence also alters the meaning of the Christian religion. Whereas Hegel prided himself upon having transcribed the entire content of revelation in terms of his philosophy of religion, Feuerbach countered that this accomplishment, if successful, canceled any claim of Christianity to embody truths revealed by some transcendent source. Whatever can be adequately derived through a strict philosophical method, has neither need nor leeway for invoking supernatural authorization. Furthermore, humanity is no longer constrained to project its own conception of absolute perfection into some heavenly, other-worldly being. There is now sufficient moral strength and devotedness among men to dispense with a transcendent God and to rely solely upon the inspiration and instruments which man furnishes himself. Theologism can henceforth be reduced safely to anthropology, the new universal science. In accord with this pronouncement, D. F. Strauss applied to Scripture the identification of God with humanity's highest interests and ideals. The figure of Christ must be taken in a thoroughly "humanistic" way, as an embodiment of human aspirations and only in this sense as divine. It was only a short step for Marx to locate "the really human man" not in an idealized moral individual but in the social fabric, woven by men working together in the technical exploitation of nature. So understood, the human situation allows no room for religion as a bond with a transcendent God, who is above nature and man. Salvation is the work of our own hands—the harmonious society which our labor and the weight of history will inevitably bring forth.[2]

Kierkegaard kept abreast of the scriptural and philosophical radicalization of Hegel's teaching, and to some extent was also familiar with the socialist replacement of religion by worldly zeal and mass endeavors. Just as his view of existence was advanced against Hegel's theologizing metaphysics, so his category of the individual and the analysis of Christianity were intended as an answer to the new philosophical anthropologies. On one point, indeed, he agreed with the Hegelians of the Left, as against those of the Right. If it be granted that Hegel succeeds in incorporating Christianity into his System, then the inferences drawn by the radical Hegelians do follow with inexorable logic. God, man, and their relationship must then be reinterpreted according to the requirements of a purely immanent and rationalistic set of principles. The unavoidable conclusion is the substitution of humanity for God and the claims of temporal society for the obligation of religion. In this respect, orthodox Hegelian theologians remain orthodox Christians, only in virtue of their muddleheadedness. But these radical results obtain, *only if* the original premise about Hegel's success is sound—and this Kierkegaard (unlike the Hegelian divines) denied on the basis of his analysis of existence and the individual.

The truths of Christian religion are existential; that is, they concern the order of real becoming, freedom, history, and individual striving. As such, they resist inclusion in a System of philosophical idealism, just as vigorously and effectively as does the act of existing itself. What Kierkegaard established about the incompatibility between Hegelianism and the sphere of existence is also applicable here. Hegel's treatment of revelation is based upon an embarrassing *ignoratio elenchi*, since it is an attempt to apply Systematic principles to a region which, by nature, falls outside their province.[3] What misleads idealistic theologians is their haste in explaining dogma in terms of Systematic concepts, without first inquiring whether or not Christian truth can validly be "mediated" and transferred to so foreign a terrain. This failure to criticize the suppositions of idealistic philosophy of religion suggested to Kierkegaard that the professed defenders of Christianity may be as mistaken about its real nature as are its detractors on the Left.

A similar double-barreled criticism of the Hegelians follows from Kierkegaard's view of the individual. When he states that an appreciation of the individual person cannot be gained from the absolutist standpoint, he means both that atheistic humanism and socialism are inhumane and that idealistic theology has lost sight of the genuine human subject of redemption. The former group does not see that man retains his authentic proportions only as living in God's acknowledged presence, whereas the latter compromises man's distinction from God and God's gracious freedom in saving man. Neither approach respects the dignity of the individual man or the transcendent element in Christianity. But it is better to confess openly to atheism and disdain for the mere individual than to pretend to be a strong supporter of Christianity and personal rights, and then to betray them both by one's method.

Kierkegaard's constructive thoughts on natural religion are set down in the many discourses which accompany his pseudonymous books and which are published under his own name. These discourses deal largely with the common foundations of religiousness and its ethical aspects. Here, he stresses the indispensable undergirding of all religious life: a valuing of God above all the goods and fortune of temporal existence, a recognition of one's own dependence on God and unworthiness before Him, a willingness to convert oneself effectively from self-interest to His service, a frank admission that everything we achieve is God's gift and we ourselves His handiwork. Instead of exploring the possibility of a philosophical basis for these meditations, however, Kierkegaard is directly interested only in securing the distinction between natural and revealed religion. The viewpoint on existence, as set forth in the *Postscript*, emphasizes not only its non-systematic character but also its connection with faith, as a paradoxical affirmation of the presence of the eternal in time. This provides a dividing line between all other religions and Christianity, which is founded on belief in the Incarnation.[4] This distinction between religions of immanence and the unique religion of transcendence is reinforced by an analysis of the individual and the quality of inner life. The proper nature of sin, faith, and other capacities of the human spirit remains obscure, until they are illuminated by the Christian good news of man's call to share freely in the divine life, through Christ.

From 1849 onwards until his death in 1855, Kierkegaard was occupied almost exclusively with the task of renewing the meaning of Christianity for his contemporaries. In doing this, however, he was forced to compare and contrast his religious conception with the prevailing one, which shaped the policies of the Church of Denmark. The religious books which he wrote during this period are pointed tracts for the times, rather than timeless, unpolemical expositions of doctrine.[5] Yet in large measure they avoid being unrewardingly parochial and ephemeral, for they spring from a lifetime of reflection and dialectical inquiry into the structure of the religious mode of existence. Only at the very end of his authorship—after launching the open and relentless attack on the Danish Establishment—did Kierkegaard sacrifice perspective, in order to score a hit or test the limits of his personal courage. Even then, he did not leave his latter-day readers entirely without means for righting the balance and drawing profit from his excessive moments.

2. THE SITUATION OF BEING IN CHRISTENDOM

The Christian religion was fortunate during the nineteenth century in having been critically reappraised and sometimes attacked by men of outstanding intelligence. Its power of self-reform might not have functioned so vigorously, had it not been for the lessons learned under duress from open enemies like Marx, Proudhon, and Nietzsche. Their error lay not in denouncing the compromises and deformations, which had undoubtedly crept in, but in losing hope that they could be eradicated through an internal renewal of the Christian life. Their despair led them to repudiate the traditional religious view of man and to substitute for it a secular humanism based, as they thought, on this-worldly means and aims alone. But other critics, just as lucid and merciless in their analysis of the situation, were careful to point out that the true horror of "bourgeois civilization" consists in its very claim to be Christian. Léon Bloy, calling himself the obedient servant of an alien Fury, lashed out with the studied intemperance of one who feels himself, together with the simple ones of the world, being deceived and made unclean by such a profanation.[6] He sounded the Johannine call to penance and change of heart—not in an anti-Christian direction, but toward a rediscovery of those Christian verities which have been lost from sight.

Kierkegaard belongs in the company of the latter kind of solvents of the modern religious settlement. He wanted to do away, not with Christian truth, but with the false persuasion that it has prevailed generally among Western men and that the accepted social institutions are genuinely Christian in inspiration and effect. This conviction had crystallized in the notion of Christendom: a Christian society of nations and a Christian ordering of the whole range of temporal activities. In the conduct of international and civic affairs during his own day, Kierkegaard found little to correspond to the liturgical idea of *fines Christianorum*. His attention was centered more on cultural than political matters, however, since he was chiefly alarmed by the completely secularist attitude in society and by the acute stage which the class struggle had entered, in our era. As actually organized, society provided a substitute for the conscientious management of personal life under God's law. The pressure of social forces tended to reduce individuals to an irresponsible and insignificant dead level. Only the anonymous group counted, as the bearer of values and determinant of ends, and these ends were exclusively mundane ones.

The scandal was not only that individuals were surrendering their integrity and freedom cheaply, but also that the churches condoned and were party to this betrayal, furnishing the Grand Inquisitors of Christendom. They had forgotten the correlation between personal existence and Christian perfection. It is well to bring out clearly this aspect of Christian humanism behind Kierkegaard's final polemic, since he himself sometimes obscures it, in his eagerness to defend God's right over our lives against the claims of the world. He often speaks of "the inhumane and the un-Christlike" in a single breath and, on the other hand, declares that the Christian notion of the individual is the most humane view of man.[7] One fundamental reason for his hostility to the ecclesiastical establishment is its failure to promote that maximum inwardness, liberty of spirit, and personal consecration to God, which constitute for him the chief marks of religious maturity. Hence he places the state church, as he experienced it, on a par with the state itself. Both perform a minimal function, in regulating the external relations between men, but both threaten to swamp the individual in the totality, by depreciating his unique self-responsibility. To this extent, these social forms must be severely limited and transcended by those who seek to preserve the personal religious relationship with God.

Kierkegaard did not distinguish adequately between the actual ecclesiastical order in his own land and the Church as the universal vessel and bond of grace; but there are indications in his writings that the distinction was not entirely absent from his mind.[8] Sometimes, he spoke about the Church in a quite general and ideal way, rather than as found "especially in Protestantism, more especially in Denmark." As a young man, he hazarded the opinion that, when the present age of excessive individualism (which has provoked an equally exaggerated collectivism) passes away, there will be a renascence of the idea of the *ecclesia* (just as there will be an eventual renascence of the state). The church will be restored to its rightful place, as a counterbalance to religious isolation and as a counterforce against worldliness. Indeed, the category of the individual and that of the religious congregation are complementary poles of religious existence, so that an adequate expression of Christian religiousness depends on their mutual tension and demands upon the soul. What is missing from Kierkegaard's outlook is any sense of the Church as a present actuality, as something more than an ideal to be developed later on in the concrete order, when circumstances are more favorable. He was so deeply involved in the Danish situation, with its danger of religious *Schwärmerei* in connection with the religious community, that he found no opportunity to follow up his own remark that only in the case of the Church, as the *genus electum*, *gens sancta*, does the "race" or social whole again assume a primacy over the human individual. He saw only the taint of Hegelianism in his youthful statement that Christ died for each individual, but "for me" as belonging to the "many," the company of redeemed men, joined together in organic union.

Kierkegaard pointed to no definite historical realization of the religious community. But he did meditate at great length, especially toward the end of his life, upon the contrast between medieval Catholicism and Protestantism.[9] Catholicism was not treated by him as one of the serious alternatives in our time, but only as having taught us some valuable historical lessons, which will be useful in determining the future course of Christianity. The claim of the Catholic Church to be, in every age, the *una sancta*, the sanctifying union of men in Christ's mystical body, is not examined. But within the limits of his sketchy acquaintance with the Church, Kierkegaard's reflections are usually penetrating and sympathetic. Catholicism's great virtue is to have shown the need for the communal factor in religious life, so that men may share with each other the burden of a responsible use of freedom, in regard to an eternal outcome. Sooner or later, Kierkegaard predicted, Protestantism must begin to cultivate the social aspect of religion, either in the form of small, intense conventicles ("remnants") or in a genuine church, having authority and a full sacramental order. Only the most gifted and exceptional individuals have the strength, and even the duty, to stand alone with their conscience before God.

The obligation to worship in a visible, corporate way is not unconditional for Kierkegaard, but he does not furnish the exact criteria for determining which persons are dispensed from the common duty. He would like to achieve a synthesis between the religious community represented by Catholicism (apart from any political implications of a Christendom united under pope and emperor) and the reforming vigilance of a lone, conscientious individual like Luther (apart from the state churches and supporting princes, entailed by historical Lutheranism). The former would supply the traditional objective norm of faith, the latter the corrective against human abuses.[10] In actual fact, Kierkegaard has no further recourse to the "norm" than as a foil to the situation in Denmark and as a stimulus to ideal planning. It is never consulted as a concrete standard, which is truly authoritative and compelling for him. Rather, the contrast which Catholicism erects between the Church and the world is used as a club against the Lutheran Establishment. In the more relevant Kierkegaardian sense, "Christendom" signifies the unholy alliance concluded by official Protestantism with the state, an alliance which spelled the end of the older notion of an implacable enmity between the Christian spirit and the powers of this world.

The state church is, in reality, a department of the state, and hence does not afford believers an independent foothold in their effort to secure the primacy of the spiritual. Its effect upon the mind is a confusing one. On the one hand, it counsels us to deny the world and become crucified to the world, whereas its own daily example preaches something else, which comes closer to being an amiable settlement on the world's terms. Behind his satirical and often unjust remarks about infant baptism, marriage and a married clergy, fashionable congregations and court preachers, the priesthood of all where it means nothing special to be a priest, and about attacks upon medieval asceticism made by those who enjoy comfortable "livings," Kierkegaard is agitated lest the shepherds be guilty of perpetrating a gigantic fraud, and lest the sheep be led astray into thinking that all is well in this easy-going climate. The opposition between the Church and the world, taken as the seat of evil, is whittled down and smoothed away, so that it amounts to nothing more than an inspiring renunciation made only during the weekly sermon. When sacrifices are no longer demanded, vows no longer respected, suffering no longer prized as a component of the religious life, then Christianity is being replaced by an esthetic representation of the Christian drama. This is a token that the established order has deified itself in practice, allowing no place for a transcendent God, before Whom we exist in inwardness and in fear and trembling.

The basic charge is that the established order undermines moral seriousness and the transcendence of Christianity, by secularizing the entire religious outlook of men.[11] People come to see no difference between assuming the rights and duties of temporal citizenship and being reborn in Christ. The latter seems to involve no "dying from the world," except in a poetic sense, no need to appropriate a new principle of life and a new viewpoint through costing choices, no unremitting warfare with oneself and with the corrupting influence of the world. Christendom glosses over the lines of battle, satisfies us that the victory is already won—and so hands us over to the enemy, as to a trustworthy friend. This, Kierkegaard understood to be an act of high treason, calling for his midnight cry of alarm. Salvation is not given to us automatically, when we prove ourselves to be solid pillars of worldly society, nor does it ever come wholesale but to each of us passing singly through the wicket. To be born in Christendom is a description of the *terminus a quo* of the Christian's search for life eternal, not a passport which assures effortless entry therein by its own authority.

Kierkegaard's attack upon Protestant Christendom has led some readers to turn away entirely from Christianity and others to move closer toward Catholicism. He himself followed a much less forthright course, a course which he did not propose as a model for others to follow. He took his own stand on the dangerous buttress of Protestantism, rather than in the secure building of Catholicism. He preferred to stand *in discrimine rerum*, on the razor edge of the religious situation, pointing out the "normality" of the Catholic teaching on the Church, the sacraments, and religious authority, without inquiring more closely into its claims of truth or sharing visibly in its life. His own vocation was to remain a gadfly among Protestants, reminding them that their only justification is to provide the incorruptibly critical conscience of the Christian community, and that they must not try to convert the reforming principle itself into a counternorm and countertradition. This led him to assume an ambivalent attitude toward Luther, listening with edification to the passionate and paradoxical preacher, who spoke from the depths of his personal religious experience, and satirizing the ecclesiastical politician and theologian, who set the main lines of the Protestant Establishment.[12] Not only Lutheranism but

also the back-to-Luther movement of his own day seemed
to Kierkegaard to betray a misunderstanding of Luther's
significance, as a single witness. This tendency erects an
obstacle to the integral development of the religious individual. Each man is called upon to relate himself to God unconditionally and at his own risk, rather than in terms of
neo-orthodoxy.

3. "FIRST, SEVERITY—THEN, GENTLENESS"

The "category of suffering" is employed catastrophically
in the religious sphere to dissolve the illusion of Christendom,
just as the category of the individual is used in social matters
to break the power of the irresponsible crowd. Kierkegaard's
strategy is to quote at its very highest the price of becoming a
Christian, stressing the severity of the test which must be
passed, rather than the consolation which follows. Thereby,
the contrast between what Christianity demands and what the
Establishment deems to be sufficient for salvation is made
plain, even though the distinction between the commands and
the counsels is sometimes overlooked. This accords with
Kierkegaard's earlier teaching on the need to make a break
with one's given natural state, by subjecting it to critical reflection and the test of freedom. This is an indispensable step
in the development of personality, but it is not a sufficient
one from the moral standpoint. For, one can deliberately
choose to be confirmed in evil. The moral qualification enters,
when the individual seeks to establish the *right* relation between various ends and values, giving an unconditional primacy to the absolute good. Such an ordering of interests
involves the possibility of having to relinquish certain
attachments, which conflict with one's search for the absolute.
The morally mature person must be ready to make the sacri-

fice, and must already have detached himself from every uncritical adherence to finite goods.

From his study of the various existential attitudes, however, Kierkegaard found that actual suffering is more likely to be met with at the esthetic level than at the moral, and that the presence of such suffering is an indication of the close relation between the lover, the genius and the man of religious faith. But the esthetic individual remains more or less an unwilling victim of suffering, because of his inability to grasp the full sense of his exceptional situation. Its meaning becomes clear, only when one's life is viewed religiously, in the light of God's holiness and His desire that we become perfect. Kierkegaard proposed a curious criterion for determining the true marks of religion and Christianity.[13] Find a point which is under fire by an atheist of the nineteenth century and which is also defended by a seventeenth-century man of faith—and you have found an incontrovertibly religious belief. Such is the case with suffering, which is a scandal to a Feuerbach and a matter of glory to a Pascal, but to both a distinguishing note of the Christian mode of existing.

In the degree that it promotes a meditative inwardness, Christianity makes us aware of God's supreme goodness and our own distance from, and hostility towards, His holiness. A religious sense of one's own sinfulness leads neither to morbid despair nor to rationalization. It issues in a voluntary acceptance of suffering as a way of atoning for sin to God, the just judge, and a way of approaching closer to God the redeemer. In a series of discourses entitled *The Gospel of Suffering*, Kierkegaard establishes the relation between guilt, suffering, and the triumph of faith, much after the manner of Luther's dialectical treatment of the theme of the sinner as believer. In the religious situation, we learn to regard our attempts at being autonomous as a personal offense against the majesty of God, from Whom alone we have our sufficiency. Since our original condition is one in which we do build our existence upon our own foundation and pattern, it is already qualified religiously and morally as guilty. Hence the need for "death," for a deliberate renunciation of the self-centered attitude, as a prerequisite of living in a spiritual way. Kierkegaard considers any religious teacher, who fails to emphasize the place of severity and suffering in religious growth, to be lacking in honesty or insight. Frequently, as with the Hegelian divines, it is a case of not recognizing "idolatry," a purely immanent and pantheistic view of oneself and God, where it is all too evident.[14] This misunderstanding often leads to a confusion between existential suffering on the part of a finite man and sinner, and the merely ideal operation of the dialectical "principle of negativity."

Kierkegaard placed more emphasis on the need of faith in order to recognize sin than he did on the fact itself of sin. He saw the consciousness of sin fast disappearing among men, in proportion as Christian faith is displaced by mass opinion and the rationalistic philosophies of religion. The full nature and horror of sin are grasped only by him who sees the individual man as a genuinely finite and free agent, and who relates human action to God, in the person of Christ. For the believer, Christ's life on earth is not a myth of the "creative community" nor an illustration of the workings of the absolute Concept in the world. Man as a sinner is at personal enmity with Christ, and man as a sufferer is professing the reality of the forgiveness of sin, by following in the way of Christ. Kierkegaard, who was a close student of the *Following of Christ*, reminds Christians that they are cross-bearers, who walk with Christ in the path of self-denial and acceptance of suffering for His sake. Suffering is the great training school for eternity. Its burden may be heavy, but there is no other way of learning the meaning of repentance, obedience to God and the power of faith. The Christian is no masochist, as Nietzsche supposed, since suffering is a means and a springboard, rather than an end in itself. After severity comes gentleness; after death, life. "There is in life one blessed joy: to follow Christ; and in death one last blessed joy: to follow Christ to life!" [15]

His own experiences with the press and the Establishment also taught Kierkegaard that the world, by nature, hates the principle of love and strives to suppress religious truth, whenever it can. Any softening of this opposition aroused his suspicion, and any failure to inculcate it in Christian minds seemed to him a piece of unrealism, or something worse. He came more and more to regard the Christian existence in the world as one of bearing witness even as the martyrs did, of being prepared at any time to sacrifice one's reputation, livelihood, or life itself. Of himself, he said that Denmark had need of "a dead man." Moreover, the Christian should take the initiative in the conflict, rather than wait for the world's good pleasure to bring it to his door. The converse side of suffering, then, is confidence in eternity and God's governance. Although the Christian good news is disquieting rather than tranquilizing, it also gives a man the power to "stand out" from the herd and to become "heterogeneous," in the sense of striving to realize something more than the common measure of natural human perfection. Without despising the latter, Kierkegaard refused to identify it with the Christian measure of man's capacities and duties. His own positive statement of the Christian requirement is formulated in his teaching on contemporaneity with Christ. This is the truth for which we should be willing, at all costs, to bear witness.

4. BECOMING CONTEMPORANEOUS WITH CHRIST

At the height of his polemic against the established order, Kierkegaard was supported by one central and decisive thought: that each individual believer can and must become contemporaneous with Christ. The philosophical basis for this conviction had been established a decade previously, in the *Fragments*, which is a nineteenth-century *Cur Deus Homo*, cast in the hypothetical mode. On the supposition that the Incarnation has taken place, what relations do believers of various generations sustain toward Christ and each other? The answer is framed within Kierkegaard's general teaching on the historicity of existence and the credal character of historical apprehension.[16] An event is called historical, in so far as its existence is due to a process of temporal becoming. Since becoming involves both an element of contingency or uncertainty and one of factual certainty, the historical process is correspondingly grasped only by an act of belief. Now the nature of belief will be further specified by the kind of historical becoming under consideration. In the case of an ordinary temporal event, belief "in the first degree" or the usual sort of historical acquaintance is sufficient. Here, a premium is placed upon the testimony and reliability of eyewitnesses. The probability of the assent is in proportion to the more or less exact and exhaustive accumulation of relevant facts by such eyewitnesses or later scholars, upon whom the present generation must rely, as upon intermediaries. No more than a high degree of probability can ever be obtained through such procedures.

The Incarnation is a historical fact and hence a proper object of belief. Yet it is no ordinary historical event, but the coming of the eternal in time, the assuming of mortal flesh by the infinite God, in an actual, historical situation. Hence it can be apprehended only through an act of belief "in the second degree," or religious faith in the strict sense. The divine nature of Christ is not present incognito in His human nature, in the sense that it is cleverly concealed from all but the best-trained philosophical minds. Its presence is rather an absolute mystery and paradox, being inaccessible to even the most ingenious and sublime efforts of merely natural intelligence, and yet being also available to anyone and everyone who prays for the power to recognize it. Faith lies on the other side of reason's "death" or frank acknowledgment of its essential inability to grasp this truth. Moreover, faith comes as a gift from God Himself: He gives the very condition for apprehending His incarnate presence. The situation in which an individual is given faith to confess the Incarnation, the presence of the eternal God as an individual man in history, is termed by Kierkegaard the Instant.

The meaning of contemporaneity is proportioned to the historical fact itself.[17] In the case of the Incarnation, Kierkegaard distinguishes between believers and all other interested people, maintaining that *only* the former class is contemporaneous with Christ in His full historical reality and that all members in this class are *equally* contemporaneous with Him. The only way to become contemporaneous with this theandric event is by believing in it. Thus, one might have seen and heard Christ on earth without coming to believe in Him, and hence without participating in the historical truth of the Incarnation. Such an eyewitness would be as remotely distant from the person of Christ as would any unbelieving historian or philosopher of a later age. To be contemporaneous with Christ, as with one ordinary historical event among others, is only a possible occasion for having faith in Him, the occasion which was given both to His followers on earth and to those who put Him to death. But the former became disciples only by believing in Him, and only in this way became fully contemporaneous with Him.

The special historical character of the Incarnation is also seen by comparing it with other facts which are known to men. A "fact" may convey a purely eternal truth, a purely temporal one, or one which is at once thoroughly temporal and thoroughly eternal. An eternal act is essentially not a historical fact at all. It dominates the entire historical process and can be known in all ages, simply because it is outside of time entirely and revokes the meaning of history. An ordinary historical event is completely temporal in its constitution, and knowledge of it is subject to the vicissitudes and limitations of time. Historical apprehension based on such a fact is never more than probable, although the probability may be constantly heightened through our historical studies. Now, the Incarnation neither transpires outside of history nor is wholly subject to the immanent conditions imposed by time. Because it is a genuinely historical fact, it must be approached as an existential and historical truth. But because it is also the presence of eternity in time, this fact can (and can only) be known by the act of faith, which banishes all doubt and is more certain than any immediate perception. Faith is not an act of the will, in the sense of wishful believing or sheer willfulness of credence. But it does involve the will, in so far as it concerns an existential truth, transcends the natural scope of reason by means of a "leap" of personal decision, and requires the free acceptance of the conditions of faith from God.

The main consequence which Kierkegaard drew from this discussion, concerns the difference between the various generations of believers. God Himself gives the power to share in the Instant, and God is master of the temporal process. Hence the very same condition of faith is given immediately by God to all who believe in Christ, even though they live at a later time.[18] What Christ's own earthly presence was to His first disciples—an occasion for receiving faith, but not faith itself—is now supplied by the testimony of believers, the tradition "handed down from the fathers." The power to believe, however, is God's direct gift to each individual disciple, and makes every believer, of whatever historical period, contemporaneous with Christ in His unique historical actuality. The difference is not thereby overlooked between having Christ's earthly presence as the occasion of faith and having the witness of tradition among believers. But the mystery of Christ is shared by all who join in the Instant or the actual believing, and is shared by all believers contemporaneously.

This is Kierkegaard's answer to Hegelian theologians and biblical scholars, such as Daub on the Right and Strauss on the Left. It contains one serious deficiency; but, apart from that, the advantages are many in helping to restore a sane attitude, in the wake of theological and historical rationalism. The actual truth of faith in the incarnate God is left unsettled in the *Fragments*, whereas in the religious works it is taken as the most radical existential truth. But Kierkegaard, in his concern to dissociate faith from bare rational assent and pretended philosophical demonstration of revelation, is suspicious of *any* intellectual motives of faith. Probability is removed not by an intellectually certain adherence of both mind and will to the revealed truth, but by the sheer courage and tenacity of the leap of personal commitment to a way of life. This leap combines an extreme "objective uncertainty" or absence of philosophical proof and an equally extreme "subjective certainty" or adhesion of the will and the whole personality to the demands of such belief upon our existence. In setting faith off from Speculative reason, Kierkegaard fails to give the intellect its normally full and explicit share in grasping revealed truth. He is not anti-intellectual, for he hints that if reason is confident enough in God to break through its own autonomy, it will discover itself to be in secret accord with faith.[19] But the office of reason, in laying the foundations of natural religion and in preparing for faith, is inadequately analyzed by him.

On the other hand, Kierkegaard's view of faith and history helps to correct some misconceptions, to which the procedure of Christian apologists sometimes gives rise. This can be confirmed by indicating three trends in the apologetics of his day and of later times which his views are intended to challenge and amend. (a) Necessary as it is to cultivate the historical approach to Scripture, this reconstructive work should not be taken as equivalent to a complete recapturing of the historical truth of the Incarnation or as the only path to attaining this truth. Historical studies are bound, by their nature, to treat Christ's life according to the general canons of historical research. The outcome can, however, never lay bare the heart of the divine-human mystery, although it may suggest sound reasons why we may believe. Neither can the work of unfavorable biblical critics affect the ground of faith itself. The Incarnation and life of Christ have a unique historical significance, which does not wait upon the results of biblical controversies and research in order to be apprehended, beyond doubt, by ordinary men. Sacred history contains more than the historians and critics can ever formally establish. (b) The proofs of credibility, philosophical and historical, must never be allowed to render the act of faith superfluous or a mere conclusion drawn from intrinsically necessitating premises. Similarly, the testimony of other believers and the weight of tradition must not intervene as though they constitute the formal motive of faith. In this respect, there are no disciples at second hand, although there are disciples of an earlier and a later age of Christian tradition. Kierkegaard brings again into prominence the supernatural character of faith and the need for *Deus revelans* as the sufficient motive for believing—points which were being ignored by the philosophizing apologists whom he read. As he expresses it: "The successor believes *by means of* . . . the testimony of the contemporary, and *in virtue of* the condition he himself receives from God." [20] (c) Finally, the study of the historical life of the church may sometimes lead astray, if the church is treated only in accordance with ordinary historical methods and is not viewed also through the eyes of faith. If only the first standpoint is cultivated, in an effort to prepare the groundwork of faith, there is likely to be a confusion of high probability and admiration with faith itself. Furthermore, the passage of centuries is apt to make the presence of Christ seem remote and hazy. By highlighting the contemporaneity of all believers with Christ, Kierkegaard indicates how one may arouse a lively sense of Christ's closeness to, and personal concern for, every Christian throughout history.

This explanation also fits in admirably with other facets of Kierkegaard's mind, notably his views on existential truth, equality, and the individual. The Incarnation is a historical event and hence must be treated in an existential way. For this reason, Kierkegaard always speaks of *becoming* contemporaneous with Christ and *becoming* a Christian, not in order to reduce faith to approximation, epistemologically, but as a warning that existential truth has unending consequences in one's daily conduct.[21] While a man remains in time, he cannot be said to have comprehended the mystery of Jesus or to have conformed his life adequately to the model which Jesus furnishes. Progress toward holiness is never brought to an end in history, and yet God's will is that each of us strive to become holy. Kierkegaard would have supported George Santayana's dictum that "the need of deliverance and the immediate personal possibility of it are the twin roots of the whole gospel." [22] The Kierkegaardian conception of the absolute equality of all individuals in God's sight is confirmed by the assurance that we can all become equally contemporaneous with Christ. Significant differences between men are the work of freedom, not the senseless discriminations of fate. That we make the venture of faith and continue to take faith as the guiding principle in our life, depends upon God's grace in such a way that it also engages our freedom. Faith is thus both a gift and a matter of free choice. A Christian man ought to be "freedom's ordinary," in realizing the kingdom of God on earth.

The existential conception of the individual can shed light, in two ways, on the problem of religious contemporaneity. In the first place, faith is specified as bringing a man into relation with God, precisely as with an actual, historical individual. The uniqueness of Christianity is founded on the personal presence among us of the eternal being as a temporal existent. This incarnational closeness of Christ the individual should elicit in our hearts a singular wonder, humility, and devotion. The immanence of God to His creation, which Kierkegaard is inclined to pass over in his more speculative and polemical writings, is nonetheless firmly established at the base of his position on Christian faith. It does not receive due emphasis, because of his dread of pantheism and lack of a philosophical theory of God's power and presence. Kierkegaard is unnecessarily hostile to the "undialectical," Franciscan type of piety, which dwells upon Christ's sacred humanity and His nearness in all things to us.[23] This is traceable to his mistaken fear that familiarity and childlikeness in religion will cancel out the tremendous mystery of the Incarnation, the supernatural quality of faith, and the need of suffering. His constant self-torture before the Hegelian element in his own breast thus prevented Kierkegaard from developing all the implications of the correlation between faith and individual existence.

The problem of the individual enters in a second way, from the side of man the believer. From this angle, the formula of Christianity is expressed as the relating of oneself as an individual to God. The Instant is present whenever a man ceases to be thoughtlessly dominated by the herd instinct and when, as an individual, he turns from exclusive care for himself to care for God's majesty and holiness. This turning or conversion of mind and will to God is an inalienable affair of "the single one," since it constitutes a free, personal conse-cration to God. But Kierkegaard infers that, therefore, each individual has his relation to God only in isolation from other believers. Inadvertently, he is laying down the conditions of union with God, instead of accepting them integrally from Him. Both as an individual act and as one which reduces all human accessories to the status of occasions, the Kierke-gaardian act of faith gives little significance to the Church. Each believer enjoys his peculiar relation to the historical Incarnation in such a way that, although this is the common lot of all believers, still it does not lead to a mutual sharing of religious life, except as a prospect for the future.[24] Kierke-gaard is troubled by the idealistic totality, especially Hegel's "folk religion," which would suppress the personal response or sublimate it into something impersonal and necessitated. He gives little thought to the possibility that Christ may have provided more definite conditions and means of union with Him, so that we are to become jointly contemporaneous with Him in the Church, as the prolongation in history of His in-carnational presence. The religious community which Kierke-gaard envisages would be more the work of men in the future than of the Holy Spirit in the present.

5. EDUCATION IN RELIGIOUS EXISTENCE

The German literati, philosophers, and theologians whom Kierkegaard consulted, were at least agreed on the importance of education in the formation of men and the advancement of civilization. Kierkegaard did not enter into their disputes about the orientation and organization of the university, but in his characteristic way gave attention only to the problem of the religious education of the individual. The deliberate narrowness of his approach here, as in other cases, is meant as a protest against the neglect of certain issues and as the most practical way of exploring them, within his limited resources. The religious books of his last period are all contributions toward "training in Christianity" (as the title of one of them announces). Kierkegaard used the pseudonym "Anti-Climacus," lest he appear presumptuous and thus turn attention from the pressing question: how should I train myself? to the less important one: who is telling me to do this? In his old role of poet and thinker, he tried to evoke the Christian ideal as a pitch of perfection not reached by himself, but yet laid upon all professing Christians to strive toward.[25] Like a detective who has gained the confidence of delinquents through his own unassuming ways, Kierkegaard sought, by a fresh reading of the original documents, to expose the forgery of those who have been tampering with the text of Christian existence. His restatement of the Christian call to perfection rests on three major Biblical themes: becoming sober, taking Christ as one's model, and loving God with all one's heart.

Christian Sobriety

Jean-Paul Sartre takes as a fundamental datum and point of departure for his analysis of man, the "fallen" or "abandoned" quality of human experience. In doing so, he has done violence to one aspect of Kierkegaard's religious thought and of the Christian tradition in general. Kierkegaard would dispute their right to regard this condition as an original, essential deliverance of existence. For him, man's feeling of aloneness and his dizzy lack of orientation are the results of a sinful decision to abandon God, rather than original and necessary traits of existence. Our life cannot but be out of joint and the world a frightening maze, as Kafka described them, once the relation with God is suppressed.[26] This can be done either by a postulatory atheism or by open revolt or by the slow, grinding process of compromise and forgetfulness. St. James warns against this, in speaking about the man who beheld himself in a mirror and then forgot what manner of man he was. When the bond with God is broken or neglected, the human predicament takes on a senseless, frustrated, and wounded aspect.

Various philosophical measures for dealing with this situation have been proposed since Kierkegaard's day. The existentialist prefers to depict in lucid hopelessness the absurdity of man and the world (Camus), to propose a new *mystique* of the superman spinning out his own fine web of rationality and purpose (Sartre), or to appeal to a vague, poetic attitude based on a cultivation of the tragic sense of life (Unamuno). From the opposite quarter, the pragmatic naturalist makes a show of common sense and daylight reasonableness, by admitting as genuine problems only those which arise in a specific social context and which admit of practical solution, through recognized scientific methods. This would systematically discredit beforehand the whole discussion about dread (which arises precisely because of the essential risk of freedom), guilt (which refuses to be explained away in a nonethical way), death (which is not resolved through any practical course of action, no matter how much it may be in our concern) and suffering (which is there, not only to be alleviated but also to be embraced and sought). One advantage of Kierkegaard's religious standpoint is that it saves him both from merely bathing in the flow of existentialist sentiment and from turning his back upon the many levels at which the difficulties of existence present themselves to us. In contrast to the anguished cry of existentialism and the bland surgery performed upon man by naturalism, his answer is crisp and yet comprehensive: Be ye therefore sober.[27]

Like all basic Christian counsel, this injunction, taken from the Apostle Peter, has a paradoxical, arresting quality about it. For, no one is more assured of his levelheadedness and closeness to the facts than the man who pays no worship to the living God or who does so quite discreetly and without personal strain. Yet he is also the man found unprepared to meet the crises of personality-development meaningfully and maturely. Existential courage, naturalistic efficiency, and bourgeois shrewdness, are purchased at the cost of a blinkered acquaintance with man. By hugging so closely to the shores of the finite, such a training leaves a person unprepared for the deeper shocks of existence; for it does not inform him that there is no effective recourse to oneself, without the acknowledged concourse of God. An education of this sort does not help a man evaluate himself properly or meet the unavoidable test of living in the presence of the infinite. At every moment, he is at the crossroads of moral and religious choice, without admitting the need of making a decision for or against God or the sacrifice involved in such a choice.

To become sober in a Christian way is not to be exempted from the common human situation, but only to become fully appraised of its seriousness and to seek God's help in meeting it. It is a case of understanding oneself as being nothing, when cut off from God, and yet as being under an unconditional obligation to obey and trust Him. This does not mean a blunting of intelligence and enterprise; it does require the dissociation of our confidence in our human abilities from the additional assertion of self-sufficiency. Kierkegaard considers the fear of the transcendent to be the most formidable enemy of human sanity and dignity in the modern world. It relies, for its appeal, upon a specious disjunction between the utmost use of our own resources and reliance upon God. The former can be achieved, only when these resources are realistically assessed and when man does not hesitate to raise questions about his ultimate placement in existence. When this is done, there is occasion for admitting our creatureliness and for placing ourselves unreservedly on the side of God's power and governance.

We are become sober in Christian faith, for here we seek to know ourselves in the light of God's appraisal of us and our own foundation in His being. The obverse side of contemporaneity with Christ through faith is contemporaneity with oneself, a grasp of the individual as the point of intersection for temporal and eternal interests. Where this integral view is lacking, these two sets of values are in unresolved conflict or "drunkenness." This condition undermines the personality, even when the rights of eternity are denied. Irresolution and a cloven mode of being are the alternative to the believer's self-mastery. Kierkegaard supports St. Augustine's warning that a return to God must be accompanied by man's own restoration to himself.

Christ the Pattern

Kierkegaard agrees with the existentialists in underlining "this tremendous danger in which man finds himself by being man." [28] Man is a warring field for good and evil, but if it were not for the danger in which freedom places him, there could be no question of salvation. The worldly wise live as though there were no such risk and choice, but then they cannot be drawn up to Christ. For He will neither seduce nor drag men to Himself, but only draw them as responsible selves, through the discipline of freedom. He asks every man first to enter into himself, so that in his own inwardness he may conform with the Pattern. To do so, is to become a follower of Christ, one who is on the road to perfecting the likeness and presence of God in him.

There are two escape routes for evading the Pattern, without making an outright denial: to approach Christ Speculatively and to do so in a merely esthetic way. What Kierkegaard discovered about the general inadequacy of the Speculative and purely esthetic relationships to existence, applies forcibly in the case of the most existential situation. He compared his opposition to the scientific-professorial attitude toward Christianity with Luther's protest against an extreme calculus of good works. But what was for Kierkegaard's Luther a personal passion for faith and God's freedom, soon became ossified as a doctrine of *sola fides*, which meant in effect the abandonment both of good works and of the demands of faith. Hence the new stress upon the following of Christ was proposed by Kierkegaard as a reinstatement both of faith and of the activities to which faith and love impel the Christian. These works of charity are forever postponed, when faith in Christ is treated as a Speculative problem, still awaiting solution by the Hegelian professors of theology (the supplanters of the apostles, martyrs, and doctors of old). As long as everything is still "in suspense, under consideration," there is an indefinite delay in the task of modeling one's life upon that of Christ. One is always awaiting the outcome of further investigation—and in the meantime, it is most prudent to drift along with the current, in the most comfortable fashion.

The difference between abstract and existential truth is reaffirmed by Kierkegaard in a religious context.[29] To heed the words of Christ "in truth," does not mean merely to ascertain his message as a theoretical proposition. The saving truth is not a reduplication of being in the mode of thought alone, for then it would be sufficient to think correctly or to have bare faith, without an overflow in charity and its works. There is required a reduplication of being in the mode of one's own way of existing, so that truth in this sense is present only when one's *life* corresponds in some way to the example of Christ. This is a moral-ontic view of truth, rather than a strictly noetic one. The difference lies in the application or nonapplication of will, a difference which also marks off the following of Christ from esthetic admiration of such an enterprise. Whereas the follower is one who is personally involved and pledged to imitate what he admires, the mere admirer remains personally aloof and uncommitted. The admirer is related to the Pattern through the medium of imagination only, dreaming about this ideal perfection but without making a proportionate response in personal conduct.

In visualizing this moral and religious perfection, imagination works under a twin handicap. It experiences difficulty in picturing the sufferings which may be entailed by a wholehearted dedication to the life proposed by the Pattern, and it is inclined to underestimate the force of the world's opposition. Yet Kierkegaard was unwilling to exclude imagination completely from the education of a religious personality. The importance of the esthetic factor in his own formation was sufficient to deter him from eliminating it entirely. Moreover, the attitude of admiration from a distance is easily transformed, on the religious level, into one of adoring distance, even in the midst of intimate love of God. This reminder of our creatureliness compensates for the ethical tendency toward self-identification with the moral ideal within one. In justification of a limited role of imagination in religious training, Kierkegaard pointed out that Christ the Pattern attracts us to Himself gently and gradually. We first approach Him as an ideal placed on high, giving little thought to the intervening distance marked by our own deficiencies and our failure to pass the test of everyday fidelity. Moral resolution is needed to persevere in the effort to follow our model, precisely under the stringent conditions imposed by temporal existence. Then, we find that He is not only beckoning to us "from on high" in His exaltation, but also helping at our side and behind us, through the redemptive power of His earthly life.

Religious growth depends upon our meeting the God-Man

on His own terms: in His lowliness as well as His glory, in a lifetime of following as well as the Instant of consecration. The trial of suffering is not due to any harshness on Christ's part, but to the fact that we remain in the world, even when we follow in His steps. We belong to the *ecclesia militans*, the church militant, in that each of us must express in a hostile environment what it means to be a Christian.[30] By the very definition of the Christian vocation, then, the religious person must reproduce in his life not only unlikeness but opposition to the world, and must, in turn, expect a similar aggressiveness from the world's side. Faithfulness to God's will on the part of His servants cannot avoid leading to conflict, any more than did the faithfulness of Christ. Yet we must accept this consequence of the imitation of Christ voluntarily, and with the possibility that it will cause scandal to those who admire Him from afar.

Kierkegaard's recounting of Christ's life is austere and highly selective. He passes over in silence those portions of the Johannine Gospel which record Christ's solicitude and effective prayer for unity and community among believers, lest they weaken his insistence that the spiritual combat is an individual, solitary struggle. In the presence of Christ's gentler sayings and relations with people, he is uncomfortable and displays considerable ingenuity in explaining such occasions away as accommodations to Jewish piety or to the childlike and esthetic factor in human nature. Kierkegaard fears lest people will mistake comprehensive balance for compromise, consolation for dispensation from taking up one's cross. Yet his papers include many consolatory prayers, devotional meditations, and stray hints which are of aid at least to later generations in filling out his religious standpoint. In his reflections upon the love of God, Kierkegaard comes close to the motor center of the following of Christ and the religious spirit among men.

The Love of God

Kierkegaard confessed that, Christianly speaking, there is no more religious value in melancholy, cultivated for its own sake, than in lightmindedness.[31] This holds true also of the contrast between severity and gentleness, if they are divorced from a radical love of God lying deeper than either alternative. Kierkegaard took advantage of the ambiguity in the phrase, "the love of God," which signifies both the loving nature of God and the response which we make to Him. That God is loving and providential, was a conviction implanted in him as a child by his father, a conviction which helped to modify the rigorous, almost terrifying, account of the Redemption which was also taught him. The thought of God's loving care for us certainly gave him a good deal of personal consolation amidst his own tribulations, and provided the theme for many of his finest religious discourses. Our trust in God and obedience to Him are grounded in a recognition of His goodness toward us. If we are visited with opposition and suffering in the world, we are also able to take heart from the love which He has for us and from His coming in the flesh for us.

The fact that God's omnipotence is that of a divine lover, is also the foundation of our religious freedom. If God had not created us out of infinite love as well as infinite power, He could not and would not have "held back," have given us a certain initiative in coming freely to Him or turning away. That we should freely want to give our love to God is, for Kierkegaard, first of all a deep expression of our utter need for Him. In infinite measure, He is our creditor, whereas our only valuable possession is the disposition of our freedom. It is through Christ that we can approach God as a loving person as well as creator. Hence Kierkegaard sometimes observes that Christ is not only the Pattern but also the Redeemer, the one who gives us access to God, as well as power and grace to conform to His example throughout temporal existence. A favorite text is the sentence that all things work for the good of him who loves God.[32] For all his sternness and dialectical play upon this theme, Kierkegaard does convey a sense of utter confidence in God, our friend, and free dedication of service to Him under all conditions. This is the only kind of "free man's worship" which is both free and worshipful.

Religion is a search after kinship with God, and this is most intimately attained in Christian existence. Christian doctrine is itself based upon the person of the God-Man. Christian existence is one of sharing in the divine life, through brotherhood with Christ. Despite a harassing fear of the "sentimental, bourgeois" corruption of this keystone of faith, Kierkegaard places it at the pivotal place in his conception of religious life. To exist religiously means to become united individually with Christ, and to strive to impenetrate our temporal life with His loving presence and power. This is also the ultimate lesson which the study of existence in its entire range teaches us.

Chapter Eight

Kierkegaard and Christian Philosophy

KIERKEGAARD gave a good deal of thought to the fate of his own lifework and reputation, at the hands of posterity. He wanted to avoid scholarly embalmment and discourage the growth of a Kierkegaardian cult, but on both counts his wishes were denied him. Minute scholars and enthusiasts have found him a fair subject for their attentions. There is certainly room for both scholarship and enthusiasm in any assessment of his mind and personality. But if these qualities are divorced from critical independence of outlook, they serve only to betray him and give us a false impression. Kierkegaard could never tolerate personal adulation or an indiscriminate reception of his message. Like Bergson and Marx, he repudiated in advance any attempt to attach an "ism" to his name. Kierkegaardianism seemed as ridiculous to him as Socratism, since both thinkers located truth in the personal relation of man to man. Similarly, his conception of truth as demanding an individual, responsible decision about the meaning of one's life, led him to warn against a merely disinterested analysis of his teaching. This does not rule out a legitimate study of his mind in accord with the canons of historical research. But Kierkegaard requested the historian of philosophy and religion to present his thoughts in such a way that they may be seen to have relevance for contemporary problems.

Nevertheless, Kierkegaard looked forward to the advent of both his poet and his critic. The former personage would be one possessing sufficient insight and sympathy to grasp the meaning of his life and convey to others something of its original venturesomeness. To a man whose own days were spent in the shadow of misunderstanding, this hope of an eventual transparency before men, as well as before God, was a great support. He did not conceive his poet's function as one of vindicating all his moves but as one of securing an honest hearing for all the evidence and motives, upon which he himself had acted. One consideration which conditioned all of Kierkegaard's actions was the idea that, like Luther, he was called upon to be a corrective of the peculiar cultural and religious situation of his own day. Hence he consistently refused to regard his position as an ultimate standard, but only as the standard which was most needed during his lifetime. This does not mean that he denied permanent norms of thought and conduct or that he tried to disregard them. It is rather an acknowledgment of his own limitations, his proclivity towards the one-sided and paradoxical, and the specially unbalanced condition of his own world. Thus he felt the need for more than a poet. He expected that there would be a critical sifting of his convictions and an integration of them with a norm, i.e. a normal outlook.

It is unlikely that any single individual can successfully claim to be *the* poet or *the* critic hailed from afar by Kierkegaard. The work of understanding and evaluating him is a co-operative one, one which may be carried out in several different ways. This is evident from a survey of his various critics. The great majority of them can be classified among either the existentialist philosophers or the crisis theologians. In their different ways, they have called attention to his general importance and to many particular points of interest. Their estimates of his mind, however, often stand in sharp mutual contrast, leaving open the question of his basic contribution to the human search after truth. Some of the chief existentialists want a Kierkegaard from whom the sting of living one's life before God and eternity has been removed. But the atheistic, temporalistic interpretation is forced to discard or explain contrariwise all the convictions which he considered most valuable and unambiguous. For their part, the crisis theologians have retained most of his religious beliefs. But they have failed to deal with other levels of his mind. Moreover, they have not weighed sufficiently his own objections against the usual interpretations of the confessions of faith. Consequently, they have remained helpless before most of the philosophical and theological difficulties which he raised but could not solve, on the basis of his own premises.

The upshot of this conflict between schools of Kierkegaardian interpretation is the widespread opinion that one must choose between his detached philosophico-psychological insights and his religious views. This is one either/or which the master of such dilemmas might challenge. It seems more sensible to admit the coherence of these two areas of thought in his own mind, and to weigh the *whole* outlook in a critical way. This involves an implicit criticism of the approaches of both atheistic existentialists and crisis theologians to Kierkegaard. Their method has been one of picking and choosing, and it is only to be expected that very little of the original subject remains after such arbitrary dissection. When one or another set of partial statements is advanced as the authentic Kierkegaard, the result for most readers can only be skepticism about ever making sense out of the man or reaching a settlement about his intrinsic worth.

The surer course is to accept all that he has to offer and

attempt criticism of his beliefs in the light of a comprehensive philosophy, which can give a positive evaluation and also supply for his shortcomings. The claim that this or that body of doctrine is indeed capable of assimilating and evaluating the whole Kierkegaard can never be made in an a priori way. One must first proceed on the hypothesis that such is the case, and then abide by the actual results of the undertaking. This procedure can be followed in making comparisons between Kierkegaard and the Christian wisdom of Augustine and Aquinas, who in their turn sought to rescue the best in Greek thought. No foolish claim is made that the Danish thinker falls within the category of an Augustinist or a Thomist philosophy. But the total view of life which these thinkers represent, does aid one in appreciating and weighing the many sides of Kierkegaard's genius. Direct comparisons are rendered difficult by the fact that he lacked first-hand acquaintance with many sources of Christian philosophy. Through Luther, however, Kierkegaard was led to read a good deal in Augustine. His thought displays significant points of contact with the Augustinian tradition, as it extends down into the modern world of Luther and Pascal.

The connection with Aquinas is much more indirect, although no less real. It is to be found in their mutual respect for the metaphysical realism of Aristotle. Despite the wide differences in their intellectual milieus, Aquinas and Kierkegaard are united in an appreciation of the Greek approach to the problems of being and becoming. St. Thomas, however, retains the interests of the professional theologian and philosopher, seeking to cast his views into a formal, scientific mold. Hence it is inevitable that, even on those questions where there is fundamental agreement, he would be obliged to correct and extend the position of Kierkegaard. The latter always remains an informal religious thinker and poet, whose thought-processes shy away from complete scientific formulation and comprehensiveness. It is a definite test of Thomism to evaluate Kierkegaard's resistant and elusive attitude, without transmogrifying it into that Systematic Speculation so dreaded and detested by him. Five concrete instances are selected for brief illustration of this comparative problem. These test cases are: the starting-point of cognition, the modes of being, the nature of systematic speculation, the integrity of man, and the relation between faith and reason.

I. THE STARTING POINT OF COGNITION

Kierkegaard voices the general dissatisfaction, felt during the eighteen-forties, about Hegel's attempt to philosophize on the basis of a purely undetermined notion of being. The human mind is not so constructed that it can make a presuppositionless beginning. Although it may start a process of demonstration and exposition at some definite point, this is a first step only in the methodological sense. Actually, this starting point has been prepared and determined by previous activity of an intellectual sort. Moreover, understanding always comes after the fact. "The fact" refers to the total matrix of knowledge, including both the knower and the surrounding world in their status as existent beings. Some transaction between these poles at the pre-cognitive level is supposed, before knowledge becomes actual. Cognition is one form of motion or becoming. As such, it requires an initial movement of actualization, which is not itself cognitive but which naturally leads to knowing. There is also something irreducible and inexhaustible about that which we come to know through this process of fecundation by the existent world. We draw upon its resources more than idealists and pragmatists are ready to admit. We are existentially affected by the thing, as a condition for knowing it and for using or transforming it to suit our practical purposes.

Kierkegaard's defense of the creaturely conditions of knowledge is a reminder that religion is not forced to choose between the pantheistic God of idealism and the finite, developing God of pragmatism. The latter conception has been constructed as a curative against the popular image of a remote, vengeful deity, as well as against the more sophisticated Absolute Mind of the idealists. But neither of these notions of the infinite God has any standing in the main body of the Christian philosophical tradition: they are poles removed from the Augustinian and Thomistic doctrines on God and the world. Kierkegaard saw the need for a realistic basis of religious belief; he also recognized that a man can worship only a God Who retains infinite majesty and goodness of being. There was no conflict in Kierkegaard's mind between a realistic view of knowledge and the transcendence and perfect actuality of God. This suggests that the empiricist proponents of a finite deity have been proceeding on a false alternative. Kierkegaard sought to make return both to realism *and* to a theistic view of God as infinite and transcendent.

That he did not complete the integral recovery of realism is evident, even in regard to the present question. He made only casual mention of whether knowledge should start with the world about us or with man. A sound instinct told him that there is no genuine disjunction here, even though his Augustinian leanings led him to give actual preference to man. He began with man, and yet he did not begin with man in the manner of recent Cartesians. He would not concur with Sartre's choice of the abstract, fugitive consciousness, as the foundation for existential meditation. It is rather man the concrete exister, who serves as the priming point for Kierkegaard. What attracted him to this pole of existential act is the notable fact that, in man, existence and cognition are inextricably bound together. Man is an *inter-esse*, a synthesis of being and knowing. Or rather, he exists in such fashion that his highest act is one of knowing and modifying in a free way his own existent condition. In the human mode of being, Kierkegaard saw the most convincing proof and basis of realism. Thought and reality are not confused in man, and neither are they alienated from each other. Neither idealism nor phenomenalism translates the human situation in a faithful way. Thought bears a reference to reality, because the thinker first exists and because his cognitive acts themselves belong to the realm of existence. Their function is to bring being to the perfection of self-awareness and self-determination. This is man's calling and one basis of his claim to dignity.

Existentialists like Sartre have gone a step beyond this, by systematically excluding the non-human world as a basis for speculation. This has led them to develop a man-centered ontology, in which the modes of human being become the dominant modes of being generally and the constructive laws of each man's projection of his own world. Kierkegaard himself would not agree to this further inference. He was unable to explain how an existential knowledge of the world can be acquired, but at least he allowed that the essential determinations attained through the sciences do belong to the public realm of intersubjective knowledge and do describe the real universe. Furthermore, one of his major contentions against Hegel implied a wider scope to existential knowledge than he recognized. The only way to show that the self-movement of the dialectical Idea is logical, rather than real, movement is to appeal to sense perception of the physical world. Kierkegaard accepted the Aristotelian dictum that real change is first grasped through the senses; it is a given factor which cannot be generated by pure thought alone. He agreed with Feuerbach that the apprehension of real change as such is the accomplishment of the understanding, acting in co-operation with the senses. Only the negative aspect of this thesis was exploited against Hegel, namely, that his pure logic does not deal properly with real change. But it has as its positive side the admission that understanding, functioning in its properly human mode along with sense perception, apprehends an existential process independent of man. With the aid of the senses, some knowledge can be gained about existential acts other than that of the reflective, moral subject.

Kierkegaard's appeal to the senses admits of one further inference. Since thought by itself cannot grasp change and the existent, a certain primacy must be accorded to our sense acquaintance with the world of natural things. It is indispensable for every existential cognition, including that of the human self. Kierkegaard's inability to achieve a lasting synthesis between body and soul is due, not only to psychological reasons, but also to a failure to work out this implication. The empirical bias of Aristotle and Aquinas is a pointed corrective of this deficiency. These philosophers recognize that self-knowledge is conditioned by knowledge of the physical world. Our knowing powers are awakened in an existential direction, through sensuous perception of natural things. There is no independent, purely intellectual apprehension of the soul: we only become aware of the fact of its existence concomitantly with the exercise of our knowing powers in respect to material things. All of our subsequent reasoning must be brought back eventually to the criterion of sense perception, for it is here that the intellect first meets existence. We need not follow Hume in consigning all metaphysical inferences to the flames, but we should cast off all such reasonings as have *no* warrant whatever in the evidence provided by the sense world. The quarrel of the theists with naturalistic empiricists is not over the indispensable character of sense experience, but over its implications.

2. THE MODES OF BEING

It is a commonplace among contemporary existentialists that "existence" is derived from "ex-sistere," to stand out from. They go on to explain that the existent is that which asserts itself in the face of the naught. Remarkably enough, this etymological prologue is often followed by a thoroughly idealistic dialectic of being and nothing. This transition could not have been made so easily, had these existentialists really respected the mind of Kierkegaard, who does not contrast the existent primarily with unqualified nothingness. This opposition is occasionally found in his thought, but it comes too close to Hegel's pairing of "being" and "nothing" to serve as the basic contrast. Much more pertinent is the fact that existential act stands out from both pure thought and possibility. The opposition between existence and pure Systematic thought enables Kierkegaard to distinguish existence from *every* moment in the Systematic dialectic, including the initial antithesis between "being" and "nothing." He sets the existential order off from the pure concept of "being," just as definitively as from the Speculative explanation of the naught. To exist is to exercise a mode of being totally distinct from the entire Speculative play upon the concepts of being in-itself and for-itself, *en soi* and *pour soi* (to employ Sartre's terms).

Even within the realm of real being, however, there is a contrast between existence and mere capacity for existence. Kierkegaard appropriates for himself the Aristotelian distinction between actual and potential being, with the added precision that the ultimate act of a concrete nature is the act of existing itself. Until it has received this ultimate and unique perfection, the thing is still comprised within its causes. It cannot be said to be, in a plenary way, until it exists in its own right and on its own foundation. In this sense, existence is a mark that the thing has passed from potential to actual being, that it subsists as an individual entity. This involves a standing forth from one's causal principle, as well as from the potential mode of being. For Kierkegaard, there is no contradiction between being an existent thing and a caused thing. In fact, his analysis of the historicity of existence reveals that the only way in which an existent emerges, is by means of a passage from potential to actual being. Such a transition can be made only under the active influence of a cause, which confers the act of existing upon the thing in process. One of the main objections leveled against absolute idealism is precisely its suppression of the efficient cause of change, in favor of the ground-consequent relation between concepts. For Kierkegaard, existence is the mode of being proper to a thing that has a first cause and a temporal duration.

The temporal, historical nature of the existent means that it has come to be by way of passing from potency to act, through the operation of an efficient cause. Gilson's research has established that the close association between existing and having a temporal origin from a cause was the characteristic Christian view of existence, until the modern period. Augustine and Aquinas would have understood Kierkegaard's assertion that God does not *exist*, He *is*.[1] Kierkegaard liked to reflect upon the Biblical saying that in God there is no shadow of alteration, and hence he denied to God a mode of being which signifies change. To Augustine as well, the divine immutability is a distinctive attribute, setting off the eternal way of being from that of temporal things. One way of expressing the divine transcendence is to deny to

God a manner of being which involves change and causation. Aquinas respects this meaning of existence and occasionally refers to God as *non-existens*. On the other hand, he also observes that change and causation are only associated with existence because of the finite way in which it is present in creatures, not because of an intrinsic connection. Being caused and subject to change are not identical with the act of existing itself, but are only the means whereby finite, historical beings gain access to existential act. These traits define the conditions of finite participation in existence. Although the created conditions and limitations of existence do not apply to God, He does realize in its full perfection the act of existing. He alone is a subsistent act of existing, unmixed with any shadow of change and causation. He is *esse super omne ens*, the supreme act of existing not subject to the conditions under which finite entities share in the perfection of the existential order. What Kierkegaard and Augustine call God's eternal being is metaphysically designated by Aquinas as His subsistent act of existing. In this way, some analogical knowledge can be acquired about the purely actual being of God, with the aid of that which exists by coming to be in a caused, historical way.

This conception of existence also provides a solid theoretical basis for Kierkegaard's belief in the hierarchy of beings. He was not much concerned about determining all the aspects whereby man differs from other beings in the material world. All of his attention was concentrated upon the polar relation between God and man, eternity and history. The great divisions of real being are into potential and actual, existential and eternal.[2] The presence of eternity to time illuminated all of his meditations and trials, for the distinction between man and God does not lead to God's banishment from the sphere of time. God's immanence to creation, indeed, is secured only by His infinite perfection, since only a being of unlimited actuality and power can be effectively present to others, without tending to displace or flatten them. The divine omnipresence is a generous, creative one and, in the casé of man, it is the very condition for the use of created freedom. The fresh note sounded in Kierkegaard's doctrine on the human individual is the refusal to found individual integrity upon a rhetorical claim to self-sufficiency. Instead, man's freedom is proportioned to his acknowledgment of the majesty of God and his own ordination to a share in eternal life.

The naturalistic assumption that a theory of grades of being is inevitably derogatory of man and sapping of his initiative, has seldom been subjected to critical examination by the naturalists themselves. It was elevated into a truism in Kierkegaard's day by Feuerbach, and has continued to remain unquestioned in Marxian and Deweyan naturalism. But the recognition of higher forms of being need not entail a devaluation of lower forms. Man's place in the cosmos must first be determined on grounds of present fact, before we consider the consequences. Some sort of hierarchy is present in a universe which permits of wider sharings in value and more adequate embodiments of the traits of experience. Because he admitted that temporal existence is ordained to eternity, Kierkegaard did not therefore counsel men to flee from their historical, mundane responsibilities. Rather, he asked them to face these problems with awareness of an added dimension, provided by God's demand upon our exercise of freedom.

3. SPECULATIVE AND SYSTEMATIC KNOWLEDGE

Kierkegaard's commitments concerning being and existence stand in uneasy relation to his anti-Speculative and anti-Systematic campaign. His speculative analysis of existence is at odds with his general attack upon philosophical speculation. He resembled Marx both in proclaiming the downfall of philosophy and in contributing a good deal toward its advancement. Neither thinker could bring an era of philosophical speculation to an end, without helping to generate a new phase in its history. Kierkegaard's tragedy was that there was no philosophical movement on the horizon which could find a place for his deliverances. After a shrewd appraisal of contemporary tendencies, he concluded that, at its worst, philosophy degenerates into the Hegelian "pure thought" and, at its best, remains an analysis of essential forms. He saw no way of incorporating his existential insights into any of the systems of his day. This forced him to give his convictions an exclusively religious connotation and to depreciate their metaphysical consequences, except for polemical purposes.

Yet, in his writings, there is observable a definite strain of sustained, speculative reasoning. His actual practice belies his words, and compels us to distinguish between the historical forms of philosophy with which he was acquainted and other possibilities for philosophy. Kierkegaard does not leave entirely unexplored the alternative routes to philosophical wisdom. For instance, he reproaches Hegel for introducing the readers of his *Philosophy of History* straightway to particular trends of events, instead of giving a careful explanation of historical process and knowledge as such.

Why at once become concrete, why at once begin to experiment *in concreto?* Was it not possible to answer this question in the dispassionate brevity of the language of abstraction, which has no means of distraction or enchantment, this question of what it means that the Idea becomes concrete, what is the nature of becoming, what is one's relationship to that which has come into being, and so forth? [3]

Save for the name, this is asking why Hegel does not examine more exactly the metaphysical problems underlying philosophy of history. Most of the above-mentioned questions

are treated in a quite formal and technical way by Kierkegaard himself. In turn, we can interrogate him as to whether
his own stand on the modes of being has only an abstract, essentialist significance. An admission that his position does
convey some knowledge about the universe in its existential
character, paves the way for a *philosophical* theory of being
as existent. Such a doctrine can avoid absolute idealism, without restricting itself to a phenomenological description of
essential structures.

A few philosophies have addressed themselves primarily to
the problem of existence. One of these is that of Aquinas. It
is orientated to the study of existence, precisely because it is
a philosophy of being. As the science of being as such, metaphysics is directed primarily to the most radical principles of
being: essence and existence. The beings of our experience are
constituted, not only by a determinate nature, but also by an
ultimate act whereby this concrete subject is enabled to be
in the existential order.[4] In virtue of the act of existing, the
individual takes its place among the actual entities of the
world. Since a thing is not a being in the full sense, until it
exercises this existential act, a philosophy of being must have
special regard for the existential order. The intelligible structure of the thing is secured by its essence, whereas its fruitful sharing in the community of the actual universe requires a
decisive posing of this essence through the existential act.
There is no basis for Sartre's charge that classical metaphysics
favors essence over existence. It is not a question of favoring
one over the other, but of giving due recognition to the contribution of each principle to the concrete being. This enables
us to take account of experience both as intelligible and as
urgently existential.

Two features of the Thomistic "existential communication"
are relevant here. In the first place, it is elaborated in a strictly
theoretical and systematic fashion; secondly, it entails a sharp

delimitation of the scope of speculative and systematic thinking, in view of the existential nature of the real world. It
accepts Kierkegaard's justifiable strictures against the Hegelian
conception of philosophical science, without surrendering the
rights of a scientific treatment of being as existent. Allowance
is made for a more practical and homiletic discussion of existence, although the latter is not given exclusive competence.
This is the proper function of a metaphysical norm, when
confronted with the Hegel-Kierkegaard debate.

The meaning attached by Hegel to speculation is peculiar
to his standpoint of absolute idealism. His method and his doctrine stand in circular relation to one another, so that if the
one is undermined, the other collapses. Apart from his conception of Absolute Mind or Spirit, there is no reason for regarding the speculative process as a self-enclosed, autonomous
method. Unless one is already convinced that philosophizing
is an expression of the dialectical growth of Absolute Spirit
itself, there is no ground for robbing the finite individual of
its proper significance, inalienable freedom and responsibility.
By attacking this absolutist prejudice, Kierkegaard prepared
the way unwittingly for a renaissance of that kind of speculation which displays a truly humane character. The goods of
human life are not jeopardized by a speculative activity op-
erating within a realistic and theistic context. Here, the speculative method is not antagonistic to subjective interests or
practical understanding; rather, it underlies these other aspects
of the human spirit as their reliable foundation and guide. To
speculate means to engage in a quest of the truth for its own
sake, but without any implication that the relation of the
knowing subject to the truth is unimportant or that our work
as men is completed, once we gain a knowledge of what
things are. Speculative truths are self-justified, in the sense
that a knowledge of them satisfies the desire of our intelligence
simply to know the nature and existential act of things. But

these truths also have a paramount bearing upon our practical outlook and upon praxis itself. Metaphysics tends to become wisdom, not only as a contemplation of the widest truths about the traits of being, but also as a regulation of the whole order of goods and actions. The aim of the wise man is to realize the most intimate synthesis between practical and theoretical understanding, and to order action in the light of this unified insight. Speculative wisdom is at the service of the whole man.

A similar problem is presented by the ideal of systematic construction. There is a minimal and neutral sense in which every thinker of any caliber must be systematic. He must try to furnish an explanation on the basis of reliable principles, consistent inferences and ever more inclusive evaluations of experience. It is supposed that the object of inquiry is, to some degree, intelligible to us and patient of being expressed in a unified body of knowledge or a system. But absolute idealism adds considerably to this minimum. It interprets the systemic enterprise in terms of an organismic theory of reality and the mind's relations to things. Being is said to be not only intelligible in itself but, in principle, completely available to the philosopher. The idealistic proportion between mind and thing is founded on a view that the existent world is an "estranged" product of Mind, and is destined for complete return to the conceptual state. The mind can totally comprehend nature, because nature is the state of Mind-in-estrangement-from-itself. Whatever resists assimilation to the philosophical concept, is thereby shown to be caught in illusion and to stand in need of "sublation" to a higher level. The philosophical system in its conceptual interconnections is an adequate transcription of the world, considered as a dialectical organism. In the face of this set of Hegelian claims, Kierkegaard was led to rebel despairingly against all systematic thinking. Most non-idealistic philosophers would agree with him in repudiating the Hegelian notion of a system, but they would do so without prejudice to the more restrained statement of the need for systematic organization of thought. St. Thomas adds a metaphysical reason why the extreme Hegelian view is untenable. In the speculative order, we cannot legislate about the human condition but must accept it as we find it. The human mind is not divine, and its concepts not creative. By means of our concepts and empirical investigation, we can attain to some understanding of the structure of being through its experienced traits. But we are not equipped to gain an exhaustive insight into essences, such that they might be completely assimilated to a system. The perfection of human knowledge is achieved in the judgment about existence, since this is the way in which the mind expresses to itself the perfect act of being. The existential judgment affirms that the thing exercises its own act of existing, that it stands forth from the realm of concepts and possibles. By implication, this judgment also affirms that the being of the thing remains other than, and more than, the judging act and its conceptual factors. The human intellect acknowledges, but does not ingest, the existing world. To understand the existent is to make a conquest, whose ground is a confession of humility before the given.

Not only at the beginning of the philosophical enterprise but also at every subsequent phase, we are striving to grasp that which can never be transferred in its entirety into the order of concepts and judgments. The individual being remains other than philosophical thought, in virtue of the act of existing. Hence it furnishes the philosopher with constant nourishment, mystery and incitement to make further discoveries. Its otherness is not a self-deception on the part of an Absolute Mind, but the integrity which every individual existent demands for itself. An existential philosophy must be an open enterprise rather than a closed, circular discipline, a system always in the making and always subject to revision and unexpected advance. In this way, it escapes the force of Kierkegaard's ironical comment that the System must already be completed in principle, on pain of not being a System at all.

4. THE WHOLE MAN

The Thomistic theory of man is a remarkable instance of the application of existential principles to a specific domain of being. In main part, Kierkegaard's ideas on man can be incorporated into Thomistic anthropology, without detriment to the general structure. Among Kierkegaard's major contentions are that man is finite, a body-soul complex whole, and a passional creature. These three points can serve as a frame of reference in showing the relation between metaphysics and existential meditation.

What makes a thing to be a created, finite being? Aquinas departs from some earlier traditions by explaining finiteness in terms of essence and existence, rather than matter and form. There might be beings (such as the angels) which would be free from matter and yet be finite. What is distinctive about the finite mode of being, is the presence of really distinct and radically constitutive principles of being: essence and existence. These factors compose with each other as a concrete subject and its ultimate actuation. The perfection of existence is proportioned to the determinate subject which is actuated, since there is a strict, mutual adaptation between the essential principle and the act of existing. The concrete essence is itself a limited capacity for receiving the existential act. The actual being constituted by the union of these mutually proportioned potential and actual principles is a finite existent. Not only its essential nature and mode of existing, but also its powers and operations partake of this limited sharing in being. It is thoroughly and permanently a finite being, even though it can progressively gain control over its field of experience.

Men are finite beings in this sense. It may be true, as Hegel states, that finitude as such is a category of the understanding, but this does not apply also to the individual, finite acts of being, which are the real foundation for the category. They are not mere concepts of the understanding which feign to be independent of mind and distinct from the Absolute. Finite beings are other than the categories whereby they can be classified and analyzed. Similarly, they affirm, by all that is real within them, their decisive otherness from an infinite being, in which no real distinction can be drawn between essence and existence. The divine essence has no limits, since it is nothing other than the very act of existing, in its unrestricted perfection. Finite things are caused by the infinitely actual being: they are not masked developments of this being. Each of them is a unique and rich act, an integral whole rather than a moment in a dialectical process. This is most evident in the case of human persons. The person is aware of himself as an inalienable center of existence and freedom. He cannot be assumed into any higher state of being; that which could be so assumed, would never have been a person. The individual is terminated in itself, and the human individual seals this termination with an affirmation of his own selfhood and self-mastery. He is not only made to exist: he deliberately asserts himself as an existent and a moral character, which cannot be attributed to another entity.

In describing the nature of the human person, Kierkegaard makes a deliberate return to the threefold division of body-soul-spirit, so dear to the Fathers of the Church and other spiritual writers. Not only as a weapon against Hegel, but also as a means for describing the interior struggle that accompanies the birth of a mature personality, he found this trichotomous conception of man a useful one. It is a division also recognized by Aquinas, who usually tries to find a place for the empirical data and spiritual tools of the Fathers. Hence, he notes that what is ordinarily referred to as the rational, human soul is at once a soul and a spirit.[5] It is a soul, in so far as it communicates life to matter, and this function it shares with all other life principles in the material world. But what elevates it above the others is its own spiritual character. The human soul not only informs matter but has its own subsistent mode of being, which is not intrinsically dependent upon matter. It can receive and exercise the act of existing in its own right, so that it does not perish in the extreme case when the body is dissolved. This is the metaphysical aspect of its spirituality.

Nevertheless, this same spiritual principle is also the enlivening soul of matter. The existential act is not only received by the human soul but is naturally communicated by it to its proper matter, in the formation of the body. The soul is a part of human nature and has its complete natural perfection, only as united with its matter. Soul and matter are joint principles, specifying the structure of human nature: were they not both present, we would not be the kind of beings we indeed are. The genuine human individual, the person in the proper sense, is the individual composite whole of soul and matter. In their union is found the mode of being, distinctive of man. This is our only safeguard against assimilation to the angels on the one side and mere things on the other. From the former we are set off by the material factor in our being, and from the latter by the immaterial nature of our soul or formal principle. Metaphysically regarded, the human spirit is not a third something, superadded to soul and body: it is the soul itself, regarded in its distinctively human status as an immaterial act of being.

Kierkegaard gave short shrift to theological speculations about the "rectitude or state of integrity" of the human soul before the Fall. Yet he might have profited by a reading of the pages devoted by St. Thomas to this topic.[6] St. Thomas inquires whether a perfect subjection of the body to the soul and its government belongs to our natural equipment. He replies in the negative and adds that, since the Fall, the soul's task of securing order and unity in the person has been made more difficult. Its aim ought not to be the suppression of the bodily side of man but its proper ordering, so that the entire man may share in material and spiritual goods, in due proportion. The primacy of the spiritual principle in man is to be established, not its exclusive rights. It is a question of subordination and synthesis, not of suppression and elimination of man's material aspects. Here is where the problem of man ceases to belong solely to the speculative sciences. There are moral and religious difficulties standing in the way of a harmonious development of personal life. Kierkegaard's interpretation of spirit can be inserted at this place in a discussion of humanism. For, it concerns the manner in which personal existence is orientated to good or evil, in accord with a dominant ideal.

Both man's finite nature and his composite character as a soul-body complexus have a bearing upon the problem of the "passions." This problem is taken here, in the broad Kierkegaardian sense of securing the real distinction between the cognitive and the conative aspects of human nature. Hegel did not require Kierkegaard's tutelage to instruct him about the power of the passions, in determining human affairs. One of the leitmotifs in the Hegelian philosophy of history is the passional aspect of man, his all-consuming concern for his proper, subjective interests. But Hegel regarded this moment of passion as a trick played upon us—and eventually upon itself—by Absolute Spirit, as a ruse of the dialectic for attaining its own ends, despite our egoism. Not the existence and importance of the passions, but their noncognitive and nonabsolutist character, is the point at issue. Kierkegaard found no evidence which would warrant reducing the passions to aspects of knowledge and the march of the Absolute Spirit through time.

In a realist philosophy of creaturely, participated being, it is impossible to confuse the two orders. To know a thing, does not forthwith place us in full possession of it. The knowledge must be followed through with desire, decision and effort, if the relation is to be made more intimate. This is due to something more than a defect in our knowledge. It cannot be said that, if we did have sufficient knowledge about the object, nothing more would be wanting in the order of desire. That something over and above the cognitive possession of the thing *is* demanded, follows from our finiteness. We still yearn for a fuller grasp, because of the limits of our nature and its exigency for other goods. Man is related to things not only as objects to be known but also as goods or ends to be pursued. He would be deluding himself, if he hoped to maintain a purely theoretical attitude in the face of the world of experienced goods, for he needs to go out to them and obtain them in their own actuality. Nor can knowledge pass through the human mind in a purely impersonal and disinterested fashion, as information passes through a complex calculating machine. In us, knowing is a personal act, which must be appropriated in a personal way and ordained to the good of man, under the rule of prudence.

Since man is not pure mind and will, he also experiences bodily desires or passions, in the ordinary sense. Kierkegaard's esthetic individual is entangled in the network of the passions, and yet he is not sufficiently passionate to assume mastery over his own life. The paradox is resolved by recalling that the will is regarded by Kierkegaard as a major natural passion. To be lacking in passion is to fail to achieve the synthesis of psycho-physical powers, under the guiding discipline of what

Aristotle and Aquinas call "rational desire" or "desiring reason." But little is said by Kierkegaard about the bodily passions, in reference to moral and religious life. He is so preoccupied with a description of such spiritual-passional states as dread, despair and faith, that he often loses sight of the total person and the problem of integrating all the passional drives. A narrow approach of this kind is dangerous, since it leaves the individual exposed to sudden waves of bodily passion, which cannot be correlated with the spiritual aims of the person. Conflict and disorder are the consequences for moral life, instead of a progressive unification of tendencies.

Methodologically, the Thomist approach to man stands midway between that of Kierkegaard and that of contemporary naturalists. It has in common with the latter a program of studying man along with the other beings in the material universe, for the sake of discovering their common features. Man is a changing, material, striving existent, to whom applies all that can be gathered about the general cosmic traits of process, purpose, vital function and value. Kierkegaard would include all the evidence gathered by this method under the heading of objective or essentialist truth, but it also has existential significance, in view of the fact that theoretical judgments about existence are possible. Kierkegaard is justified, however, in insisting (against naturalism) that man represents a distinctive embodiment of the notes of existence, and that this requires a causal as well as a descriptive explanation of human reality. He helps one to strike a balance between a description of the different modes of existence and a causal account of these differences. Man exists in a distinctively personal way, as a reflective and free agent. His culture and moral personality are the work of freedom and—Kierkegaard would add—of divine government. Man's way of existing rests on a recognition of his placement in the existing world and his vocation to participate in the source of existence.

· 263 ·

5. FAITH AND REASON

Being a hundred years removed from Kierkegaard, we sometimes make inferences from his stated position which he himself would not admit. Because one of his pseudonyms preached the scandalous crucifixion of reason on the tree of faith, we are ready to conclude that he is anti-intellectual or, more subtly still, that he is engaged in discrediting religious faith indirectly in the eyes of intelligent men. His actual intent is much less forbidding and devious than is sometimes supposed. He was confronted with a peculiar sort of rationalism, not one which outlawed faith as nonsense, but one which clasped it so vigorously to itself that faith was suffocated in the embrace. Consequently, there was no more effective, temporary strategy than to proclaim the utter irreconcilability between religious truth and an absolutist brand of reason. Kierkegaard hesitated to say anything in human tongue about Christian faith, under these circumstances. He had his pseudonym, Johannes Climacus, advance a distinction between *doctrine* or philosophical exposition of faith and an *existential communication*, after the manner of a subjective truth.[7] It seemed to him that the ordinary doctrinal treatment fails to arouse practical response, and that ordinary apologetical methods betray a lack of confidence in faith.

For his part, St. Thomas kept the distinction between his sermons and his theological treatises, but he also held that theology is the one science which is both speculative and practical. Sacred doctrine should not be treated in a purely speculative way, since it is formally concerned not only with God but also with directing human actions to the vision of God. Hence it fulfills in the highest degree the requirements of wisdom, which judges and orders all matters in the light of man's final end. On the other hand, Aquinas made the fullest use of reason, in examining the content of faith. This he did, without any implication that it is due to the weakness of his belief or to a compromise between natural and supernatural orders of assent. The theological use of human reason rests on an acceptance of man as he is. Just as we cannot decree man into becoming a phase of Absolute Mind, so we cannot decree that faith and reason will have no commerce in him.

Man is a being who knows in part and believes in part, but both believing and knowing help to perfect his one personal outlook. He has a native tendency to unify the truths to which he assents, bringing the deliverances of faith to bear upon the life of reason and, conversely, exploring the groundwork of faith with the aid of reason. Augustine and Anselm set the pattern for this view of the normal intercourse between faith and reason, when they formulated the guiding axiom of Christian wisdom: I believe so that I may understand, and I understand so that I may believe. The purpose of a Christian wisdom is not to erase the distinction between understanding and believing, but to keep open the lines of communication and mutual aid.[8] St. Augustine compared this polar activity, in the cognitive order, to the moral dialectic of coming into possession of finite goods so that one may desire the supreme good all the more intensely. Truth is ultimately one, not only in its primary source, God, but also in the final tendencies of believing and understanding. Reason is strengthened in its operation by the direction it receives from faith. The latter, in turn, draws upon the resources of reason, in order to make intelligible that which has been revealed. If faith seeks after direct insight into the grounds of supernatural truth, it specifies as its goal not philosophical cognition but the sheer vision of God, face to face.

St. Thomas customarily distinguishes between two sorts of

truth in the content of revelation. Some truths are of a
strictly supernatural sort, which could in no way be discovered by unaided reason; other truths do not surpass the intrinsic capacity of natural reason but nevertheless have been
revealed, because of their importance for our salvation and
the weakness of our mind in its actual condition. In this way,
the mysteries of the Trinity and the Incarnation are set off
from revealed assurances about immortality and providence.
Because he did not make this distinction, Kierkegaard took
needless scandal at every sort of philosophical treatment of
man's immortality and God's existence and providential care.
It seemed to him that these matters could not be handled
philosophically, without reducing the entire content of faith
to the level of natural reason and philosophical criteria. But
from the fact that both faith and reason can deal with these
truths, it only follows that there are some revealed truths
which can be believed at one time and known at another, or
believed by one individual and known by another. In regard
to the mysteries of faith which are entirely above our natural
power of proof, however, Kierkegaard is justified in protest-
ing against efforts to provide philosophical demonstration.
Revelation is not, as Fichte dreamed, a sort of *Volksausgabe*
or popular version of what reason will later establish in a
philosophical way. Neither is our saving adherence to revealed
truth an exclusively intellectual act, isolated from the affective
side of man's life. Kierkegaard's analysis tells also against the
rationalistic theologians, who had forgotten the influence of
will upon intellect in the free and supernatural act of believing. There is a close resemblance between the dialectic which
Augustine noted between love and understanding, in the
growth of faith, and Kierkegaard's appeal for renewed co-
operation between passion, will and interested reason. Both
these Christian thinkers were only recalling, each in his own

generation, the Biblical conception of *fides caritate formata*, faith quickened and warmed by love of God above all.

Crisis theologians like Emil Brunner have followed Kierkegaard in locating faith formally in the subjective act of believing and in personal encounter with Christ.[9] It is a welcome reminder that all the roads of Christian existence lead to the person of the Word of God made flesh. But it was difficult for Kierkegaard to avoid correlating what older theologians called the act of believing—*fides qua creditur*—with the truths and the personal Truth revealed for our assent and adhesion—*fides quae creditur.* Taken by itself, a theological science which concentrates upon the latter is apt to issue in dead formalism and to be insensitive toward devotional life and personal sacrifice for the sake of revealed truth. But the believing act, if cultivated in isolation, leads to mere sentimentality and undisciplined enthusiasm, consequences which were equally repugnant to Kierkegaard. Both aspects of faith belong to the foundation of Christian life, since they both lead men to the person of Christ.

The difficulty of maintaining intimate contact and balance between dogma and devotion, creed and cult, suggests that the problem of faith cannot be resolved merely from the standpoint of the individual believer and an invisible company of the faithful. It is also a matter of joint concern to a Church or visible body of believers. Faith incorporates one into the wider religious community in its incarnate form, as a Church. It makes the demand that we acknowledge God not only in the privacy of our hearts but also in a public and corporate way, along with our fellow believers. The movement of existence impels the man of faith toward visible and social confession of that faith and a corresponding communal act of worship. Kierkegaard hesitated to make this inference, however, lest it commit him once again to the Hegelian organismic whole.

Having criticized the latter as being destructive of the individual, he remained forever wary of visible expressions of the social aspect of religion. This is a final instance in which it would be fatal for us to lend unconditional normative weight to his criticisms. In faithfulness to Kierkegaard himself, we can acknowledge the normal development of religious existence in the visible Church, as well as in the private oratory.

Bibliographical Note

The Danish edition of Kierkegaard's *Samlede Vaerker* is edited by A. B. Drachmann, J. L. Heiberg and H. O. Lange. Second edition, 15 vols. Copenhagen, Gyldendalske Boghandel, Nordisk Forlag, 1920-36. The Danish edition of his *Papirer* is edited by P. A. Heiberg, V. Kuhr and E. Torsting. Second edition, 11 vols. in 20 parts. Copenhagen, Gyldendalske Boghandel, Nordisk Forlag, 1909-48.

The following are the English translations of Kierkegaard used here, together with the abbreviations used in the Notes.

1. *Either/Or, A Fragment of Life.* Volume One translated by David F. Swenson and Lillian Marvin Swenson; Volume Two translated by Walter Lowrie. 2 vols. Princeton, Princeton University Press, 1944. Cited as: *Either/Or.*

2. *Repetition, An Essay in Experimental Psychology.* Translated by Walter Lowrie. Princeton, Princeton University Press, 1941. Cited as: *Repetition.*

3. *Fear and Trembling, A Dialectical Lyric.* Translated by Walter Lowrie. Princeton, Princeton University Press, 1941. Cited as: *Trembling.*

4. *Stages on Life's Way.* Translated by Walter Lowrie. Princeton, Princeton University Press, 1940. Cited as: *Stages.*

5. *The Concept of Dread.* Translated by Walter Lowrie. Princeton, Princeton University Press, 1944. Cited as: *Dread.*

6. *Edifying Discourses.* Translated by David F. Swenson and Lillian Marvin Swenson. 4 vols. Minneapolis, Augsburg Publishing House, 1943-46. Cited as: *Edifying Discourses.*

7. *Philosophical Fragments or a Fragment of Philosophy.* Translated by David F. Swenson. Princeton, Princeton University Press, 1936. Cited as: *Fragments.*

8. *Concluding Unscientific Postscript.* Translated by David F. Swenson. Princeton, Princeton University Press, 1941. Cited as: *Postscript.*

9. *The Present Age and Two Minor Ethico-Religious Treatises.* Translated by Alexander Dru and Walter Lowrie. New York, Oxford University Press, 1940. Cited as: *Present Age.*

10. *The Point of View.* Translated by Walter Lowrie. New York, Oxford University Press, 1939. Cited as: *Point of View.*

11. *Purify Your Hearts!* Translated by A. S. Aldworth and W. S. Ferrie. London, C. W. Daniel Company, 1937. Cited as: *Purify.*

12. *Consider the Lilies.* Translated by A. S. Aldworth and W. S. Ferrie. London, C. W. Daniel Company, 1940. Cited as: *Consider.*

13. *The Gospel of Suffering and The Lilies of the Field.* Translated by David F. Swenson and Lillian Marvin Swenson. Minneapolis, Augsburg Publishing House, 1948. Cited as: *Suffering.*

14. *Works of Love.* Translated by David F. Swenson and Lillian Marvin Swenson. Princeton, Princeton University Press, 1946. Cited as: *Love.*

15. *Christian Discourses.* Translated by Walter Lowrie. New York, Oxford University Press, 1939. Cited as: *Christian Discourses.*

16. *The Sickness unto Death.* Translated by Walter Lowrie. Princeton, Princeton University Press, 1941. Cited as: *Sickness.*

17. *Training in Christianity.* Translated by Walter Lowrie. New York, Oxford University Press, 1941. Cited as: *Training.*

18. *For Self-Examination and Judge for Yourselves!* Translated by Walter Lowrie. New York, Oxford University Press, 1941. Cited as: *Self-Examination.*

19. *Attack upon "Christendom," 1854-1855.* Translated by Walter Lowrie. Princeton, Princeton University Press, 1944. Cited as: *Attack.*

20. *The Journals.* Edited and translated by Alexander Dru. New York, Oxford University Press, 1938. Cited as: *Journals.*

In the English language, there is a small but reliable company of books that will help the reader become acquainted with Kierkegaard. Walter Lowrie's *A Short Life of Kierkegaard* (Princeton, Princeton University Press, 1942), presents the basic biographical information in a concise and lively way. The same author's earlier and larger work, *Kierkegaard* (New York, Oxford University Press, 1938), covers the same ground but in much more detail, with numerous quotations and critical evaluations, as well as a useful synopsis of Kierkegaard's writings and a glossary of his distinctive terms. There are two sympathetic guides to Kierkegaard's personality and thought: *Kierkegaard the Melancholy Dane*, by H. V. Martin (New York, Philosophical Library, 1950), and *Introduction to Kierkegaard*, by Régis Jolivet, translated from the French by W. H. Barber (New York, E. P. Dutton, 1951). Martin gives a brief, elementary sketch of Kierkegaard as "the Morning Star of a New Reformation in Christian Theology," whereas Jolivet makes a more systematic study of the various facets of his mind, from a Catholic standpoint. A good beginning can be made in the direct study of the sources, with the help of Robert Bretall's well-edited *A Kierkegaard Anthology* (New York, The Modern Library, 1959). The selections are illustrative of Kierkegaard's many levels of communication and are accompanied by pertinent editorial comments. See also, W. H. Auden's edition of *The Living Thoughts of Kierkegaard* (New York, David McKay, 1952).

The pioneer American philosophical work on Kierkegaard was done by David Swenson, who was publishing articles on him long before his name became generally known in our country. These papers have been collected under the unassuming title: *Something About Kierkegaard*, edited by Lillian Marvin Swenson (second, revised ed., Minneapolis, Augsburg Publishing House, 1945). Swenson's explanation of Kierkegaard's existential dialectic and the three stages on the way of life is especially valuable. For a more detailed analysis of Kierkegaard's views on music, the possibility of philosophy, the nature of dread, and other topics, consult T. H. Croxall's *Kierkegaard Studies* (London and Redhill, Lutterworth Press, 1948). The final part of this book examines Kierkegaard's remarks on the Holy Trinity. Two notable works are devoted to a special consideration of Kierkegaard's religious position: *Lectures on the Religious Thought of Søren Kierkegaard*, by Eduard Geismar (Minneapolis, Augsburg Publishing House, 1937), and *Kierkegaard's Philosophy of Religion*, by Reidar Thomte (Princeton, Princeton University Press, 1948). Geismar gives a general orientation to Kierkegaard's religious world; Thomte discusses the particular problems and arguments underlying this outlook.

The impact of Kierkegaard upon the European mind of the last generation can readily be gauged through a reading of two little monographs by one of his German translators and expositors, Theodor Haecker. In *Søren Kierkegaard*, translated by Alexander Dru (New York, Oxford University Press, 1937), Haecker meditates upon Kierkegaard's mission to Europe and his relevance for contemporary philosophers, theologians and literary critics. Haecker's essay, *Kierkegaard the Cripple*, translated by C. Van O. Bruyn (New York, Philosophical Library, 1950), deals with the delicate question of Kierkegaard's physical constitution and its effect upon his psychological attitude and his approach to religious problems.

Out of the vast ocean of European literature on Kierkegaard, the following eight books are chosen for their penetrating contribution to an understanding and appreciation of Kierkegaard's significance. A broad, synoptic account is given by Torsten Bohlin: *Søren Kierkegaard, l'homme et l'oeuvre*, translated from the Danish by P.-H. Tisseau (Bazoges-en-Pareds, Chez le traducteur, 1941). *Søren Kierkegaard: Seine Lebensentwicklung und seine Wirksamkeit als Schriftsteller*, by Eduard Geismar, translated from the Danish by E. Krüger and Madame Geismar (Göttingen, Vandenhoeck and Ruprecht, 1929), is the fundamental twentieth-century study of the genesis of Kierkegaard's thought and personal vocation. Of equal stature and interest is Emanuel Hirsch's *Kierkegaard-Studien* (2 vols., Gütersloh, C. Bertelsmann, 1933), which circumstantially follows Kierkegaard's development as a writer and religious thinker. A comprehensive analysis of Kierkegaard's religious standpoint and its historical connections is given in Walter Ruttenbeck's *Søren Kierkegaard: Der christliche Denker und sein Werk* (Berlin and Frankfurt, Verlag Trowitzsch, 1929). Two major attempts have been made to pierce the enigmatic relationship between the esthetic and the religious strains in Kierkegaard's mind: *Søren Kierkegaard: Der Dichter des Religiösen*, by Martin Thust (Munich, C. H. Beck'sche Verlagsbuchhandlung, 1931), and *Le vrai visage de Kierkegaard*, by Pierre Mesnard (Paris, Beauchesne, 1948). The special worth of Jean Wahl's *Études kierkegaardiennes* (second edition, Paris, J. Vrin, 1949), lies in its concise summaries of previous research and its perceptive comparisons between Kierkegaard and contemporary existentialists. Finally, the Italian translation of Kierkegaard's *Journals* contains a noteworthy introduction, notes, glossary and various indexes by the editor, making this edition an excellent research tool and point of comparison with Catholic theology. The *Diario* is translated from the Danish and edited by Cornelio Fabro, C.P.S. (3 volumes, Brescia, Edizioni Morcelliana, 1948-51).

For other Kierkegaardian studies, the bibliographies in Lowrie, Bretall and Wahl provide the essential leads. Most helpful for the student is the separate bibliographical essay on Kierkegaard in the *Bibliographische Einführungen in das Studium der Philosophie*, under the general editorship of I. M. Bocheński, O. P. Fascicle four in this series is Régis Jolivet's *Kierkegaard* (Bern, A. Francke Ag. Verlag, 1948), a 33-page analytic and annotated bibliography. A description of Scandinavian research is furnished in Aage Henriksen's *Kierkegaard Studies in Scandinavia* (Copenhagen, Ejnar Munksgaard, 1951); see also, *Søren Kierkegaard, Bidrag til en Bibliografi*, edited by E. O. Nielsen, in co-operation with N. Thulstrup (Copenhagen, Ejnar Munksgaard, 1951). Surveys of current world-wide literature on Kierkegaard appear regularly in *Meddelelser fra Søren Kierkegaard Selskabet* (1948 ff.).

Bibliographical Supplement

The second Danish edition of Kierkegaard's *Samlede Vaerker* has been reissued (20 vols. Copenhagen, Gyldendal, 1963-64), with improved annotations by P. Rohde and a revised edition of J. Himmelstrup's terminological dictionary as vol. 20. N. Thulstrup has edited the correspondence and documents: *Breve og Aktstykker vedrørende Søren Kierkegaard* (2 vols. Copenhagen, Munksgaard, 1953-54).

The list given above of English translations of Kierkegaard's writings can now be extended with three more works:

21. *The Concept of Irony.* Translated by Lee M. Capel. New York, Harper and Row, 1965.

22. *Johannes Climacus or, De Omnibus Dubitandum Est.* Translated by T. H. Croxall. Stanford, Stanford University Press, 1958.

23. *On Authority and Revelation: The Book on Adler, or a Cycle of Ethico-Religious Essays.* Translated by Walter Lowrie. Princeton, Princeton University Press, 1955.

There are also two freshly translated selections made from the many prayers and meditations composed by Kierkegaard: *Meditations from Kierkegaard* (Philadelphia, Westminster Press, 1955), translated by T. H. Croxall, and *The Prayers of Kierkegaard* (Chicago, University of Chicago Press, 1956), translated by Perry D. LeFevre. A complete revision of the translation of Kierkegaard's *Philosophical Fragments* (number 7 above) has been made by Howard V. Hong (Princeton, Princeton University Press, 1962), who enhances the value of the work by also including a translation of the Introduction

and Commentary to the *Fragments* done by Niels Thulstrup.
Paperback editions have been issued of several books by
Kierkegaard. The Harper Torchbook series includes the books
listed above as numbers: 2, 6 (selections), 9, 10 (revised), and
20 (selections).* The Doubleday Anchor Books series includes
the books listed above as numbers: 1 (considerably revised),
3-and-16 (together). Number 15 is in the Oxford University
Press Galaxy series, while number 19 is a Beacon Press Paperback. There is also a revised edition of Lee M. Hollander's
Selections from the Writings of Kierkegaard in the Doubleday
Anchor series.

The 1955 centenary of Kierkegaard's death was marked by
two international collections of essays by leading scholars. *A
Kierkegaard Critique* (Chicago, A Gateway Edition) is
edited by Howard A. Johnson and Niels Thulstrup; *Studi
kierkegaardiani* (Brescia, Morcelliana, 1957) is edited by Cornelio Fabro, C.P.S. The collections illustrate the worldwide
appeal of Kierkegaard and the way in which many lines of
research intersect in the examination of his thought.

There are three recent books which give an informed general account of Kierkegaard the man and the thinker. Frithiof
Brandt's *Søren Kierkegaard, 1813-1855: His Life—His Works*
(Copenhagen, Det danske Selskab, 1963) reflects the emphasis
of modern Danish scholars upon the biographical and cultural
aspects. These same aspects are developed more at length in
Johannes Hohlenberg's *Søren Kierkegaard* (New York, Pantheon Books, 1954), which nevertheless avoids psychologizing
away the ideas. Anna Paulsen's *Søren Kierkegaard, Deuter
unserer Existenz* (Hamburg, Wittig Verlag, 1955) highlights
the dialectic of communication, presenting Kierkegaard in
the light of his threefold dialogue with his fiancée, the cultural
age, and the church. It is good to have Walter Lowrie's great

* Harper Torchbooks also contains the Steere translation of number 11 (entitled here *Purity of Heart*) and the Hong translation of number 14.

work, *Kierkegaard*, made available in a two-volume Harper Torchbook paperback edition.

The theological literature on Kierkegaard in English is notably strengthened by four books. In *Kierkegaard as Theologian* (New York, Sheed and Ward, 1963), Louis Dupré works out the main themes of sin and grace, faith and the following of Christ. The techniques of linguistic and conceptual analysis are employed by J. Heywood Thomas, *Subjectivity and Paradox* (New York, Macmillan, 1957), to explore the personal and objective sense in which Kierkegaard speaks about the being of God and the existence of Christ, in relation to the strivings of human existence. The anthropological dimension, along with the answer to the Kantian question of what may I hope for, are the central topics in George Price's *The Narrow Pass: A Study of Kierkegaard's Concept of Man* (New York, McGraw-Hill, 1963). The value of T. H. Croxall's *Kierkegaard Commentary* (New York, Harper and Row, 1956) lies in its sensitivity to the problem of esthetics and faith, as well as in its sharp concentration upon the major Kierkegaardian terms which attempt to elucidate this problem.

Further bibliographical details can be obtained by consulting the working list prepared by J. Himmelstrup: *Søren Kierkegaard. International Bibliografi* (Copenhagen, Nyt Nordisk Forlag, 1962).

Bibliographical Note (1983)

A thoroughly reliable and helpful fresh translation of Kierkegaard's works is now being published by Princeton University Press. Howard V. Hong is General Editor of *Kierkegaard's Writings*, which will consist of 25 volumes and a separate cumulative index. The entire project is scheduled for completion in 1988. Each volume directly translates Kierkegaard's text from the best Danish edition. It also provides a historical introduction, relevant materials from Kierkegaard's own journals and papers and from other contemporary sources, detailed editorial notes, and its own index. The following volumes have been published to date, as numbered in the series.

VI. *Fear and Trembling/Repetition* (1983), edited and translated by Howard V. Hong and Edna H. Hong.

VIII. *The Concept of Anxiety* (1980), edited and translated by Reidar Thomte, with Albert B. Anderson.

XIII. *The Corsair Affair* (1982), edited and translated by Howard V. Hong and Edna H. Hong.

XIV. *Two Ages* (1978), edited and translated by Howard V. Hong and Edna H. Hong.

XIX. *The Sickness Unto Death* (1980), edited and translated by Howard V. Hong and Edna H. Hong.

XXV. *Letters and Documents* (1978), edited and translated by Henrik Rosenmeier.

Much of Kierkegaard's vast behind-the-scenes writing is presented in the English translation made and edited by

Howard V. Hong and Edna H. Hong: *Søren Kierkegaard's Journals and Papers* (7 vols. Bloomington: Indiana University Press, 1967-1978). Volumes 1-4 arrange thematic materials from the twenty-two-volume Danish edition under alphabetically ordered topics. Volumes 5-6 give a chronological ordering to Kierkegaard's autobiographical papers and letters, while volume 7 is an index and composite collation of concepts and names. His skill at using stories to illuminate and motivate stands forth in Thomas C. Oden's *Parables of Kierkegaard* (Princeton: Princeton University Press, 1978), a selection of about ninety parables and a reference list of the others.

Under the general editorship of Robert L. Perkins, *International Kierkegaard Commentary* is being published by Mercer University Press. Each volume will contain historical, interpretive, and critical articles on the corresponding source volume in the Princeton edition of *Kierkegaard's Writings*. Thus the *Commentary* will provide scholarly and reflective guidance for studying each newly translated work of Kierkegaard.

An essential tool for using the Danish edition of Kierkegaard's *Collected Works* and for collating it with the English and other translations is Alastair McKinnon's *The Kierkegaard Indices* (4 vols. Leiden: Brill, 1970-1975, distributed in U.S.A. by Princeton University Press), a computer-generated series of reference books. Volume 1 makes a collation by page and line between the Danish text and (the older) English, French, and German translations. Volume 2 is a concordance between 586 basic words in the Danish edition and corresponding words in the three translations. Volume 3 is an *index verborum* to Kierkegaard's *Samlede Vaerker*. Volume 4 gives a rank list and an alphabetical list of Kierkegaard's terms, together with computer analyses of the frequency and distribution of recurring words. Another tool is Julia Watkin's *A Key to Kierkegaard's Abbreviations and*

Spelling/Nøgle Til Kierkegaards Forkortelser Ag Stavmade, edited by Alastair McKinnon (Montreal: Inter Editions, 1981).

Four introductory books furnish distinctive perspectives. Ronald Grimsley, *Kierkegaard: A Biographical Introduction* (New York: Scribner, 1973), brings out the intimate connections between Kierkegaard's life, mode of writing, and attitudes toward man and God. Gregor Malantschuk, *Kierkegaard's Thought*, translated by Howard V. Hong and Edna H. Hong (Princeton: Princeton University Press, 1971), traces the central dynamism in each of Kierkegaard's stages of existence, along with the corresponding orientation evoked in the careful reader. Josiah Thompson, *Kierkegaard* (New York: Knopf, 1973), probes critically into the moods, motivations, and crosscurrents underlying Kierkegaard's writings and life decisions. Alastair Hannay, *Kierkegaard* (Boston: Routledge and Kegan Paul, 1983), introduces us to the unified intellectual pattern of Kierkegaard's philosophy. A critical inspection is made of Kierkegaard's main problems, basic intellectual principles, and modes of argumentation whereby he organizes the wealth of his experience, thought, and imagination.

Henning Fenger, *Kierkegaard, The Myths and Their Origins: Studies in the Kierkegaardian Papers and Letters*, translated by George C. Schoolfield (New Haven: Yale University Press, 1980), issues a caveat against any uncritical reading of Kierkegaard's letters and autobiographical reports. Imagination, self-justification, and polemic color these accounts. In ongoing debate among Danish psychiatrists about Kierkegaard's personality structure, Ib Ostenfeld, *Søren Kierkegaard's Psychology*, edited by Alastair McKinnon (Waterloo, Ontario: Wilfrid Laurier University Press, 1978), argues (against Hjalmar Helweg) that Kierkegaard is not manic-depressive but is ultrasensitive to family and social stresses. The ways in which Kierkegaard contributes to the study of the self and human attitudes are specified by: Kristen Nordentoft, *Kierkegaard's Psychology*, translated by B. Kirmmse (Pittsburgh: Duquesne University Press, 1978); Vincent McCarthy, *The Phenomenology of Moods in Kierkegaard* (The Hague: Nijhoff, 1978); Adi Shmuëli, *Kierkegaard and Consciousness* (Princeton: Princeton University Press, 1971); and by several philosophers and psychiatrists in original essays, edited by Joseph H. Smith, *Kierkegaard's Truth: The Disclosure of the Self* (New Haven: Yale University Press, 1981).

Kierkegaard blends an analysis of moods with a religious conception of our capacity for communication and love. Underlying this hopeful synthesis are his views of temporality and being. Their contributions toward human maturation are explored respectively by Mark C. Taylor, *Kierkegaard's Pseudonymous Authorship: A Study of Time and the Self*, and by John W. Elrod, *Being and Existence in Kierkegaard's Pseudonymous Works* (both published by Princeton University Press, 1975). Taylor correlates the modalities of time with those of the human self, as it moves from possibilities to actualizations of freedom. Elrod examines the necessary relationship between Kierkegaard's spheres of existence and their underlying ontological structures, which relate the human quest ultimately to God. Kierkegaard refers to the existential stages of life as instruments in our education or gradual self-awareness, a theme whose synthesizing power is shown in Ronald J. Manheimer's *Kierkegaard as Educator* (Berkeley: University of California Press, 1977). Kierkegaard's art of using all his imaginative gifts and communicative skills in service to the continued enhancement of all spheres of human life is the central theme of Louis Mackey's *Kierkegaard: A Kind of Poet* (Philadelphia: University of Pennsylvania Press, 1971).

Kierkegaard's approach to human moods, attitudes, and life spheres is not only descriptively psychological and ontological but also normative. George Stack, *Kierkegaard's Existential Ethics* (University, Alabama: University of Alabama Press, 1977), explicates the ethical demands upon the self and its freedom arising from the analyses of anxiety and despair. Countering the view that Kierkegaard is concerned solely with the individual's moral life, John W. Elrod's *Kierkegaard and Christendom* (Princeton: Princeton University Press, 1981) probes the social dimensions of his ethical thought. This study of Kierkegaard's later ethical and religious writings (especially *Works of Love*) focuses on his critique of the individualistic state and the church establishment, leading to his call for social therapy and political transformations. For similar findings see David B. Fletcher, *Social and Political Perspectives in the Thought of Søren Kierkegaard* (Washington: University Press of America, 1982).

Valuable factual information on Kierkegaard's actual acquaintance with and attitudes toward, various types of Christian religious life is supplied in *Kierkegaard's View of Christianity*, edited by Niels and Marie Thulstrup (Copenhagen: Reitzel, 1978), a collection of eleven specialized essays. There are two concise general accounts of his own religious and theological approach: Gregor Malantschuk, *Kierkegaard's Way to the Truth* (Minneapolis: Augsburg, 1968), and Robert L. Perkins, *Søren Kierkegaard* (Richmond, Va.: John Knox Press, 1969). For Kierkegaard's acquaintance with the sectarian style of radical pietism and the Brethren, consult Vernard Eller, *Kierkegaard and Radical Discipleship* (Princeton: Princeton University Press, 1968), describing the anti-establishment religious alternative. The several religiously pertinent meanings of "reason" are distinguished by F. Russell Sullivan, *Faith and Reason in Kierkegaard* (Washington: University Press of America, 1978).

Niels Thulstrup, *Kierkegaard's Relation to Hegel*, translated by G. L. Stengren (Princeton: Princeton University Press, 1980), describes Kierkegaard's actual study of Hegel, Danish Hegelianism, and the latter's theological uses of Hegel. A thorough comparative study of similarities and differences between the Hegelian and Kierkegaardian conceptions of the natural-esthetic, ethical, and religious realizations of the human spirit is made by Mark C. Taylor, *Journeys to Selfhood: Hegel and Kierkegaard* (Berkeley and Los Angeles: University of California Press, 1980). Concerning the critical opposition between Hegel and Kierkegaard on prospects for religion and philosophy, see Stephen Crites, *In the Twilight of Christendom: Hegel vs. Kierkegaard on Faith and History* (Missoula, Montana: Scholars Press, 1972). The Marxian component in this comparison is added by Robert Heiss, *Hegel, Kierkegaard, Marx* (New York: Dell, 1975).

Anthologies of recent articles include: *Kierkegaard: A Collection of Critical Essays*, edited by Josiah Thompson (New York: Doubleday Anchor, 1972), with bibliographical supplement: *Essays on Kierkegaard*, edited by Jerry H. Gill (Minneapolis: Burgess, 1969); *Kierkegaard's Presence in Contemporary American Life*, edited by Lewis A. Lawson (Metuchen, N. J.: Scarecrow Press, 1970); and *Materialien zur Philosophie Søren Kierkegaards*, edited by M. Theunissen and W. Greves (Frankfurt: Suhrkamp, 1979).

Three bibliographical aids are: F. H. Lapointe, *Søren Kierkegaard and His Critics: An International Bibliography of Criticism* (Westport, Conn.: Greenwood Press, 1980); Aage Jørgensen, *Søren Kierkegaard-litteratur 1961-1970* (Aarhus: Akademisk Boghandel, 1971); and for current publications, *The Philosopher's Index*, s. v. "Kierkegaard."

There are two excellently stocked American centers for doing Kierkegaard research. They are the Kierkegaard Library of St. Olaf College, Northfield, Minnesota (Howard V. Hong, Director); and the Kierkegaard-Malantschuk Library Collection of McGill University, Montreal, Canada (Alastair McKinnon, Director). They contain the various editions of Kierkegaard's publications and collected works, translations of his writings into various languages, international studies on Kierkegaard, and pertinent writings by Kierkegaard's contemporaries and background sources in Denmark and other countries.

Notes

In these Notes, the secondary works mentioned in the Bibliographical Note are cited according to the author's name alone. In every case, "Lowrie" refers to Walter Lowrie's larger book, *Kierkegaard*. Haecker's two books and Geismar's two books are cited by title as well as author. For all other books cited in these Notes, full bibliographical information is given the first time the book is cited. The translations of Kierkegaard's own works are cited as indicated in the Bibliographical Note.

Notes to Chapter One. Kierkegaard the Man

1. *Point of View*, 76-92.
2. Consult the chapter on "the great earthquake," in Lowrie, 68-76.
3. See the long note in the *Journals* on "My relation to 'her'": *Journals*, entry 367 (pp. 91-96).
4. An interesting and full account of the *Corsair* incident is given by Johannes Hohlenberg, *Søren Kierkegaard*, translated into German by Maria Bachmann-Isler (Basel, Benno Schwabe and Company, 1949), 202-37.
5. These documents are collected in *Attack*. For the events leading up to this outburst, cf. Lowrie, 487-588, and Geismar, *Søren Kierkegaard*, 555-639.
6. Recorded by Kierkegaard's friend, Emil Boesen, and transcribed in *Journals*, p. 551.
7. R. Friedmann, *Kierkegaard* (London, Direction Series, 1949), 59. For other refutations in the same vein, cf. T. M. Knox, in *Giornale di metafisica*, I (1946), 224, and T. D. Weldon, in *Mind*, N. S., LVIII (1949), 111.
8. *Journals*, entry 142 (p. 48, note); cf. entry 1294 (pp. 490-92). The remainder of the present chapter gives a close paraphrase of the entries for the years 1834-36.
9. *Ibid.*, entries 4, 16, 335, 784 (pp. 1-2, 7, 86, 249). At the outset of his second *Meditation*, Descartes announced that he was seek-

ing for the Archimedean point of a single indubitable truth; cf. *Meditations concerning First Philosophy*, translated by Laurence J. Lafleur (New York, Liberal Arts Press, 1951), 21. Descartes' point of rest was a speculative truth, whereas Kierkegaard's was a practical one.

10. For a concise introduction to the Romantic thinkers, see Hinrich Knittermeyer, *Schelling und die romantische Schule* (Munich, Ernst Reinhardt, 1929).

11. Hirsch, 5-60, 566-602; cf. Geismar, *Søren Kierkegaard*, 75-88.

12. *Journals*, entries 20, 212, 289 (pp. 12-14, 60-61, 75). Compare Fichte's exalted mood, in the closing pages of *The Vocation of Man*, translated by William Smith (LaSalle, Illinois, Open Court Publishing Company, 1946), 160-76.

13. In *Søren Kierkegaard's Pilgrimage to Jutland*, translated by T. H. Croxall (Copenhagen, Danish Tourist Association, 1948), Arthur Dahl describes traveling conditions in the Denmark of Kierkegaard's day and transcribes the sections from his *Journals* dealing with the trip to Jutland. Kierkegaard agreed with the Romantic philosopher, Novalis, that philosophy is nostalgia or a yearning to be at home, but he came to interpret the feeling of nostalgia in terms of the wayfarer status of our present life and our longing to return to our fatherland, with God.

14. *Journals*, entry 22 (p. 15); cf. *Either/Or*, II, 294. Truth always has this practical and individual connotation for Kierkegaard. For the comparison with Pascal, cf. Denzil Patrick, *Pascal and Kierkegaard* (2 vols. London and Redhill, Lutterworth Press, 1947).

15. *Journals*, entry 88 (p. 35). For an example of how crisis theologians of our own day have transmuted sacred history and dogma, this time in the name of the creative mythology of existential consciousness, consult the third section of Charles Kean's *The Meaning of Existence* (New York, Harper, 1947). Kierkegaard certainly set an example for this later trend, with his "psychological" exegesis of original sin, in connection with the nature of dread. But still, he did see the limitations of his approach and was ready to defend the independence of theology and the historical act of faith.

16. *Journals*, entry 96 (pp. 38-39). This conviction became a cornerstone in Kierkegaard's defense of human freedom against the determinism of the Hegelian dialectic.

17. *Ibid.*, entry 88 (p. 35). Kierkegaard tried to restore the word to its proper function as an appropriate expression and tool of the

human person's search after the meaning and order of existence. This aspect of his thought inspired the work of Ferdinand Ebner: *Das Wort und die geistigen Realitäten* (Innsbruck, Brenner-Verlag, 1921).

Notes to Chapter Two. The Spheres of Existence and the Romantic Outlook

1. The main esthetic books are: *Either/Or, Repetition, Trembling, Stages* and *Dread*.
2. *Journals*, entry 140 (p. 47). On Nietzsche's deliberately cultivated ambiguity, see H. A. Reyburn, *Nietzsche, The Story of a Human Philosopher* (London, Macmillan, 1948), chapter 23, "The Man of the Masks," 356-69.
3. *Postscript*, 225-66; *Point of View*, 13-14, 39-42. Judicious discussion of this question will be found in Geismar, *Søren Kierkegaard*, 133-40, and Ruttenbeck, 107-30.
4. In *Either/Or*, I, 7-8, this is recognized as a typically esthetic and Romantic trait. Curiously enough, one of Kierkegaard's pseudonyms adopted the same motto as did Descartes: *Bene vixit qui bene latuit* (*Stages*, 34).
5. *Postscript*, 552.
6. *Point of View*, 39-41. John Keats once wrote to his friend, John Hamilton Reynolds, that "axioms in philosophy are not axioms until they are proved upon our pulses. We read fine things, but never feel them to the full until we have gone the same steps as the Author." *The Letters of John Keats*, edited by M. B. Forman (2 vols., Oxford, Oxford University Press, 1931), Letter 61, I, 154. Kierkegaard's pseudonyms make sure that we do follow in his footsteps.
7. Etienne Gilson's Aquinas Lecture on *History of Philosophy and Philosophical Education* (Milwaukee, Marquette University Press, 1948), stresses the indispensable need of making a personal appropriation of philosophical wisdom and achieving the habit of wisdom.
8. *Point of View*, 24-31.
9. For an exposition of this doctrine, cf. Swenson, 159-77; Harry Broudy, "Kierkegaard's Levels of Existence," *Philosophy and Phenomenological Research*, I (1941), 294-312.
10. Compare *Journals*, entry 121 (p. 44), with *Postscript*, 242-43, 400-04. It is the contention of Mesnard, 462-63, that, to the end of his life, Kierkegaard governed his personal relationship to

Christianity under the sign of humor. This opinion confuses the attitude of humor with that of religious humility, which never claims to have already realized Christian principles but only to be engaged in trying to put them into practice. The distance between religious principle and practice leaves room for constant "becoming" or improvement, but this is not the same as the uncommitted distance between the humorous mind and Christian truths.

11. See the annotations of Walter Lowrie to his translation of *Stages*, 335-36, note 132.

12. *Point of View*, 18; *Journals*, entry 367 (p. 95).

13. *Postscript*, 261.

14. *Journals*, entry 49 (p. 26). For Kierkegaard's indebtedness to, and criticism of, the Romantics, cf. G. Niedermeyer, *Søren Kierkegaard und die Romantik* (Leipzig, Quelle und Meyer Verlag, 1909). Kierkegaard's theory of art is discussed by G. Vecchi, "Il problema dell'arte nell'esistenzialismo di Kierkegaard," *Rivista di filosofia neoscolastica*, XXXVIII (1946), 61-69, but with an overstatement of the conflict between rationalism and irrationalism in Kierkegaard. F. de W. Bolman, Jr., "Kierkegaard in Limbo," *Journal of Philosophy*, XLI (1944), 711-21, is enthusiastic about Kierkegaard's esthetic insights and psychological views, but wants to detach them from the general framework of his authorship.

15. *Either/Or*, I, 70-74. Cf. E. Susini, *Franz von Baader et le romantisme mystique*, vols. II and III: *La philosophie de Franz von Baader* (Paris, J. Vrin, 1942), for the "mystical" notions of the Romantics. Kierkegaard got many of his views on the Romantic outlook on nature and mysticism from Baader, but eventually was repelled by Baader's fantastic, pantheistic speculations on God and nature. It was Kierkegaard's misfortune to find an acceptable philosophy of nature neither in the empiricists nor in the Hegelians nor in the Romantics. This influenced his own exclusive concentration upon problems of human nature.

16. *Journals*, entries 488, 753 (pp. 133, 238-39); *Either/Or*, II, 150-63; *Stages*, 159.

17. *Either/Or*, II, 138-42. The entire edifying discourse, *Purify Your Hearts!*, expresses the inability of a purely esthetic standpoint to bring unity and purpose to the human personality: only the undivided will of the religiously dedicated man can ultimately achieve integration of ideals and decisions. In terms of an atheistic existentialism, Albert Camus, *Le mythe de Sisyphe* (eighteenth edition, Paris, Gallimard, 1943), 97-106, regards the

Don Juan story as a symbol of man's tragically absurd situation in a Godless universe.

18. *Either/Or*, I, 169-71; *Journals*, entries 107-09 (pp. 41-42).

19. *Ibid.*, entry 115 (p. 43). Here, Faust is also compared with Kierkegaard's beloved Socrates, who unshackled himself from the weight of Greek society, although (unlike Faust) he did not break with God.

20. The constructive nature of ethico-religious reflection is portrayed concretely in *Edifying Discourses*, I, 100-03; III, 39-40; IV, 29-40 (the dialectic between the first or immediate, esthetic self and the inner or deeper, ethico-religious self).

21. *Trembling*, 148-52, 166-72; *Stages*, 219; *Journals*, entries 242, 508-09 (pp. 66, 137; Kierkegaard himself as a daimonic "police spy" in the service of divine justice, one of "God's spies," after the manner of Shakespeare's King Lear). Walter Rehm, *Kierkegaard und der Verführer* (Munich, Hermann Rinn, 1949), is so impressed with Kierkegaard's insight into, and preoccupation with, the daimonic attitude, that he regards Kierkegaard himself as a daimonic man, who never overcomes esthetic categories or reaches religious faith. Like Mesnard (see above, note 10), Rehm fails to see that a perceptive understanding of esthetic attitudes and a constant inner struggle to integrate them are compatible with a fundamental religious dedication of oneself to God.

22. *Journals*, entry 88 (p. 33); *Either/Or*, II, 177-78.

23. *Journals*, entry 26 (p. 21); on esthetic despair, cf. *Either/Or*, II, 162-77. The anatomy of despair is fully examined in the later treatise, *Sickness*. For an analysis of Kierkegaard's views on despair, consult B. Meerpohl, *Die Verzweiflung als metaphysisches Phänomen in der Philosophie Søren Kierkegaards* (Würzburg, Becker, 1934).

24. *Repetition*, 36-71, 94-95.

25. On the relation between Kierkegaard's notion of irony and his estimate of Romanticism, cf. Wahl, 58-69; Geismar, *Søren Kierkegaard*, 87-88; Mesnard, 117-79 (on his use of Romantic sources).

Notes to Chapter Three. The Ethical View and Its Limits

1. A brief exposition of this work is given in Swenson, 182-85. On the ethical sphere of existence as such, see Jolivet, 134-42; Paul L. Holmer, "Kierkegaard and Ethical Theory," *Ethics*, LXIII (1953), 157-70.

2. Cf. the programmatic statement by Abraham Edel, "Naturalism and Ethical Theory," *Naturalism and the Human Spirit*, edited by Y. H. Krikorian (New York, Columbia University Press, 1944), 65-95. A critique of the naturalistic conception of ethics is made by Eliseo Vivas, *The Moral Life and the Ethical Life* (Chicago, University of Chicago Press, 1950), with frequent reference to Kierkegaard.

3. *Journals*, entries 562, 617-19, 1036, 1054 (pp. 151, 181-86, 363, 373-74).

4. *Either/Or*, II, 173, 192.

5. Yet Kierkegaard agrees with the Romantic mind (*ibid.*, II, 87-88), that the individual human person must be respected and that we should not serve universal standards in such a way that we deplete ourselves or violate the proper reserve of individual selves. Kierkegaard's observations about esthetic concealment and ethical openness may be compared with the remarks of Bergson and Scheler on closed and open types of personality, as well as with Gabriel Marcel's contrast between the unavailable and the available self.

6. *Either/Or*, II, 39-52.

7. For Kant's moral rationalization of dogma and sacred history, cf. *Religion Within the Limits of Reason Alone*, translated by T. M. Greene and H. H. Hudson (Chicago, Open Court, 1934), especially 129-38.

8. What Kierkegaard establishes about faithfulness in married life (in part two of *Either/Or*) and about loyalty to the dead (in *Works of Love*) may be compared with the similar observations in the plays and journals of Gabriel Marcel.

9. *Either/Or*, II, 116.

10. In *Stages*, 157-63, Kierkegaard advances some deliberately flimsy proofs of the ethician's claim and, in describing the way in which women make the transition from the esthetic to the moral sphere, he has satirical recourse to a vague and pretty myth.

11. *Either/Or*, II, 179. This passage is left almost bare of any explanation, for instance, when it is quoted by Denzil Patrick, *Pascal and Kierkegaard*, II, 188.

12. Another reason is that ethical deliverance comes from deliberately choosing despair, rather than remaining its melancholy victim.

13. For Sartre, *Existentialism*, translated by Bernard Frechtman (New York, Philosophical Library, 1947), 19-25, the chooser is responsible for all men, since his choice constitutes "his world,"

of which the other individuals are elements. This is a theory of moral solipsism, precisely because of the way in which one's choice determines other agents.

14. *Either/Or*, II, 181-82, 210. The notion of a "created creation" or free origination of acts on the part of an intelligent, secondary cause is developed in *Edifying Discourses*, I, 67. Cf. Louis Lavelle's masterly analysis of created freedom and participation, in *De l'Acte* (Paris, Aubier, 1946), 179-99.

15. A representative statement of his main position is given in Brunschvicg's Sorbonne lectures for 1921-22: *La philosophie de l'esprit* (Paris, Presses Universitaires, 1949).

16. *Stages*, 107.

17. H. J. Paton, *The Categorical Imperative: A Study in Kant's Moral Philosophy* (Chicago, University of Chicago Press, 1948), has made a strong case for revising the ordinary view that Kant's ethical doctrine is vitiated by an excessive formalism. Kierkegaard's own emphasis upon the material or experiential aspects of ethical problems gave impetus to the approach of Max Scheler and other phenomenologists.

18. *Dread*, 15-18; cf. *Journals*, entry 7 (p. 3).

19. *Either/Or*, II, 253-56, 274-75; *Stages*, 165-77. In the latter text, Judge William analyzes four main varieties of exceptions: the intellectual temperament, the celibate under vow, the melancholy person, and what he terms the justified exception (involving love and marriage).

20. *Repetition*, 110-13, 121-34; *Edifying Discourses*, II, 7-26. On the significance of Job and Abraham for Kierkegaard, cf. Thust, 82-126.

21. *Trembling*, 79-187.

22. *Ibid.*, 105. St. Thomas emphasizes that God Himself is the *mensura suprema et excedens* of all human acts and their moral worth (*Summa Theologiae*, II-II, 17, 1, c.).

23. Jacques Maritain, *Existence and the Existent*, translated by Lewis Galantiere and Gerald B. Phelan (New York, Pantheon Books, 1948), 56-59, criticizes Kierkegaard for separating universal law and individual conscience. Kierkegaard's actual intent is not to oppose these two, but to make sure that both of them are related to God's wisdom and justice. He rejects any *theory* of universal law that makes it a wholly autonomous rule or a substitute for the creator-creature relationship. Maritain's own remarks on the need to interiorize the natural law and appropriate it as the principle of one's individual conduct come close to the solution at which Kierkegaard ultimately aimed.

Notes to Chapter Four. The Attack upon Hegelianism

1. An excellent sketch of the intellectual world into which Kierkegaard entered is given by Ruttenbeck, 42-100.
2. For the theological situation in Denmark during Kierkegaard's student days, cf. the initial chapter of Torsten Bohlin, *Kierkegaards dogmatische Anschauung* (Gütersloh, Bertelsmann, 1927).
3. *Journals*, entries 78, 125 (pp. 30, 45). A similar criticism of Schleiermacher was made by the later German theologians, Ritschl and Otto; cf. Robert F. Davidson, *Rudolf Otto's Interpretation of Religion* (Princeton, Princeton University Press, 1947), 36.
4. The qualification "Hegelian" should be attached to each of these terms. Wahl, 174-75, regards Kierkegaard's attack upon Hegel as being formally extended to a repudiation of all philosophy. Kierkegaard certainly did not examine all the historical types of philosophy and declare them to be invalid. But his historical situation prevented him from recognizing how philosophy can be developed in non-Hegelian ways. For a discussion of non-idealistic ways of systematic thinking, see Paul Weiss, *"Existenz* and Hegel," *Philosophy and Phenomenological Research*, VIII (1947-48), 206-16.
5. *Journals*, entries 88-96 (pp. 32-39). Hirsch, 32-39, calls attention to the significance of these fragments. Kierkegaard's progress in Hegelian studies is minutely charted by Hirsch, 451-827.
6. *Prolegomena to Any Future Metaphysics*, translated by Paul Carus (Chicago, Open Court Publishing Company, 1902), 150, note 1.
7. Hirsch, 556-63, also mentions two minor anti-Hegelian projects of 1838: a comedy about the types of men bred in the Hegelian atmosphere, and a satirical essay on "the higher lunacy" (see *Fragments*, 2, 38, note 3).
8. *Dread*, 19, note. On Schelling's last period, see Horst Fuhrmans, *Schellings letzte Philosophie* (Berlin, Junker and Dunnhaupt, 1940). Kierkegaard's debt to Schelling, as well as their joint defense of the rights of reason within the objective, essential sphere, is brought out by Maximilian Beck, "Existentialism, Rationalism, and Christian Faith," *The Journal of Religion*, XXVI (1946), 283-95.
9. *Dread*, 53, note (against Schelling); *Postscript*, 111 (against Schelling and I. H. Fichte).

10. See especially, *Logische Untersuchungen* (third edition, 2 vols., Leipzig, S. Hirzel, 1870), I, 36-129. American readers will find a translation of Trendelenburg's *Die logische Frage in Hegels System* in our earliest philosophical journal: "The Logical Question in Hegel's System," translated by Thomas Davidson, *Journal of Speculative Philosophy*, V (1871), 349-59; VI (1872), 82-93, 163-75, 350-61. Kierkegaard's observations (*Stages*, 106) on the relation between Hegel's two books, the *Phenomenology of Spirit* and the *Science of Logic*, show his familiarity with the argument of Trendelenburg and Feuerbach that Hegel could not have started his *Logic* with the concept of being, had he not already presupposed the sensuous intuition studied in the *Phenomenology*. This argument told against the absolutist claim to make a completely presuppositionless beginning in thought. For Feuerbach's position, cf. *Sämmtliche Werke* (10 vols., Leipzig, Otto Wigand, 1846-66), II, 204 ff., 211 ff., 312 ff.

11. A Soviet account of Lenin's use of Trendelenburg to interpret Aristotle and to supplement the usual formal logic is presented by P. S. Popov, "The Logic of Aristotle and Formal Logic," *Philosophy and Phenomenological Research*, VIII (1947-48), 1-22.

12. Karl Löwith has studied the anti-Hegelianism of Marx and Kierkegaard, in *Von Hegel bis Nietzsche* (Zurich, Europaverlag, 1941), 185-233. These two thinkers had no direct contact, but both studied Feuerbach's criticism of Hegel and both completed their academic theses against Hegel in the same year (1841).

13. Wahl, 136-55, underlines Kierkegaard's debt to Hegel.

14. *Either/Or*, II, 144-48. The very title of this work challenges Hegel's assertion that "either/or" is merely the illusory password of finite understanding and must give way before the "both/and" of infinite, dialectical reason, which does not recognize any unyielding, permanent oppositions. Cf. *The Logic of Hegel*, translated by William Wallace (second edition, Oxford, Clarendon Press, 1892), section 65, p. 128. When Kierkegaard designates his standpoint that of "faith" and "finite understanding," he is repudiating Hegel's claim that these must be sublated into infinite, dialectical reason. Kierkegaard is "antirational," as far as this claim is concerned.

15. John Wild, "Kierkegaard and Classical Philosophy," *The Philosophical Review*, XLIX (1940), 536-51, notes that Kierkegaard's return to the realistic, Aristotelian theory of change also entails

a criticism of the Cartesian-Lockean view that the mind is concerned primarily with the idea of change, rather than with changing things.

16. *Philosophy of Right*, translated by T. M. Knox (London, Oxford University Press, 1942), sections 129-41 (pp. 86-104; especially pp. 92-93).

17. *Trembling*, 104-05.

18. *Dread*, 9-13. On the Hegel-Kierkegaard relationship, cf. Geismar, *Søren Kierkegaard*, 251-330, and Wahl, 86-171.

19. *Postscript*, 34, note.

20. Kierkegaard's exact words are as follows: "Altsaa: *a) et logisk System kan der gives; b) men der kan ikke gives noget Tilvaerelsens System.*" *Afsluttende Uvidenskabelig Efterskrift (Samlede Vaerker*, 1901-06 edition, VII, 88). The English translation reads: "(A), a logical system is possible; (B), an existential system is impossible." *Postscript*, 99. In his pamphlet, *Johann Georg Hamann, An Existentialist* (Princeton, Princeton Theological Seminary, 1950), 8, Walter Lowrie points out that Kierkegaard uses the word *Tilvaerelse* here, instead of the word *Eksistens*. Lowrie then maintains: (1) that Kierkegaard seldom uses the word *Eksistens*, and never uses it with special significance; (2) that by keeping a rigid distinction between *Tilvaerelse* (German, *Dasein*) and *Eksistens* (German, *Existenz*), Kierkegaard's responsibility for existentialism can be lessened. But (1) as far as the *Postscript* is concerned, *Eksistens* and its variants are used frequently and with crucial meaning for philosophical discussion. The table of contents for Book Two of the *Postscript* stresses *den subjektive existerende Taenker* (the subjective existing thinker). In the texts under consideration (compare Danish edition, VII, 99-102, with English edition, 110-12), there are numerous references to *Eksistens* and *den existerende Subjektivitet*. These references are multiplied precisely at this point in the work, so that Kierkegaard can establish an equation between *Tilvaerelse, Eksistens* and *Virkelighed* (German, *Wirklichkeit*). This is the masterstroke of his entire critique of Hegel, since the latter assigned an inferior role to contingent *Existenz*. It was subordinated dialectically to *Dasein* and *Wirklichkeit*, in which there is explicit recognition of the law of necessity and the identification of subjective and objective factors. Kierkegaard's point is that the existing individual never becomes a necessary being and never discovers a dialectical identity between himself, the things known and the absolute spirit. For the

individual man, there is no higher sort of *Dasein* and *Wirk-lichkeit* than that of contingent *Existenz*. It is in Kierkegaard's interests to maintain a strict equivalence between these terms, as far as they apply to man. (2) Although Kierkegaard would not subscribe to existential-ism or any other "ism," there still remains the question of the quality and extent of his influence upon the existentialist philosophers. This cannot be settled, how-ever, by means of the distinction between the terms *Tilvaerelse* and *Eksistens*. Unlike Kierkegaard, the existentialists seek to stress the difference between *Dasein* and *Existenz*, but they do so in various ways. For Jaspers, *Existenz* is more important than *Dasein*, whereas Heidegger centers his investigations on the modes of *Dasein*. From this it cannot be concluded that Heideg-ger has a closer affinity for Kierkegaard than does Jaspers, but only that all such comparisons must respect the great difference in historical situation between Kierkegaard and the present-day existentialists. Lowrie's pamphlet brings out the close resemblances between Kierkegaard and Hamann, "the Magus of the North."

21. The conventional charge of irrationalism is preferred against Kierkegaard, for instance, by G. de Ruggiero, *Existentialism* (New York, Social Sciences Publishers, 1948), 43-44, and by H. Kuhn, "Existentialism and Metaphysics," *The Review of Meta-physics*, I (1947), 37-38. Kuhn thinks that Kierkegaard went far-ther than Kant by denying even the intrinsic rationality of reality, thus confronting man with the abyss of the nought. This is read-ing backwards into Kierkegaard some existentialist theses and for-getting about Kierkegaard's distinctive historical position. Kierke-gaard only denied that reality can be "thought," in the Hegelian sense of being completely comprehended by philosophical reason and ultimately identified with a phase in the development of the absolute spirit. The distance separating Kierkegaard from strict irrationalism can be measured by these three considerations: (a) he admitted the rights of reason in the nonexistential fields of the empirical sciences and logic; (b) he allowed to man some moral and religious understanding of the order of existence and subjectivity, a region which is intelligible in its own nature; (c) he championed the omniscience of God and the correlative intelligibility of all aspects of being (which are known compre-hensively or "systematically" by God and which will be known by us in a systematic way, when we pass from time to eternity). But he protested against the effort of absolute idealism to amalga-mate points *a* and *c*, on the supposition that a human mind can

eventually discover its identity with the absolute mind and hence comprehend reality with a divine breadth of vision. Kierkegaard's own weakness centers around point *b*, above. Because of his total preoccupation with the idealistic formulation of the problem of knowledge, he overlooked the alternative of a thoroughly finite and realistic way of grasping the order of existence through the *speculative* judgment of existence. To this extent, Kierkegaard was an occasion for later irrationalist currents of thought. He wanted to save as many of the universal human characteristics as possible, including the domain of the understanding (*Journals*, entries 364, 366; p. 91), but he did not have the realistic philosophical equipment to carry out this project in the speculative order. He was concerned religiously, lest the Christian faith be subsumed as an inferior stage within the development of Hegelian reason; cf. Cornelio Fabro, C. P. S., "Foi et raison dans l'oeuvre de Kierkegaard," *Revue des Sciences Philosophiques et Théologiques*, XXXII (1948), 169-206.

22. *Postscript*, 292. Etienne Gilson, *Being and Some Philosophers* (second edition, Toronto, Pontifical Institute of Mediaeval Studies, 1952), 142-53, gives the best philosophical account of Kierkegaard's relationship with Hegel, comparing it to St. Bernard's with Abelard, and to Pascal's with Descartes. It is somewhat misleading, however, to formulate the major contrast between Kierkegaard and Hegel as that between subjective existence and objective, abstract knowledge. Kierkegaard directed his fire against "pure thought," rather than against abstract thinking and objective knowledge as such. He was opposed to philosophical abstraction only when it claimed to give an exhaustive, systematic account of the real. In the latter case, he explicitly observed that he was rejecting "abstract thought" precisely as the equivalent of Hegel's "pure thought" or "pure being." Cf. *Postscript*, 270; the Danish text brings out the Hegelian reference in an unmistakable way: "i Abstraktionens Sprog, i den rene Taenken og den rene Vaeren." *Afsluttende Uvidenskabelig Efterskrift* (*Samlede Vaerker, ed. cit.*, VII, 261). Only a general disregard for these distinctions can account for the remark by Marjorie Grene, *Dreadful Freedom, A Critique of Existentialism* (Chicago, University of Chicago Press, 1948), 22, text and note 14, that Kierkegaard opposed and rejected: abstraction, logic and all consistency, generality, objectivity and the law of contradiction.

23. *Postscript*, 279. For Hegel's description of *the* philosophical System, based on pure thought, cf. *The Logic of Hegel*, sections 14-15 (pp. 23-25); *Phenomenology of Mind*, translated by John Bail-

lie (second, revised edition, New York, Macmillan, 1931), 85-88, 797-98, 805.

24. *Postscript*, 101-06. See *The Logic of Hegel*, sections 12, 86 (pp. 19-22, 158-59). Commentators are sometimes puzzled by the fact that in certain passages Kierkegaard rejects the notion of beginning with the immediate, whereas elsewhere he defends making a beginning with the immediate; cf. Bretall, 197, note. In the former context, Kierkegaard has in view the Hegelian doctrine on a dialectical immediacy, whereas in the latter context he regards existing things themselves as the immediate beginning of our thinking. See the texts cited in note 25.

25. *Postscript*, 103, 219, 517.

26. These standpoints are constantly interchanged in the *Phenomenology of Spirit*, especially in the crucial, final sections on religion and absolute knowledge. For a criticism of Hegel's procedure, consult Theodor Haering, *Hegel: Sein Wollen und sein Werk* (2 vols., Berlin and Leipzig, Teubner, 1929-38), II, 513-17. Kierkegaard repudiates this idealistic exploitation of the principle of identity and appeals once more to the realistic, Aristotelian principle of contradiction: man is *not* the same as God or the same as the things he knows (*Postscript*, 295, 377).

27. *Ibid.*, 108, 195, 296.

28. *Ibid.*, 99-101, 271-74. As one investigator has phrased it, the most concise formula for stating the opposition between Kierkegaard and Hegel is: motion as an act of historical freedom versus dialectical mediation or transition as an expression of logical necessity (and of freedom, only as being one with this necessity). Cf. J. Sperna Weiland, *Philosophy of Existence and Christianity* (Assen, Van Gorcum, 1951), 40, note 50.

29. *Fragments*, 60-62. Compare *The Logic of Hegel*, sections 142-47 (pp. 257-67).

30. *Postscript*, 119-47. From a purely cultural and even atheistic position, Friedrich Nietzsche warned against the debilitating, dehumanizing effects of the excessive cultivation of the "historical viewpoint" on issues that require personal decision and effort (*The Use and Abuse of History*, translated by Adrian Collins [New York, Liberal Arts Press, 1949], 36-61). Long ago, Francis Bacon dryly remarked that, in the theater of man's life here below, only God and the angels can remain onlookers; cf. *The Advancement of Learning*, Book II, in *The Philosophical Works of Francis Bacon*, edited by John M. Robertson (London, George Routledge, 1905), 135.

31. *Postscript*, 138-40.

Notes to Chapter Five. The Meaning of Existence

1. *Postscript*, 169-224. In reading the *Fragments* and the *Postscript*, it must be borne in mind that Kierkegaard issued them under the pseudonymous authorship of "Johannes Climacus." On most matters pertaining to the structure of existence and the refutation of Hegel, Johannes accurately represents the standpoint of Kierkegaard himself. But when Johannes deals with the nature of religious faith and Christianity, he writes from a non-Christian viewpoint and sometimes fails to express Kierkegaard's own ultimate convictions. That Johannes gives an accurate report on Kierkegaard's attitude toward objective truth and existential truth can be ascertained from *Edifying Discourses*, III, 71-72.
2. This is Hegel's argument in the early sections of the *Phenomenology of Mind*, 149-78, on sense certainty and perception of things.
3. Sartre argues that, because contingent facts of existence cannot be deduced from any essential principles, the realm of being-in-itself has no intelligible nature; cf. James Collins, *The Existentialists: A Critical Study* (Chicago, Henry Regnery, 1952), 55.
4. In *Søren Kierkegaard*, 27, Theodor Haecker notes that Kierkegaard is interested primarily in the person-to-person relation, rather than in the thing-to-thing relation of scientific investigation. Nevertheless, Swenson, 237-38, also observes that Kierkegaard never shows any scorn for the objective validity of the sciences, but only challenges the properly philosophical position that the report of scientific objectivity is the supreme one, even in existential affairs.
5. *Postscript*, 173. On the relation between existence and truth, see Wahl, 258-88. Although Wahl (275, note 1) regards only the historical sciences as approximative, Kierkegaard himself extends this note of approximation even to the logico-mathematical sciences, in so far as their systematic inclusiveness does not embrace existential realities. On the neglected human factor behind the objective procedures of mathematical physics, cf. Vincent E. Smith, "Toward a Philosophy of Physical Instruments," *The Thomist*, X (1947), 207-33.
6. This is in direct contradiction of Hegel's prescription that philosophy should beware of being edifying (*Phenomenology of Mind*, 74). On ethico-religious truth as subjectivity, see Thomte, 110-20.
7. *Postscript*, 175-82. These characteristics imply that a different sort of approximation-process is encountered in the sphere of ex-

istential truth than the approximation proper to objective, scientific truth. The latter is approximative, in the sense that it never attains to the existing subject and his practical tasks. Ethico-religious truth is approximative, in the sense of being concerned with the finite, existing individual and his endless work of approaching toward the eternal perfection of God. Not all that is said about existential truth, as a human condition, applies to God's eternal truth. God does not need to appropriate truth or strive toward eternal perfection, in an unending temporal effort. Kierkegaard remarks that, at its maximum, the inwardness and subjectivity of truth coincide with a perfect objectivity or fullness of being; cf. *Journals*, entries 1021, 1376 (pp. 355, 533-34). As applied to God, this means that He knows and loves His own eternal being in a perfect way, so that there is no real distinction between His selfhood and His interior possession of selfhood in knowledge and love. Applied analogically to the man of faith, it signifies that the virtue of faith inclines him to worship God in spirit and truth, in conformity with the spiritual nature and infinite majesty of God Himself.

8. *Postscript*, 181.
9. *Ibid.*, 314.
10. *Fragments*, 29-38.
11. Kierkegaard was familiar with Lessing's *Wolfenbüttel Fragments* (1778) and with Jacobi's *Letters to Moses Mendelssohn Concerning the Doctrine of Spinoza* (1785).
12. In the *Journals*, entry 1027 (pp. 357-58; cf. *Postscript*, 297-98), Kierkegaard contrasts the positions of Spinoza-Hegel and Kant concerning the ontological argument. Spinoza thinks that essence necessarily involves existence, since he deals only with existence as signified in a concept. Kant, on the other hand, insists that existence adds nothing in the order of concepts and essences, since his concern is for the empirical act of existing, which is irreducible to concepts and underivable from pure essential principles. For his own part, Kierkegaard agrees with Kant that existence lies outside of, or at least is not reducible to, a concept. His cautious language is due to his unwillingness to assign existence to some region of utter unknowability, where it might escape even God's knowledge and providential care, as well as our existential apprehension. Hence he finds himself in full agreement neither with Spinoza nor with Kant, and yet is in possession of no *philosophical* way of saving our knowledge of existence. There is a "quiet despair" about his assignment of existential truth to the province of ethico-religious subjectivity alone.

13. The Kierkegaardian distinction between the eternal being of God and the existence of the God-Man bears comparison with St. Augustine's reflections on God as He Who Is—the eternal and immutable being—and as the God of Abraham, the God Who has become incarnate in the temporal, changing order for our salvation. Consult Etienne Gilson, *Philosophie et Incarnation selon saint Augustin* (Montreal, Institut d'Études Médiévales, 1947). But Kierkegaard fuses the two questions of whether God exists as a real being (*Deum esse*) and what is the meaning and intrinsic nature of God's existence or real being (*Dei esse*). Because the latter transcends our natural intelligence, he disqualifies natural intelligence from demonstrating the former. Added to this is his identification of the latter question with that of the Incarnation of the Son of God.

14. *Prolegomena to Any Future Metaphysics*, 134.

15. *Fragments*, 37.

16. *Postscript*, 267-322. In portraying the subjective thinker, Kierkegaard had in mind not only his ideal conception of Socrates and Lessing, but also Hamann. For the latter's personality, cf. Walter Lowrie's pamphlet, mentioned above, chapter IV, note 20. Paul Tillich, "Existential Philosophy," *Journal of the History of Ideas*, V (1944), 44-70, points out that the contrast between the systematist and the existential thinker is a commonplace with the first generation of anti-Hegelians, especially Feuerbach, Marx and Kierkegaard (53-55).

17. *Postscript*, 184, text and note; cf. *Repetition, passim*, for Kierkegaard's opinions on Greek philosophy.

18. *Postscript*, 282-87. Jean Wahl, "Freedom and Existence in Some Recent Philosophies," *Philosophy and Phenomenological Research*, VIII (1947-48), 538, suggests that Kierkegaard places a kind of necessity—of divine grace and of repetition—at the core of possibility, in the sense of freedom. But in the *Journals*, entry 1051 (pp. 371-72), Kierkegaard is contrasting a purely theoretical reflection on the meaning of free choice and the very act of free choice. Only the former is eliminated in the human decision. The act of free choice vindicates free actuality over both necessity and a mere possibility which fails to realize itself in a definite act of choice.

19. See the suggestions of Jacques Maritain, *Existence and the Existent*, 10-35, and of Etienne Gilson, *Being and Some Philosophers*, 190-232.

20. See James Collins, *The Existentialists: A Critical Study*, 65-67, 147, 220-22, on transcendence in Sartre and Marcel.

21. *Postscript*, 345 ff.

22. *Ibid.*, 493-98.

23. As Kierkegaard expresses it: the watchword of existence is *Forward!* (*Ibid.*, 187; cf. 368). This has influenced Heidegger's analyses of the hurtling-forward and being-thrown aspects of human existence.

24. This point is brought out clearly by Thust, 362-68, who notes that there is a correlation latent in Kierkegaard between the highest type of subjectivity and recognition of an objective, transcendent order of truth, communicated by God to us. But Kierkegaard tends to keep the objective correlate in the shadows, because of polemical reasons, springing from his fear lest faith be reduced to mere speculative assent and passive acceptance of a creed.

25. See Karl Löwith, *Kierkegaard und Nietzsche oder theologische und philosophische Überwindung des Nihilismus* (Frankfurt, Vittorio Klostermann Verlag, 1933). For Nietzsche's repudiation of Christ and Christianity, cf. Walter A. Kaufmann, *Nietzsche: Philosopher, Psychologist, Antichrist* (Princeton, Princeton University Press, 1950), 295-341.

26. *Journals*, entry 1054 (p. 374). This serves as a reminder of the practical and religious orientation of Kierkegaard's entire discussion of the meaning of existence.

27. Consult *Fragments*, 47-49, 62-73; *Postscript*, 512-13. Kierkegaard allowed for a philosophical interpretation of world history, as long as it respected the limits of the objective, essential sciences and did not pretend to penetrate the domain of human subjectivity and freedom.

28. In his Introduction, Fabro, I, xlii-xliv, indicates that Kierkegaard's criticism of the Hegelian conception of history is in conformity with his general attack on Hegel's method and theory of actuality. Kierkegaard's emphasis upon belief as the mode of apprehension proper to historical realities is in reaction to Hegel's claim to provide a superior synthesis of faith and science in the idealistic philosophy of history.

29. In the *Journals*, entry 1044 (p. 368), Kierkegaard refers to Christ unqualifiedly as "the historical," just as he calls Him "the existential" (see above, note 26). The summits of existential truth and historical apprehension are reached simultaneously in the act of religious faith, in which Christ is acknowledged as the God-Man. Once more, the *how* of existential truth is meaningless apart from its determining *what*.

30. In so far as faith is something distinct from essential insight and a purely speculative sort of knowledge, Kierkegaard says that it is not knowledge or cognition but a passion, a free act (*Frag-*

ments, 68-69). Faith requires a free act of the will and hence a practical sort of assent. Once this assent is made, however, all dispute and doubt are removed. Just as becoming in general removes mere possibility, so the process of believing removes the special form of possibility which expresses itself as the attitude of disputing and doubting.

Notes to Chapter Six. *The Nature of the Human Individual*

1. Kierkegaard's views on journalism are examined in Swenson, 186-206.
2. The present chapter deals mainly with the following books: *Present Age, Point of View, Purify, Consider, Suffering, Love, Christian Discourses,* and *Sickness* (which was published in 1849 but rooted in the same spiritual soil as the other books).
3. *Point of View,* 111-12, 139.
4. *Journals,* entry 1027 (p. 358), a basic realistic thesis.
5. *Point of View,* 124. Following other commentators, Mesnard, 421, suggests that the Danish term *Enkelte* is better rendered as *singular* than as *individual. Singular* brings out the sense of being strange and exceptional—extra-ordinary—as well as being concrete and particular. This aspect comes to the fore in Kierkegaard's religious reflections on the "heterogeneity" of the Christian man with the world and on the need for every man to "stand out from the crowd," in order to achieve his own manner of existing and his own vocation. In the English translation of Martin Buber's *Between Man and Man* (New York, Macmillan, 1948), the translator (Ronald Gregor Smith) prefers to translate *Enkelte* (German, *Einzelner*) as *Single One,* in order to bring out the spiritual requirements setting it off from the natural-biological condition of being merely a distinct organism (cf. 207, note 9).
6. The post-Hegelian movement in social philosophy was outlined by Sidney Hook, *From Hegel to Marx* (New York, John Day, 1936), and by Herbert Marcuse, *Reason and Revolution: Hegel and the Rise of Social Theory* (New York, Oxford University Press, 1941; 262-67, on Kierkegaard).
7. *Journals,* entries 85, 563, 657, 663, 867-69 (pp. 31, 151, 204, 206-08, 282-90); *Present Age,* 28-31. For an analysis of Kierkegaard's social philosophy, cf. W. Stark, "Kierkegaard on Capitalism," *The Sociological Review,* XLII (1950), 87-114. For Marx's attitude toward the revolutions of 1848, see A. Cornu, *Karl Marx et la revolution de 1848* (Paris, Presses Universitaires, 1948).

8. He voiced this fear during his audience with King Christian VIII, who consulted Kierkegaard for his shrewd observations on practical affairs and public opinion in Denmark (*Journals*, entry 868; pp. 284-85). On the opposition between Christian equality and class warfare, see *Present Age*, 37; *Purify*, 168-69; *Love*, 60-61.

9. *Present Age*, 28. Kierkegaard's observations should be compared with the twentieth-century existentialist report by Karl Jaspers, *Man in the Modern Age*, translated by E. Paul (London, George Routledge, 1933).

10. Nietzsche was anxious to keep the mob in place, so that the higher personal life might flourish among a select few; cf. George A. Morgan, *What Nietzsche Means* (Cambridge, Mass., Harvard University Press, 1941), 190-92. But he lost hope that "the Christian dynamite of man's equality before God" could achieve a universal transformation of all human individuals—a hope which remained Kierkegaard's mainstay throughout his social criticism.

11. *Love*, 117.

12. *Present Age*, 32-36; *Sickness*, 196-99.

13. In *Postscript*, 68-69, the pseudonymous author, Johannes Climacus, argues that a religious individual cannot have direct communication with others but only an indirect communication. Kierkegaard himself gradually came to see the insufficiency of this view and the need for a direct religious testimony, given by a witness to the Christian faith. In *Trembling*, 107, 112-13, the pseudonymous author holds that, although individuals can become equal before God, they must remain solitary with respect to each other. Kierkegaard viewed the Hegelian theory of society as a substitute for personal responsibility and conscience, and as a universal entity, into which the individual is subsumed and thus ethico-religiously lost. He expended his energy in opposing these consequences, rather than in exploring the positive ways in which the community may develop in such fashion as to respect personal existence.

14. *Trembling*, 155; *Journals*, entry 1063 (p. 377).

15. *Ibid.*, entry 1319 (pp. 503-04). Yet Kierkegaard (like Nietzsche) owed a considerable debt to Schopenhauer, for insisting upon the importance of individuals and their quality of willing, in opposition to what Schopenhauer called Hegel's pantheistic preference for mass movements and visible results. Cf. Schopenhauer's *The World as Will and Idea*, translated by R. B. Haldane and J. Kemp (fifth edition, 3 vols., London, Kegan Paul, Trench and Trübner, 1906), III, 404. Schopenhauer liked to observe that, whereas every philosopher is faced with the problem of some remainders for

which his doctrine cannot account, Hegel has as his remainders the entire order of individual existents.

16. *Love*, 58-60. From a Marxist standpoint, Theodor Wiesengrund-Adorno, *Kierkegaard: Konstruktion des Ästhetischen* (Tübingen, J. C. B. Mohr, 1933), 52-54, tries to explain Kierkegaard's social views in terms of his petty-bourgeois social antecedents. But Kierkegaard is critical of all social classes and their spiritual attitudes.

17. *Edifying Discourses*, II, 45-66, where the dialectic between temporal differences among people and their equality of love before God is worked out in moving fashion. Kierkegaard's personal devotion to the thought of our absolute equality before God is comparable to Proudhon's dedication to the idea of justice, although the French social thinker chose the ideal of justice at the expense of belief in God. Cf. Henri de Lubac, S. J., *The Un-Marxian Socialist: A Study of Proudhon*, translated by R. E. Scantlebury (New York, Sheed and Ward, 1948).

18. Individual human existence, like Plato's Eros, is an integer or synthesis of wealth and poverty, being and becoming, a given nature or necessity and the risk of freedom (*Postscript*, 85); see *Edifying Discourses*, II, 67-87, on what it means "to acquire one's soul in patience."

19. On these two directions for the ideal of equality, cf. Christopher Dawson, *The Modern Dilemma* (New York, Sheed and Ward, 1933), 28, 55-58.

20. It is significant that, in *Sickness*, 78-119, Kierkegaard first gives a phenomenological description of the varieties of despair and then characterizes the entire attitude of despair as one of weakness and sin. Against the despairing view of man, he proposes the good news of individual human existence, as impregnated by Christian faith and hope.

21. *Love*, 215-20. Martin Buber, *Between Man and Man*, 50-65, severely criticizes Kierkegaard for limiting the I-Thou relationship to the individual and God, cutting the individual off from social connections with other men. Kierkegaard did see that love of neighbor or the human *thou* must be rooted in love of God. But his fear of the autonomous, apotheosized social organism prevented him from accepting the *visible and corporate* forms which the I-Thou relationship assumes at the level of human community.

22. Kierkegaard both denies (*Love*, 99) and affirms (*ibid.*, 48, 274; *Journals*, entry 487, p. 133) that God is the third party or middle term in human relations. What he denies is that God is merely a disinterested, external onlooker or an accidental party to the

social union. On the contrary, he affirms that God is intimately and radically involved in every attempt to establish personal relations among men, since He is the love and the object of love that binds men together. Kierkegaard is constantly skirting the problem of *eros* and *agape*, which is probed in depth by Martin D'Arcy, S.J., *The Mind and Heart of Love* (New York, Henry Holt, 1947).

23. *Present Age*, 32-33; *Point of View*, 88, note. On Grundtvig's thought and work, cf. Hal Koch, *Grundtvig*, translated by L. Jones (Yellow Springs, Ohio, The Antioch Press, 1952); K. Malone, "Grundtvig's Philosophy of History," *Journal of the History of Ideas*, I (1940), 281-98.

24. Once this revision in the notion of the universal is made, Kierkegaard is quite ready to laud "the great fellowship of existence" (*Consider*, 39), and to admit what is "common to men," the "universally human" aspects (*Purify*, 127, 149). He looks forward to the realization of "the true humanity" (*Point of View*, 110), which is "Christian humanity: the highest is the common possession of all men" (*Postscript*, 261). This is Kierkegaard's answer to the frequent charge that he has denied the category of the general and hence cannot speak rationally to other men about their common situation in being; cf. R. Arnou, S.J., "L'existentialisme à la manière de Kierkegaard," *Gregorianum*, XXVII (1946), 82-83. For Kierkegaard, it is not a simple alternative between solipsism and generality, but a problem of determining the general factor in such a way that it does not disintegrate the individual existent.

25. *Consider*, 48-50; *Edifying Discourses*, I, 100-03; IV, 142.

26. *Dread*, 109. There are two important consequences of this definition. (a) One does not become a man, in the pregnant sense, except by reaffirming the fleshly, finite, temporal, animal principle in human nature. Hence a truly human man must always be related in a thoroughly finite and creaturely way to God: only as a finite spirit, can he lift up his heart to the Infinite Spirit. This sort of humanism avoids any identification of man with God. (b) When soul and body are synthesized by spirit, there is also a synthesis of time and eternity. Man attains to spiritual maturity only when he becomes aware of the presence of the eternal in time, and relates his own freedom to eternity. But since the Instant is also the synthesis of time and eternity, man achieves his full humanity only when he passes from the state of being in dread before eternity to the act of Christian faith in the abiding presence of the eternal to man in the person of Christ, the God-Man.

27. *Sickness*, 127; *Point of View*, 130.
28. Hence Kierkegaard regards "the guilty man" as a distinctive category of the individual; cf. *Dread*, 54, 69-70; *Postscript*, 517; *Sickness*, 195-200. This is not said out of morbidity or gloom, but simply because the sinful man attains this condition through the inalienable exercise of his individual freedom, rather than through some dialectical process undergone by humanity as a global whole. Gerard Manley Hopkins made a similar appeal to the sense of sin, as providing one safeguard against the illusion of a pantheistic identification of man and God. "My shame, my guilt, my fate are the very things in feeling, in tasting, which I most taste that selftaste which nothing in the world can match." *The Note-books and Papers of Gerard Manley Hopkins*, edited by H. House (New York, Oxford University Press, 1937), 313. Hopkins displayed as lively an opposition to Hegel as did Kierkegaard. Both men regarded sin as an act of free finitude which resists inclusion within any monistic system of the absolute. For his part, Hegel castigated the category of the finite as being the most stubborn and stiff-necked of all the notions of the understanding, and declared that his idealism rested on the proposition that the finite is of ideal nature and has no authentic being of its own. Cf. *Science of Logic*, translated by W. H. Johnston and L. G. Struthers (2 vols., New York, Macmillan, 1929), I, 142, 168.
29. *Journals*, entry 1089 (pp. 388-89). "It is true for the first time in Christ that God is man's goal and measure." *Sickness*, 186.

Notes to Chapter Seven. Becoming a Christian in Christendom

1. J. Hyppolite, *Genèse et structure de la Phénoménologie de l'Esprit de Hegel* (Paris, Aubier, 1946), 525, text and note 1, remarks that Hegel tends to assimilate God to man in a kind of absolutist humanism and to eradicate the Christian distinction between the here-below and the beyond-the-world, by limiting all transcendence to the "horizontal" sort, directed only toward the temporal, historical process. Kierkegaard criticizes the Speculative reduction of the distinction between the "here" and the "hereafter," in *Postscript*, 505-06. The best American example of an idealistic interpretation of religion and revelation in exclusively philosophical terms is Josiah Royce's *The Problem of Christianity* (2 vols., New York, Macmillan, 1913).
2. For Marx's criticism of Hegel and Feuerbach, as well as a sketch of his own naturalistic humanism, cf. "Critique of the Hegelian Dialectic," *Three Essays by Karl Marx*, translated by Ria Stone

(New York, Pioneer Publishers, 1947), 28-42. Kierkegaard criticized Hegel and Feuerbach for failing to take account of the Christian teaching that, in Christ, there is not a union of God and humanity-at-large but of God and this concrete human nature (*Training*, 84, 123). For an analysis of Kierkegaard's belief in Christ as the God-Man, cf. Croxall, 193-309.

3. For a criticism of the circular assumption that Christianity is equivalent to the Speculative interpretation of Christianity, see *Postscript*, 335-40. On Kierkegaard's own basic view of Christianity, cf. Geismar, *Lectures on the Religious Thought of Søren Kierkegaard*, 63-79; Bohlin, 166-99.

4. The distinction between the religions of immanence ("religiousness A") and the Christian religion of transcendence ("religiousness B") is examined by Thomte, 87-96.

5. The main writings are: *Two Minor Ethico-Religious Treatises* (contained in *Present Age*), *Sickness, Training, Self-Examination,* and *Attack*.

6. A comparison between Kierkegaard and Bloy is suggested by Frank O'Malley, "The Passion of Léon Bloy," *Review of Politics,* X (1948), 101-04.

7. *Love*, 61; *Training*, 92; *Postscript*, 219. Such texts must be kept in mind, when one also reads that Christianity often seems to be hostile to man (*Training*, 119).

8. Cf. *Postscript*, 492, note; *Point of View*, 153, note; *Journals*, entries 85, 121, 141, 192 (pp. 31, 44, 47, 67).

9. Cf. Erich Przywara, *Das Geheimnis Kierkegaards* (Munich and Berlin, Verlag von R. Oldenbourg, 1929), 60-113; Fabro's Introduction, I, lxxx-lxxxiv.

10. *Journals*, entry 1327 (pp. 509-13).

11. "The deification of the established order is the secularization of everything. . . . The established order desires to be totalitarian, recognizing nothing over it, but having under it every individual." *Training*, 92.

12. He called Luther an important patient for Christianity, but not its proper doctor (*Journals*, entry 1325; p. 508). On Kierkegaard and Luther, see Jolivet, 206-18.

13. *Stages*, 409, 415-16.

14. The relevance of Luther's concept of idolatry for Kierkegaard's view of religion and his criticism of Hegel is noted by Paul Ramsey, "*Existenz* and the Existence of God: A Study of Kierkegaard and Hegel," *The Journal of Religion*, XXVIII (1948), 157-76. Kierkegaard develops the theme of the idolatrous nature of

the Stoic and Hegelian conceptions of religious worship, in *Sickness*, 108-11.

15. *Suffering*, 20; see also, the entire second series of *Christian Discourses*, devoted to the relation between suffering and Christian joy.

16. This interpretation of dogma within the context of the historicity of existence has made a deep imprint upon crisis theology; cf. M. Chaning-Pearce, *The Terrible Crystal: Studies in Kierkegaard and Modern Christianity* (New York, Oxford University Press, 1941).

17. *Fragments*, 44-58, 70-72, 83-88.

18. Polemical use of this consequence is made in *Training*, 67-70, and *Attack*, 239-43, 280-81, against those who think that two thousand years of church history dispense us from receiving the condition of faith directly from the revealing God.

19. Cf. *Fragments*, 38, 43, 47, where faith is described obliquely as bringing about a good understanding between reason and the paradox of the eternal-in-time, once a man has actually believed in the Incarnation. In his essay, "Foi et raison dans l'oeuvre de Kierkegaard" (cited above, chapter IV, note 21), Fabro notes that, once reason acknowledges its limitations by admitting its inability to give a philosophical demonstration of the truth of the Incarnation, it regains its sympathetic accord with faith. But Kierkegaard stresses the struggle and the leap required before reason foregoes its Hegelian claim to omnicompetence. Throughout his discussion of faith and reason, his point of reference is to the Hegelian notion of reason as sovereign, self-sufficient and inclusive of faith, which is an inferior moment in rational knowledge. The Catholic Church, in condemning Bonnetty's traditionalism, reaffirmed the mutual help of faith and reason, and pointed out that a philosophical use of reason need not lead to pantheism and naturalism, as Kierkegaard feared. Cf. *Enchiridion Symbolorum*, edited by Denzinger-Bannwart-Umberg (twenty-sixth edition, Freiburg i. B., Herder, 1947), paragraphs 1649-52 (pp. 462-63). For a careful, textual defense of Kierkegaard against the charge of fideism and irrationalism, see V. Melchiorre, "Kierkegaard e il fideismo," *Rivista di filosofia neoscolastico*, XLV (1953), 143-76.

20. *Fragments*, 87. Ruttenbeck, 218-75, has collated Kierkegaard's remarks on faith (including those of his pseudonyms), emphasizing the objective and dogmatic aspects.

21. Indeed, Kierkegaard's customary statement of his ideal is: "To become and to be a Christian" (*Training*, 190, 219), i. e. to be a

Christian in an existential way through the continued exercise of freedom, as a constant striving to become in actuality what one professes in principle. The human mode of being is never divorced from the process of becoming and moral struggle.

22. George Santayana, *The Idea of Christ in the Gospels* (New York, Scribner, 1946), 70-71.

23. See the mocking attack on "childish Christianity," *Postscript*, 520-37.

24. Kierkegaard maintains both that the goods of the spirit are by nature communicable through love (*Christian Discourses*, 121) and that intercourse with God is absolutely nonsocial (*ibid.*, 334), an individual responsibility higher than any fellowship now possible (*Training*, 218). The fellowship of the Church is, for him, still an ideal that has no present actuality.

25. Kierkegaard usually insisted that the genius and the exceptional individual, as such, do not possess the plenary power of religious authority (*Myndighed*, the Biblical *exousia;* cf. Hirsch, 318-35), which lies only with Christ and the Apostles. See his ethico-religious treatise: "Of the Difference between a Genius and an Apostle," *Present Age*, 139 ff.

26. For a theistic reading of Kafka, see Walter Ong, S. J., "Kafka's Castle in the West," *Thought*, XXII (1947), 439-60.

27. This is the theme of Part I of *Judge for Yourselves!*, which is in continuity of the first part of *For Self-Examination*.

28. *Christian Discourses*, 345; cf. 227. On Christ as the Pattern of religious existence, consult the second part of *Judge for Yourselves!*, and *Training*, 231-50. In the latter text, there is a dialectic between the aloof esthetic admirer and the religious follower of Christ: only the latter takes Christ as his Pattern.

29. *Training*, 201. Kierkegaard admits the legitimacy of a "Christian learning" (*Self-Examination*, 204, note), which would cultivate the natural, philosophical and theological sciences, without confusing these disciplines with religious perfection. But this Christian humanism belonged to the medieval past, is not a living attitude today, and can be reinstated only in so distant a future that Kierkegaard feels no obligation to follow up his suggestion. Here, as well as in the problem of the Church, there is a polemical narrowing down of the perspective to the immediate situation and a refusal to reckon seriously with other solutions, even though their intrinsic possibility is not denied.

30. *Training*, 194, 206-07. Kierkegaard contrasts the militant status of actual believers with the premature peace and complacency of the *beati possidentes*, who have already entered into the church triumphant with the aid of their imagination and the warrant of

absolute idealism. But existence always poses a test for genuine believers, just as the world always remains their mortal enemy—although divine governance also works for the good of men of faith (*Training*, 189, 226).

31. *Ibid.*, 154. Kierkegaard synthesizes his meditations on the love of God and neighbor in *Works of Love*.

32. This theme is developed in *Christian Discourses*, 197-209. Theodor Haecker, *Kierkegaard the Cripple*, 7, observes that Kierkegaard's first and final thought is the love of God—God's own loving nature and our loving relation with Him—without which everything in his life would have turned to despair.

Notes to Chapter Eight. Kierkegaard and Christian Philosophy

1. Cf. *Summa Theologiae*, I, 12, 1, ad 3; *In Libro De Causis*, lect. 6.

2. Richard Kroner, "Kierkegaard or Hegel?" *Revue Internationale de Philosophie*, VI (1952), 79-96, attacks Kierkegaard for siding with the tradition of Aristotle and Aquinas, in regarding God as an eternal, non-temporal being. Like Hegel and Schelling, Kroner fails to see how a purely eternal God can be living, existing and active with respect to the world. He wants to inject a temporal aspect into the eternal God, whereas Kierkegaard regards this Hegelian doctrine as a compromise of the divine transcendence and a reduction of the Incarnation (in which time and eternity are, indeed, joined in the person of Christ) to a purely natural truth.

3. *Fragments*, 64, note 1. Kierkegaard also admits (*Postscript*, 112) that his extensive use of the comical, in respect to Hegel, is a metaphysical way of dealing with metaphysical problems.

4. Not only free, human agents but all finite things participate in the perfection of existence. The rehabilitation of a realistic speculative philosophy depends on the recognition that even the non-human things in the sensible world exercise the act of existing. Hints of such a broadening of the meaning and scope of existence are not entirely lacking in Kierkegaard. In treating of the ontological argument, for instance, he makes a cardinal distinction between factual being and ideal being, "faktisk Vaeren og ideel Vaeren." *Philosophiske Smuler* (*Samlede Vaerker, ed. cit.*, IV, 209, note; the English translation of this note, *Fragments*, 33, note 2, is unsatisfactory). Non-human things in the world are contingent, undergo change, have a sort of history, and are irreducible to ideal or purely essential being. To this extent, they share in some way in factual being or existence, *til faktisk Vaeren*. This opens the

road for a realistic, speculative knowledge of these things in their existential character and hence also for a revision of Kierkegaard's exclusively practical notion of existence and existential apprehension.

5. *Summa Theologiae*, I, 97, 3, c.
6. *Ibid.*, I, 94-95.
7. *Postscript*, 339.
8. Cf. Etienne Gilson, *L'être et l'essence* (Paris, J. Vrin, 1948), 240-42.
9. Emil Brunner, *Revelation and Reason* (Philadelphia, Westminster Press, 1946), 36, 156; chapter 25 is a remarkable plea (against Barth) for a Reformed Christian philosophy along Kierkegaardian lines. For a criticism of the attitude of crisis theology and neo-orthodoxy toward natural reason, cf. L. H. De Wolf, *The Religious Revolt Against Reason* (New York, Harper, 1949).

Index

INDEX

Ibsen, Henrik, 3, 175
Idolatry, 204, 222, 296-97
Imagination, 25, 41, 55, 64, 237
Immediacy and mediation, 54-55, 58-
59, 114, 118, 126-27, 211, 286
Immortality, 104, 153, 266
Incarnation, 27, 147-48, 162-66, 167,
171-74, 212, 223-31, 299
Individual (the self), 48, 83-84, 104,
106, 111, 154-55, 175-207, 211-12,
214-16, 230-31, 259, 291, 292-93
Instant, 171-73, 225, 230, 238, 294
Inwardness (subjectivity), 141, 152-
53, 160, 205, 221, 288
Irony, 24, 44, 64-65, 106-107
Irrationalism, 284-85

Jacobi, F. H., 118, 146, 169
James, William, 147, 153
Jaspers, Karl, 44, 73, 284
Job, 90
Journalism (the press), 2, 13, 176,
223

Kafka, Franz, 200, 232
Kant and Kantianism, 68, 69, 78, 81-
82, 87-88, 90, 92-94, 101, 102, 104,
124-25, 133, 148-51, 280, 288
Keats, John, 276
Kierkegaard, M. P., 3-8, 12, 25
Kierkegaard, P. C., 7, 17
Kierkegaard, Søren Aabye
a corrective, 19, 191, 242
Journals, 20-31, 35, 38
life, 2-18
polemical nature, 29-30
pseudonyms, 34-42, 276
religious thinker and poet, 179, 232
self-isolation, 177-78, 278
Kroner, Richard, 299

Lavelle, Louis, 83, 280
Lenin, V. I., 29, 111, 187
Lessing, G. E., 146

Locke, John, 22
Love, 185-86, 199-200, 236, 239-40,
267, 293-94, 299
Lowrie, Walter, 283-84
Luther and Lutheranism, 5, 16, 205,
217, 219-20, 221, 236, 242, 296

Maimonides, Moses, 34
Marcel, Gabriel, 158, 190, 279
Marheineke, P., 11
Marriage, 76-78, 86-87, 279
Martensen, Hans L., 6, 17, 100, 101,
201
Marx and Marxism, 22, 29, 49, 70, 99,
112, 181, 182, 186-87, 190, 201, 210,
213, 231, 252-53, 282, 289
Masses. *See* Crowd
Mediation. *See* Immediacy
Mesnard, 276-77, 278
Metaphysics, 68, 121-24, 129-33, 142,
179, 253-56
Møller, P. L., 12, 13, 175
Møller, P. M., 12, 100
Motion. *See* Becoming
Mynster, J. P., 5, 17
Mysticism, 51-52

Naturalism, 69-71, 139, 140, 195-96,
233-34, 252, 263
Newman, J. H., 131
Nietzsche, Friedrich, 19, 28, 29, 34,
51, 79, 164-65, 184-85, 207, 213, 222,
286, 291
Novalis, 23, 37, 41, 54, 275

Olsen, Regine, 2, 8-11, 12, 33, 36, 56
Otto, Rudolf, 160, 281

Pantheism, 24, 27, 84, 102, 104, 191-
92, 206, 222, 230
Pascal, Blaise, 25, 29, 83, 115, 221, 244,
285
Passions, 53, 54-55, 115-16, 261-63
Peirce, C. S., 159